"My life is going to mean something to someone, somewhere..."

SHANNON O'HARA, AGE 12

MAY 28, 2011

DETERMINED TO MATTER

A Family Facing Inoperable Brain Cancer

Determined to Matter

A Family Facing Inoperable Brain Cancer

by *Jen O'Hara*

INCLUDING BLOGS WRITTEN
by DAN O'HARA

SCARLETTA  PRESS

MINNEAPOLIS, MINNESOTA

Published by Scarletta Press, an imprint of Scarletta

This book is a collaborative arrangement between Scarletta and ABDO Publishing Company.

Library of Congress Cataloging-in-Publication Data
O'Hara, Jen.
Determined to matter : a family facing inoperable brain cancer / by Jen O'Hara ; including blogs written by Dan O'Hara.
    p.   cm.
ISBN-13: 978-1-938063-22-0 (hardcover : alk. paper)
ISBN-10: 1-938063-22-8 (hardcover : alk. paper)
ISBN-13: 978-1-938063-20-6 (pbk. : alk. paper)
ISBN-10: 1-938063-20-1 (pbk. : alk. paper)
[etc.]
1. Grief. 2. Bereavement—Psychological aspects. 3. Loss (Psychology) I. O'Hara, Dan. II. Title.
BF575.G70288 2013
155.9'37—DC23
                                                                    2012038580

Book Design: Chris Long, Mighty Media, Inc., Minneapolis, Minnesota
Editors: Grace Hansen and Nora Evans • Contributing Editors: Julie Murray and Mary Beth Sinclair
Printed and manufactured in the United States
Distributed by Publishers Group West

First edition
10 9 8 7 6 5 4 3 2

DEDICATION

I am a mother, so this book is for my girls.

For Erin. You amaze and inspire me. You have lost so much, but you are stronger than you know.

And, for Shannon. I was your mother, but you were my teacher.

Table of Contents

Preface   xi

Introduction   xiii

The Penalty Box   1

Diagnosis Day   April 18–20   2

The Blog   April 21–25   10

Shannon the Cannon   April 26–May 2   19

Community   May 3–13   29

Eyes Wide Open   May 15–27   41

Family Ties   May 28–June 10   53

Sisterhood Rules   June 14–27   68

Fear Factor   June 29–July 22   80

Stubborn Streak   July 24–August 7   96

It Takes an Army   August 8–24   109

New Normal   August 26–September 15   120

The Sound of Music   September 20–October 17   133

Sports   October 19–November 4   149

Passion Found   November 7–16   158

The Rebels	November 18–December 2	165
Memphis on Broadway	December 4–13	178
St. Jude	December 14–23	193
The Dumpster	December 24–January 3	208
EIO—Born Wise	January 5–15	228
The Letters	January 17–February 26	244
Grief	February 29–March 21	274
Hope	March 24–April 18	289
Lessons Learned		305
Back to the Start		307
Epilogue: Memorials and Moving On		308
Afterword	Dr. Cynthia Wetmore	312
Acknowledgments		316
The Shannon O'Hara Foundation		319
About the Authors		321

Preface

Our bank instituted a corporate initiative to be the "happiest bank ever." At the same time, my daughter Shannon was going through radiation and chemotherapy to try to tame an incurable brain tumor. Many times, when Shannon was in therapy, I would run over to manage some banking business, and the smiley teller would attempt to engage: "How are you today?" "What are you up to today?" "Looks like you have the day off, are you doing something fun?" My mood was usually not so bubbly, and most of the time I resisted the temptation to crush her like a bug by telling her the truth.

If I have learned anything in our journey as a family living out a nightmare, it is that you just never know what someone has going on in their life. And if you really want to know, you better be prepared to stop and listen. I'm a big "Hey, how's it going?" guy. Today, I am working really hard to maintain eye contact and wait for an answer. And if there is someone looking to go deeper, I am ready to listen.

As a society, we are courteous but insincere. Shannon Anne O'Hara knew she was dying, and yet she still kept eye contact and waited for an answer.

One night late in Shannon's life, my wife, Jennifer, and I were having a rare tense moment, and some sharp words were exchanged that Shannon overheard. A few minutes later I went to check on Shannon and found her up in her loft bed crying big tears. She scolded me: "I read that 80 percent of married couples that go through tragedy end up in divorce! You and Mom *have* to take care of Erin!" The emotion contorted her face. The tears were so real. She never cried that hard when she was told cancer would take her life.

As a family of three now, we are trying our best to take care of each other. To be kind. To listen. To try really hard to get better. We know that is the right way to live. We just needed a nudge to remind us how easy it is.

DAN O'HARA

Introduction

"Seasons of Love" is one of my favorite songs from the musical, *Rent*. The song is about how we measure the passage of time:

> *In daylights, in sunsets, in midnights, in cups of coffee.*
> *In inches, in miles, in laughter, in strife.*
> *One year. 525,600 minutes.*
> *How do you measure a year in life?*

This is my family's story—one year in our life—beginning with a life-altering diagnosis for my daughter Shannon. My husband, Dan, and I wrote a blog during our journey. Much of that blog remains intact in this book. As we stated on the blog's front page, we wrote from the heart, so parental discretion is advised.

It was never my intention when the blog started to try and help others, only to communicate with family and friends and to deal with my own thoughts, worries, and pain. I am not a crusader, but along the journey, I kept hearing from people that our words helped them. So, in time, and with support from many others, I came to believe that I could—maybe even that I should—write this book.

If sharing our story can inspire others who face adversity in their lives, that's a beautiful thing. Or, if it's just a good story that reminds you of what is really important in life, that's a beautiful thing too. It's Shannon's gift to us all.

Here's our story. I hope it helps.

JEN O'HARA

Two minutes for roughing | Girls hockey
game, Rochester Rebels vs. the Dodge County
Wildcats

The Penalty Box

"She punched me!" Shannon exclaimed with eyes afire and the adrenaline pumping. Her dad was there on the bench, coaching, and he had asked her what happened out on the ice.

This was an early season match-up for Shannon's Rochester Rebels girls hockey team, and the visitors were playing very physical. Shannon was up to the challenge despite the fact she'd been battling a brain tumor for seven months. Or maybe she was just loving every minute of the game for that exact reason. She had been told she had a terminal disease, so a little scuffling on the ice wasn't going to phase her. She loved to compete.

Into the corner she went, against a girl who had six inches and sixty pounds on her. After a little extracurricular action, Shannon and the opponent were headed to the penalty box. Two minutes for roughing. That doesn't happen very often in girls hockey, where there is no checking allowed.

After the game, when we pressed her about what she had done in retaliation that had landed her in the penalty box, Shannon sidestepped the accusation. "I don't know. It's all a blur." Those big brown eyes and that playful grin told us otherwise.

Shannon had a competitive fire that burned inside her, and hockey was her passion. Our little brain-tumor patient, nicknamed Shannon the Cannon, was playing the game she loved, and reveling in every minute of this hockey season.

The day was November 13, 2011. Fifty-four days later, Shannon the Cannon would be dead.

Diagnosis Day

I will never, ever forget the look on the neurologist's face when he entered that exam room. Nothing prepares you for hearing that your child has an inoperable, terminal brain tumor. Nothing. I will be able to picture that exam room in the mental movie of my life forever. The snow falling outside, Dr. Kotagal entering the room and asking Shannon to step out ... I'm feeling sick to my stomach just writing about it.

In the week following our return from spring break, Shannon had been complaining of headaches and trouble focusing at school. One never knows what's making a 12-year-old girl feel crummy, so we gave it a few days. It didn't subside, so seven days after her first headache, we made an appointment with our family medicine doctor. That was Monday, April 11, 2011. Dr. Puffer checked Shannon over and everything looked normal to him. He thought her vision might be the culprit, so we were off to the eye doctor the next day.

Throughout the eye exam, our optometrist, Dr. Huber, and Shannon were busy chatting about hockey, trash talking even. Her vision was 20/20. But Dr. Huber caught a "bounce" in Shannon's eyes when they tracked from right to left. He called a colleague to consult and suggested we see neurology just to be sure we weren't missing something.

Off to neurology on Thursday.

Dr. Kotagal in neurology gave Shannon a full neuro exam, and it was mostly normal. But he also noticed Shannon was having trouble controlling her eye movement. Just to cover all the bases, an MRI was ordered for the following day.

Shannon was scared and asked Dr. Kotagal point blank, "Do you think I have a brain tumor?" To which he replied, "No, dear, I don't think it's that, but we need to check to be sure."

The next day, Friday, April 15, 2011, the MRI revealed the brain stem glioma tumor. We went from first appointment to diagnosis in five short days. Our world was shattered and our lives would be changed forever.

Dr. Kotagal delivered the news, but he brought in a pediatric neurologist, Dr. Keating, to talk more extensively with us. Her face and her compassion are also etched in my memory of that day. Dr. Kotagal and Dr. Keating were the first two of many medical professionals who would be a part of our journey.

We spent the evening of the diagnosis calling family. Awful, terrible phone calls. We were ruining people's nights all across the country as we broke the news. Shannon's little sister, Erin, was engrossed in a movie on the Disney Channel, so she was occupied.

Shannon, luckily, had a birthday party sleepover. She wanted to go, so we let her. Maybe she didn't completely grasp what we had been told. Maybe she didn't want to. Maybe she wanted to continue to live her life. That would become her goal, to live her life the way she wanted, no matter what, until the end. This was the first of many instances where she did just that.

We began chronicling our journey.

MONDAY, APRIL 18, 2011

(This was originally written as an email to family)

Feeling a touch overwhelmed tonight. The outreach has been amazing, exhausting. So many ups and downs to manage. Shannon just fell asleep in my arms wrapped in a new Twins fleece blanket that cousin Laurynn gave her last night. The Twins were still ahead while she was awake.

Today was another good one to check off. Jen and I met with school admin and teachers at both Willow Creek Middle and Bamber Valley Elementary. A paragraph on each meeting would not cover all the cool stuff. Shannon and Erin are loved very much at both schools. Unreal. Shannon can call her own shots to get through the year. She wants to be there as much as possible. She can take the MCA—state standards—in a conference room with some comforts afforded. When Shannon told the Willow Creek team she wanted to excel in MCA's to set herself up for flex classes in eighth grade, Mrs. Mammel (her English teacher) told her, "Shannon, I could've told you that you would've qualified for flex in October!" Shannon gave that a big smile. The principal told Shannon he too wanted Shannon to take the MCA's, because he knows it will help their performance numbers!

Erin is in great hands at Bamber Valley. She has a counselor if she needs her. She will be providing the counselor with counsel as often as she needs it. Erin continues to provide us all with wisdom on a regular basis.

Mr. Myhro, the golf coach at Mayo High School, is putting Shannon in the JV lineup for tomorrow's triangular match vs. JM. She will golf in the sixth spot on the JV. Nine holes at Eastwood. God please make the snow stay away until about 5:30 ... please. Shannon thinks that is about the coolest thing in America. Mr. Myhro knows she's at her strongest today.

Then we made it to the Mayo Clinic. Our morning consult with the hematologist and peds doctors to set the course for Shannon's treatment was tough. They laid out the plan and we're going to go hard at the tumor while Shannon is strong. Oral chemotherapy Temodar; we're hoping it can be one pill at bedtime for six weeks. Then six weeks of radiation starting Thursday. Tomorrow's appointment is a treatment planning session to make the thermo-plastic facemask that will keep her head in place while they zap the tumor. The radiation will enter her skull right about where a high ponytail sits.

We're learning that a fever and low white counts will require emergency room visits. Anytime that happens she will need a transfusion. We are learning about the side effects that will likely occur, can occur, and might occur. They feel the first couple weeks she'll feel pretty good. The cumulative effects of the chemo/radiation will eventually take their toll. I think we all know someone who has gone through this process.

If the morning consult was the bad cop, the afternoon consult was the good cop. The radiation oncologist is not only a mom, but one who plays hockey herself. She has already heard much about Shannon from her hockey-mama buddies whose daughters play hockey with Shannon. Her name is Dr. Laack. Jen taught her sons Soren and Xavier tennis at the Rochester Athletic Center (RAC). She shared a really cool story of hope at the end of our meeting. Shannon was running out of questions because she was completely focused on getting to golf practice. She made it there by 3:15.

Back at Mayo tomorrow at 8:00 A.M.

We love you all. Your attention at this time is welcomed; responses are not always possible. More updates as energy permits ... we'll try for daily ... it's good to have goals.

POSTED BY DAN

TUESDAY, APRIL 19, 2011

(This was originally written as an email to family)

Another update from Willow Lane. Things are coming together with Shannon's treatment plan, and Thursday is a massive day in her life. But until then we have a little normalcy.

Miracles are everywhere. We came in to meet with the radiation oncology team this morning at 8:00 A.M. They are pretty much all hockey moms, and they were waiting for us with hugs and tears.

So, for today's appointment to set Shannon's mask that will hold her head steady during radiation, one of the moms took Shannon away while the other one—who happens to be the dosimetrist on our radiation team—stayed with Jen and me to chat. Shannon was in and out setting the mask in about twelve minutes. We took a quick tour and saw the technology that is providing us with hope. Pretty friggin' amazing machines. I hope you never have to see one. They then brought us to the scheduling desk controlled by a sassy gal named Shanan. That Shanan will play a key role in getting our Shannon the best tee times (OK for non-golfers, treatment times).

Dr. Laack checked in and answered a couple questions, and we were out of there by about 8:40 A.M. Then we were off for Willow Creek, and Shannon was thrown in the conference room to take the MCA's, which she said went just fine! She was in school all day. Took the bus home with her friends. She got off the bus with another stuffed animal and two giant get-well banners with signatures and smart-assed middle school comments. (And random celeb signatures like Megan Fox and Adrian Peterson.)

Wednesday Shannon goes to school all day and then to golf practice ... nothing at Mayo. Today's golf match was snowed out but that frees her up to skate tonight with her spring hockey team. She's pretty jacked for that.

We had to manage through a couple complicated situations that came as a result of people caring so deeply for our family. We are overwhelmed a little by all the offers to help us and to honor Shannon. It's just a little too much too soon.

Let's get through Thursday's baseline blood draw, hematology appt, chemo scrip, surgical consult, and hopefully first doses of radiation and chemo. That's not certain, so pray for that. If we can't start Thursday, treatments will not begin until Monday. God grant me the serenity to accept the things I cannot change....

We just can't express how much we love you all. The support is amazing. Just friggin' amazing.

POSTED BY DAN

WEDNESDAY, APRIL 20, 2011

(This was originally written as an email to family)
When tragedy strikes there are so many things that come up. Things you would never consider—mostly rooted in incredible efforts of support. Tonight I am kept awake by this concept of communication. So I grabbed the iPod and the laptop and headed for the fireside recliner, and I write. I'm learning that writing is really good therapy for me. You should know, nothing is sent without Jen's blessing and her most practical and sensitive editing. That's good. No doubt—I need a filter!

Today we had a mostly great day with the girls. There was downtime to rest up for Thursday for Shannon and family around in small doses. There was a soccer practice with Erin's Fireballs that was really fun. We play our first game Saturday morning, and Jen and I—along with our good bud Bart Grafstrom (Bloomington Lincoln class of 1981, same as me)—are coaching and think we might have a really fun group. Coaching rec soccer can be a challenge. You just never know how eleven girls from all over SE and SW Rochester will blend. So the Fireballs will become part of our narrative over the next six weeks. Ironically the season will pretty much span the exact length of Shannon's radiation treatments. Our one crack at frying the shit out of this damn brain stem glioma.

We returned from Wednesday night's practice to find Aunt Connie, Grandma Gwen, and Aunt Megan folding our clothes while watching *Secretariat* with Shannon. The scene brought me to tears. So special. Honestly, just a little snapshot into our completely whacked-out new life. But there is gratitude and a new appreciation for amazing little things going on all around us.

So, back to this topic of communication. Jen and I are learning how deeply embedded we are in this community. I suppose, both of us were born here and both of us have worked in fairly high profile professions for many years in Rochester. I spent thirteen years on TV, and Jen has taught tennis to literally thousands of kids over the last twenty years, many of them sons and daughters of Mayo Clinic's brightest stars. Go figure. Jen's nearly photographic recall of names and faces of kids she has taught over the years never ceases to amaze me. Just like the other day when I shared that our radiation oncologist, Dr. Laack, came in to tell how she was going to attack Shannon's tumor, and Jen asked, "Are your sons Soren and Xavier? I taught them tennis!" I know personally, nothing softens me up like someone that tells me they know my kid. I sensed Dr. Laack was taken aback. Cool. What a blessing.

So needless to say there are a lot of people who know us. Know of us. And it seems as though they all want to know what's going on with Shannon all at the same time, and we are kind of freakin' out about how to manage the communication. How can you be mad about that? In our new whacked-out world, nothing softens me up like someone that asks me how my kid is doing.

But so many people feel compelled to tell us what they would do.

How CaringBridge was a great forum for them when so-and-so's son or dad was sick. Did you know there is CaringBridge? Did you know Mayo Clinic offers a site for you to communicate information to family and friends? We get it. And we know you want to know what's going on (not allowing a Jen-filter here), but we're not here to provide you a forum for you to feel better about yourself by posting a reply that is more profound than the one above it. We have witnessed a couple experiences with these types of forums where the site just gets hijacked by people who want to feel better about themselves by going on and on about a kid they've never met. Another risk we have learned from others is that after a couple weeks or so, if you become just too exhausted to post, then the replies come enmasse: "What's wrong?" "Is everything OK?" Still I know many others have had tremendous experiences with those sites.

That has kind of happened on Shannon's Facebook. Today she just lay around and didn't even try to keep up. Jen recognized that maybe Shannon is realizing the gravity of the situation based on the way people are posting. We hope that's not the case. We were hopeful that it would be a source of inspiration for her.

Don't be confused. We are so touched by the outreach. We are just exhausted by all of this, and tomorrow is just the beginning. In my recovery program we talk all the time about planning the action, not the outcome. I know I'm guilty of planning the outcome. So Jen and I are sounding this out.

Today's song that I love and have played over and over is Ingrid Michaelson's "Maybe." Kleenex please. Remember when you first fell in love and EVERY song seemed to have lyrics written just for you? That's where I am right now. I too have been finding Jen reclining with music in her headphones more and more here over the last few days. It is how she has been ending her day. That's great. She loves her music, and her playlists are where I find goodies like Ingrid Michaelson. Jen is so cool. My inspiration. Our leader. Shannon and Erin are just budding with confidence and self-esteem—in part because of that great security blanket they call Mom.

I'm not sure how much longer I can blubber like this; I'm not sure

I can hold up and keep finding the energy to write. But it seems as though if I just get started it all comes out. That's the other challenge; I probably will require more filtering for a publicly posted blog. That sucks. But we'll see. Once again, plan the action not the outcome, right?

So tonight we put the kids down and came up to log off, listen to some music, wind down, and prepare for a big day tomorrow. And we hear footsteps coming up the stairs; it's Shannon closely followed by E. With really bright eyes—not a hint of tearing or sadness—Shannon says, "OK, I need to know right now. Am I going to die in the next six weeks during radiation?" Oh my God. Poor little angel. We assured her that the next six weeks were going to make her feel better. That the radiation and chemo might wear her out after a few weeks, but initially she will feel really great. And then we will see. We assured her that the reason she pounded out the MCA's was to be set up for eighth grade ... we'll make choices on sports, activities, etc. based on how we are feeling at that time. Day at a time. Oh, we love that kid sooo much. She has taken on an almost angelic persona with her words and actions. God has blessed us with so much ... but son-of-a-bitch ...

Jason Mraz, "A Beautiful Mess" is now playing ...

OK, it's go time! We're coming for you, tumor ... so get your shit and get!

POSTED BY DAN

The Blog

Amidst the emotions and utter devastation we felt when given Shannon's terminal diagnosis, there were practical matters to attend to. Not the least of which was how to communicate with our families and friends as we started our journey. Dan is the youngest of nine children and my mother is the oldest of nine, so there were aunts and uncles and cousins and nieces and nephews who all wanted to be kept up to date. And word got out amongst our close friends and they told other friends and so on and so forth.

In this social-media age, starting a blog is easy. In fact, we did it from the waiting room using the Wi-Fi offered at the Mayo Clinic. Just like that, in a matter of minutes, Dan and I had a forum to communicate to our family and friends that would save us from making phones calls or sending emails each night.

That was the original intent of our blog. As Dan and I realized that writing was cathartic for us, we were more willing to share the link with a wider audience. We told friends and family to pass it on. We would see people around town who would sheepishly admit that they were following us because a friend of a friend shared the link with them. Some people admitted that they felt like they were stalkers! We always let them know that it was OK with us that they were blog followers. We wanted to share our journey.

I never imagined that it would become such a powerful tool and would reach a much wider audience. By the time we reached our darkest day, more than 11,000 people viewed our post.

THURSDAY, APRIL 21, 2011

OK, my turn to take a stab at writing these words. It's not as easy for me to put myself out there emotionally as it is for Dan. But, as we keep saying, in our "new normal" so many things are different. So here I am writing a blog for all to see ...

Today was the day that treatment began. First up, blood draw where the results showed, as Shannon said, "I am really completely healthy except for this tumor." Yep. Next appointment was back in hematology oncology with Dr. Khan for a consult and to receive the prescriptions for anti-nausea meds and the chemotherapy drug Temodar. Shannon had lost five pounds since Friday, so even though she has been attempting to eat healthy to keep her strength up, Dr. Khan said to throw in some high-calorie foods. Finally, an area I know something about. Shannon can't wait until Sunday; she gave up ice cream for lent, so once it's Easter, packing in the calories gets a whole lot easier!

We also met with a social worker for the first time, and Shannon shared some thoughts but also spent plenty of time looking at Mom and Dad to see how we were reacting and protecting us a little, no doubt. We will meet with her weekly and separately, which hopefully will give Shannon an outlet. Up to this point, Shannon has had such grace and composure through this all. I want to scream and swear and complain, and she keeps it together almost all the time. As my dear friend tells me, our kids are always showing us how to live ...

The next appointment was a first-time meeting with the surgeon, Dr. Wetjen. Despite my joke about surgeons (sorry to any of you out there reading this), Dr. Wetjen was actually very nice! But, his news was sobering, even if we had heard it before. No need to biopsy, we know what it is and it's a bad tumor in a bad place. If there was a clinical trial somewhere that gave us a better chance, he would send us, but there isn't. For the first time the thought of coming up with a Make-a-Wish idea was addressed. I ... can't ... go ... there ... yet.

Lunchtime was spent haggling with the insurance companies to get prescriptions approved so that treatment could start today. Taking the chemotherapy pill is supposed to coincide with the radiation. I'll spare you the nuts and bolts of it, but tracking down doctors to rewrite prescriptions was no easy task. In the end, the Mayo Pharmacy made it happen, hallelujah! At 3:30, Shannon was off to her first radiation treatment. One of the hockey moms who works in the radiation oncology department was there to walk Shannon through it and put her at ease. I am so grateful for people's kindness. This is a woman whose daughter has never been on Shannon's team. I knew of her daughter, but had never met the woman before Tuesday. Now, here she is answering any questions we have and being with Shannon as if she were her own child. Unbelievable.

By the time we got home, Grandma had handled getting Erin on and off the school bus, made an after-school snack, and helped with homework (except for that pesky fifth grade math that was a little beyond Grandma). Each of the next five Thursdays will look something like today with weekly check-ins with each team of doctors, the social worker, blood work, and still the daily radiation.

Tonight Shannon was absolutely exhausted, but she did share this funny story: When they made her radiation mask on Tuesday, she was smiling. So now, in order to make the mask fit effectively, she needs to smile through forty-two radiation treatments!

We enjoyed a great drop-off dinner by some hockey friends, the Pankows, and we are trying to get our arms around accepting this kind of help. Our friend Ellen Wente is managing this for us. The "new normal" includes letting other people decide what's for dinner.

Now that we have this blog up and running and are ready to share, it's going to be kind of boring for the next few days, we hope. Dan and I both need to find a way to work a little and sleep a little. Shannon will go to school for four hours a day, head to radiation, and then if she's feeling up to it, off to golf practice. Erin is gearing up for the Fireballs first soccer game on Saturday.

The world spins madly on …

POSTED BY JEN

GOOD FRIDAY
Isn't Easter all about The Miracle?
POSTED BY DAN

FRIDAY, APRIL 22, 2011

A quick note about our first day of the "new normal" schedule. It went off without a hitch, except for Mother Nature cutting golf practice short. I'll add her to the list of things out of our control.

My goodness, Shannon is strong willed (some might call her stubborn). She needed to get to school early so she could "get on the same page" with her teachers—her words, not mine. The teachers are encouraging her to cut herself some slack. She wants to do things by the book and complete all her assignments. Hmm, I wonder where she gets that … it must be from her dad.

We received nice notes from both girls' teachers and administrators today just making sure the lines of communication remain open as we go forward and that our kids' needs are being met. So grateful for that support.

Dan and I got both girls off to school, and then he managed to clean up our kitchen for the first time since people started bringing goodies to us last Saturday. Trust me, that was quite an accomplishment. It's the small things … ·

Shannon completed her now truncated school day at 12:35, including taking three separate medications at school, and we were off for day two of radiation. She already has the hang of it: check in, get your beeper, it buzzes, you go back. Put your iPod on their dock, get locked into place on the table in your mask, listen to three songs or so, and it's over. If you twitch or wiggle, the GPS makes the table adjust slightly so the radiation beam is hitting the tumor. Grab your stuff, stop at the scheduling desk, and find out what time your appointment is on the next weekday. Routine …

So, that's the "new normal," at least until further notice. Tonight, we enjoyed a short visit with some family offering support to Dan and me and company for the girls, and then it was time to call it a day. Shannon was tired tonight and her stomach unsettled. Lots of chemicals being pumped into that little body now. Perhaps the first inkling of what's ahead …

No profound thoughts from me tonight, just the facts. Time to try for some sleep. Erin's soccer team kicks off the season tomorrow at 8:30 A.M. Go Fireballs!

POSTED BY JEN

SATURDAY, APRIL 23, 2011

I'm really struggling today. With acceptance, with the April from hell, with Charter for not having the pay-per-view title we want. Just not feeling the strength I had earlier this week when I knew our fight was going to require tons of it. Our "new normal" pisses me off.

Shannon is getting an early taste of the "discomfort" the drugs and radiation will require her to endure for the next six weeks. Her stomach has really been bugging her, especially later in the day. She thinks she can feel the drugs working behind her eyeballs. Brother Tim, his wife, Suzie, and their kids, Maggie and Sean, were with us Friday night surfing around between NHL and NBA playoff games. Even the Twins rainout pissed me off since our night was built around eating pizza and watching the Twins. But listening to Shannon talk smack with cousin Sean is worth the price of admission. Seanny likes his NBA. Shannon likes hockey players. Funny stuff.

This morning the Fireballs lost 4–3. A really good building block experience for the squad. We need to work on throw-ins and corner kicks, for sure. The fifth graders had fun. But the field was soaked, and it was forty-two degrees and drizzly and someone … someone … anyone, please make the sun shine. I need to feel it on my face and find strength.

Shannon and I slept in our big bed together last night—she was beat. We both were out by 9:30. At 5:00 A.M., I awoke and she was awake. We had a good talk about the pain and the anger and the sadness, and that it's OK to let it go every once in awhile. And we did. She was just full of chatter. She felt great and had energy and was craving an Egg McMuffin from McDonald's. I think she wants to get up and get after it before taking the chemo that creates the feelings inside her that are unfamiliar and uncomfortable. So my sense is that our days will start early. I am in.

Shannon and Grandma watched Erin's game from the sidelines in about ten layers of clothes and blankets and that also pissed me off. So we are canceling our tee time at Soldiers Field to play a practice round on the front nine where Shannon will play a JV match for the Mayo girls golf team Tuesday. Oh well.

iPod to the rescue again. Cat Stevens, "Can't Keep It In." Perfect. *"I'm up for your love, love heats my blood."*

Tomorrow is Easter.

POSTED BY DAN

EASTER MORNING

Shannon is up and at 'em early again today. We had a good night last night. Erin went to her friend Emily's to dye Easter eggs and giggle. Shannon went to the rink to play hockey. For the first time since her diagnosis, she was just there to skate and play. Everybody knows now, so there's nothing new to say until something changes. And she scored. Backhand, five hole ...

Dinner at John Hardy's Barbecue, then home to lie on the couch and watch the Bruins/Canadiens game. Same as it ever was.

Everyone slept hard. OK, everyone except me. I realized late last night that for the first time since I became a mother, I didn't prepare Easter baskets for my girls. The Easter Bunny gagged. But, as my friend told me on the phone last night, I better cut myself some slack on that one. So I will.

Happy Easter, everyone.

POSTED BY JEN

MONDAY, APRIL 25, 2011

4:20 A.M. ... time for more blog therapy.

As painful as Palm Sunday was, Easter Sunday at St. John the Evangelist was wonderful. On Palm Sunday, none of us could stop crying, but Easter was incredibly uplifting and the Kleenex stayed in pocket. Fr. Mahon's homily was just what I needed to hear; people in pews everywhere have stuff, but Easter is the story of hope right NOW. We were asked if we would want to present the gifts, and Shannon said sure. I think we are pretty much committed at this point to publicly fighting this battle.

That is a source of tremendous conflict for Jen and me. Ten days into Shannon's devastating diagnosis we are still working through so many issues and emotions. How could we be parading these out in front of our world? I don't know. But I will tell you that so many of our friends—and especially family—are telling us to keep it up because it is working for them. And I know most of the time it is working for us too.

My iPod mood this morning is old school. The genius setting is finding classics: Carole King, Cat, James Taylor, Billy Joel, Tracy Chapman, old Elton John ... *"Harmony and me, we're pretty good company ..."*

Shannon's golf coach, Mr. Myhro, called to tell us the media is on Shannon's story. Someone called the KTTC tip line. Oh jeez. Mr. Myhro seems to feel Shannon's Mayo teammates are good with this—I think he is being really nice. I am super sensitive about this. I called my old friend Chuck Sibley—the greatest photog in the history of TV news—and shared our concerns and discomfort. In my opinion, if Shannon's story making the air creates even a single resentment or distraction, it's the wrong thing to do.

Shannon is in Mayo's JV line-up again for Tuesday's triangular with Lourdes and JM. KTTC wants video. Shannon just wants to play and experience the competition. KTTC has a morning show at five, six, nine, and ten and a website and an assignment editor (do they have one of those anymore?) facing tremendous pressure to get human-interest stories on the air. Live, local ... blah, blah, blah. I do get it.

Then we asked Shannon about it. She surprised me when she expressed a desire to share her story. We need to revisit this later today when she is in a different mood to be certain. Here is this confident, beautiful little person loaded with personality and she thinks she might want to tell her story. If her story lifts the spirit of one person—or one sick kid—it's the right thing to do. As a parent, I am really torn. As a sports fan, a viewer, an adult male age eighteen to fifty, I would watch.

Van Morrison, "Days Like This." (I swear these songs keep coming up exactly when I need to hear them.)

Here's what I conclude now that I've blogged it out: While Shannon is healthy, strong, and capable of expressing herself, why not? I want everyone to know her like we do. However, sounds like Mother Nature may take care of the issue for us: rain, heavy rain is predicted for Tuesday.

Brother Mike and Connie hosted the O'Haras and the Harkins for Easter. There were cousins and aunts and uncles everywhere. Ham, turkey, salads, potatoes, carrot cake and pastries from Daube's courtesy of brother Pat from Arizona … a feast … a celebration! Erin had a great time. Shannon had a great time. Jen had a great time. I had a great time … then I got kinda sad. At home later we grilled and decorated our cooler for the meal-droppers, and we laughed and I felt better. We went for a bike ride and—oh yeah, baby—we ate ice cream. Lent is over!

Being surrounded by family just feels so right at this time. But love hurts, and that's when I get sad. Just for a minute though. Then I have to buck-up because Shannon ain't got time to bleed!

OK, I gotta do some work this week. I need to run to Indianapolis for some meetings, Jen has hours to cover at the RAC, and for the first time chemo and radiation treatments will pound on Shannon for five days in a row. The Fireballs will need to have productive practices.

Life goes on. It has to. We're just getting started …

POSTED BY DAN

PROTECTING MY YOUNG

Who knew I would not only be Shannon's mother, but also her publicist? At this time, there will be no story on KTTC. No story in the *Post-Bulletin* either. Not now, not yet. In a year, hopefully Shannon is still on the Mayo girls golf team and the support from her teammates has helped her to persevere, and then maybe there's a story to tell. For all of us. But, playing in a JV match tomorrow is a personal gift from Coach Myhro and his team to Shannon to lift her spirits. And she is excited and it is bringing her joy. Now, about that weather forecast …

My dad arrived today. He drove a car back from his home in Nevada so he and my mom will have their own wheels from here on out. Over sixteen hundred miles in two and a half days. Next on the agenda is finding them a temporary Rochester home. They lived here until four years ago when they retired out west. Now they can't imagine not being here. And we need them.

I've lived in Rochester my entire life (except for the college years), and I've never needed the Mayo Clinic. Sure, my mom worked as a nurse, so it helped pay the bills in our house. And sure, we delivered our babies at Methodist and treated our ear infections and strep throats through the Family Medicine department, but we never needed it. How different would our lives be if we had to uproot everything to pursue this kind of treatment? As we walk the halls at the clinic, we see people from all over. And here we are, living in our own house, shopping at our familiar grocery store, going to our jobs. (Yes, I actually managed to teach tennis for a whole ninety minutes today!) Shannon goes to school, gets picked up at 12:35 P.M. and is done with radiation and home by 1:30 P.M. Not every kid being treated at Mayo has that. For that, we are grateful.

Another great meal appeared at our door tonight. Grateful for that too.

A few people have asked us to continue to share our musical selections. On this Monday, I've gone with an all Jack Johnson playlist. Today's favorite for me: "All at Once."

All at once, the world can overwhelm me
There's almost nothin' that you could tell me
That could ease my mind
Which way will you run
When it's always all around you
And the feelin' lost and found you again
A feelin' that we have no control

POSTED BY JEN

Shannon the Cannon

Over the course of our journey, this nickname would become well known by all our friends and followers. Shannon's buddies had bracelets made using it, and we put it on t-shirts to wear in support of her. Shannon would often comment that it was a little awkward for her to pass someone in the hall at school who was wearing a t-shirt with her name on it! For the most part, though, she took it all in stride. She certainly wasn't seeking the attention, but she appreciated the support.

The nickname—Shannon the Cannon—started in jest, early in Shannon's hockey career. Shannon was always small for her age, and her ability to shoot the hockey puck was anything but cannon-like! But, Shannon could score. She played smart and had a knack for seeing the play and being in the right place at the right time. While other girls who were bigger and stronger could really fire the puck, we'd tease Shannon about scoring cheesy goals on tip-ins and rebounds. Shannon would remind us that they all count the same, and they all help your team win.

Fair enough. Shannon the Cannon it is …

TUESDAY, APRIL 26, 2011

Shannon is just this life force right now—brightening up people's days all around Desk R at the Charlton Building. They love her! Grandma and Papa tagged along to treatment today. Oh wait, Shannon told me she doesn't like the word "treatment." She prefers we call it "healing" instead. So, Grandma and Papa tagged along to healing today and met the team that is working with Shannon every day. They saw the room where the radiation is delivered and even the radiation mask with the built in smile. They also met Shanan the Scheduler who said with great enthusiasm, "It's Shannon the Cannon!"

We consulted with Dr. Laack briefly today, and Shannon explained some of the symptoms that are causing her sleepless nights and early mornings. We are going to taper off the steroids a bit these next three days before our next appointment with Dr. Laack and see if that helps.

The golf meet was canceled again by crummy weather. Coach Myhro plans to give Shannon the opportunity to play next Tuesday now. I'm hoping it works out one of these times!

Dan managed to get on an airplane and go to work this morning. As we've said here before, life must go on. I am hoping his day is full of activity and his mind is busy and not wandering to thoughts of "missing out" on the "healing" here at home.

I'm also hoping today is a better day for Erin. She was sad yesterday. She is caught in this tornado that is our life right now, and she has even less control over what is going on than the rest of us. So, I'm hoping she comes home this afternoon and reports a normal day at school.

I seem to be doing a lot of hoping today … hope is good …

POSTED BY JEN

WEDNESDAY AFTERNOON, APRIL 27, 2011

Good morning from the home of the Indy 500, the Indianapolis Colts, the Butler Bulldogs, and the world-famous Indy O'Haras.

I need to take a second this morning to share about my employment situation. What kind of a company would send a sad dad on the road, away from his wounded and healing family? I just want to make it clear that my mini-trip to Indianapolis was my call alone. In fact, my manager and the big boss have told me to do what I have to do for my girls. If that means working from home, not working at all, or traveling as needed, whatever.

Add the good folks at EFS Transportation Services, Memphis, Tennessee, to the growing list of amazing blessings in the lives of Erin, Shannon, Jen, and Dan O'Hara.

About six weeks ago I was working in Indiana and added a couple new opportunities to my pipeline that required at least one more face-to-face meeting. These are the kinds of opportunities that will keep a sales guy's direct deposit hitting on the fifteenth and thirtieth. So, that's why I am out here this week. The airfare was booked and the appointments are set weeks in advance.

That's how it works for a sales guy: you make a connection and you pursue the connection until it dries up. If I've learned anything over my twelve years in sales, it's that relationships sell deals. Relationships are really hard to establish and grow if you are in the fetal position in the corner of your home office. So I'm out here selling. Just a couple really meaty appointments. My cold calls and prospecting can wait. I'm pretty sure I will not be out selling every week while Shannon is in treatment ... or healing.

Van Morrison, "Golden Autumn Day" ... *"And I'm pretending that it's paradise, on a golden autumn day ..."*

So I will be back on the ground in Rochester today by about 3:00 P.M. central—plenty of time for the Fireballs practice! The girls barely missed me. I saw in the forecast that Shannon's golf meet was going to be rained out again because spring is MIA, so I made my trip. But that's about to change. I sense it. Jet stream a changin'. It's comin' people!

So, I just wanted to tell you about my work situation, which is really great. I'm out here for a quick trip because that is what I do and that is what my family needs me to do. Plus, I think I might have actually sold something this week!

I checked-in to my hotel last night and took a visit from several of my Indy-O cousins and I was able to be with family. That was great. Of course, they are just crushed by our news. We are big family people, us O'Haras. Big, giant hearts, hell we cry at a good Alpo commercial. The Indy O's are a family of eleven kids ... I am the baby of nine ... you get the picture. Our other O'Hara cousins are part of a family of thirteen kids. Family reunions are held at major venues.

Speaking of, my mom and dad return to Minneapolis from Ireland tonight. They will hear about Shannon's tumor for the first time at around 8:00 P.M. Pray for Ed and Tess to have strength.

POSTED BY DAN

TEMPORARY HOUSING SECURED!

I am compelled to jump on here and post so that people know that my parents are all set on the housing front. Since I posted that they were looking for a place to live, we've had six different offers to help! People are so kind. Grandma and Papa's old neighbors arranged a housing option that is ideal. OK, as ideal as it can be in this situation. As I write, they are already moving into their new "summer vacation home"—an empty townhome on their old street just across the golf course from us. Just a short walk or bike ride away … that is, if it ever stops raining! Thanks to all of you who offered to help.

POSTED BY JEN

WEDNESDAY, APRIL 27, 2011—EVENING

As Shannon's friend Samantha would say, people's generosity is AH-MAY-ZIN. All this support gives us strength and makes us want to continue this journey with as much grace as we can muster.

But, there are moments when grace is hard to come by. Even the perpetually smiling Shannon has her moments. Last night, Shannon's mind wandered to the what if: What if I lose my coordination? What if it gets harder to be a good student? What if this is the best I ever feel again? Her tears came, and I didn't have any answers. And I'm usually in charge of having all the answers—just ask my husband!

This morning Shannon said it felt good to cry, but it feels better to smile and laugh with her friends. She had a "new normal" day of school, healing, and golf practice. Tonight another wonderful meal was delivered and then some time watching the Twins and playoff hockey. We're in good spirits tonight.

Dan's parents arrived safely back in Minnesota. Dan had a brief conversation with them, and they are exhausted from their trip and shocked about Shannon. After such a long day, it was hard for them to verbalize their emotions over the phone. Hopefully we'll find a way to get together with them in the next few days.

Tomorrow is the weekly day of appointments. Erin is going to join us so she can put some faces with names when we talk about Dr. So-and-so, Charlton Desk R, etc … This is her fight, too.

On the agenda for Thursday: weekly blood draw, weekly hematology/oncology appointment, an hour with the social worker, daily radiation, and our weekly radiation/oncology appointment. Also, we have two additional appointments tomorrow. Once a month, Shannon will do an infusion therapy to protect her lungs from infection/pneumonia because the immune system is compromised by the chemo. We also have a one-time appointment with a Radiation Oncology Educator to give us information about managing side effects of the radiation.

So, by my count, we have appointments at: 8:00, 8:30, 9:30, 10:00, 1:00, 1:30, and 2:30. Erin's going to wish she had just gone to school instead!

Week two, here we come.

POSTED BY JEN

THURSDAY, APRIL 28, 2011

Just back from our Thursday Mayo day with Shannon. Today's special guest was Erin O'Hara! It was great to have her along for our appointments with Shannon's team. It is a bit draining to go from appointment to appointment to appointment. But, Shannon would rather pack them into one day and keep the rest of the week more normal with only a radiation/healing session to manage between school and golf.

Shannon is going along nicely considering she has a brain tumor. Her neurological exams were strong, her blood work was holding solid, very few side effects so far from chemo and radiation, and she even gained a few pounds, which made us all laugh. Basically, we are eating dessert with every meal. "Yes, I will have the poached eggs with some hash browns and fruit and how about an ice cream pie, thank you." It's unreal. You people are killin' us. Keep it up!

We continue to be grateful for many of the blessings in our lives. We talked about that with our social worker today; one of the ways to transition into restful sleep at night and stay stuck in the present is to end the day by recollecting what made us happy today. I like that.

OK, to all of our friends and family who enjoy the music of our lives, I need to insist you add the Jason Mraz record *We Sing We Dance We Steal Things* to your collection. The song "Live High" represents so much good to me right now; it's all about gratitude. I've played it about fifty times this week. *"Live high, live mighty, live righteously … takin' it easy …"*

POSTED BY DAN

FRIDAY, APRIL 29, 2011

I was a bit agitated today. Overall, things went fine—Shannon went to school, Erin went to school, Dan worked, I worked, but today was just hard. People irritated me. Things irritated me. I'm sad and mad at the same time.

Shannon is really processing what she's feeling and she's being more honest about what she wants—and what she doesn't. When the day starts with a conversation on the way to school where your twelve-year-old tells you she doesn't want to end up in a hospital bed, that she wants to pursue treatment but not at the expense of quality of life, that she wants to have the ability to do the things she loves until the day she dies, well, maybe that's why I am sad and mad today. There are so many questions about what's ahead for her and us, and there are no answers. It must play out over time. Tough, tough stuff …

A group of Shannon's friends had rubber bracelets made (think Livestrong). They are lime green—Shannon's favorite color—and they say "Shannon the Cannon" on one side, and "Fight Like A Girl" on the other. A pretty cool gesture of support and we are all sporting them proudly. Shannon was going to bring one for each of her buddies at her lunch table, but by the time she saw them, each of them was already wearing one!

Shannon came home early from school today with a little nausea, but it was easily fixed by getting something in her stomach. We joked about her snacking her way through the day to keep her tummy settled. Before she jumps in the car to head somewhere, she stops at the pantry first!

Healing went well—we were in and out in fifteen minutes flat today. Not too much chitchat, as everyone wanted to get on with things and get out and enjoy the sunshine. In the afternoon, Shannon, Dan, and

Papa enjoyed the nice weather by getting out on the golf course and playing a few holes.

There will be days like today. I just have to accept that. This journey is hard and overwhelming and sometimes we struggle. But, sometimes we have enough strength to buoy the others. We take turns protecting. We take turns having perspective. Sometimes it's me, sometimes it's Dan, sometimes it's Erin, and often it's Shannon. It wasn't my turn today, but tomorrow is another chance to get it right.

POSTED BY JEN

SUNDAY, MAY 1, 2011

We were on a beautiful spot on our earth last night celebrating with our friends the Anglins who own a farm cut through a river valley in Fillmore County. The clouds cleared right around happy hour, and I promised everyone high pressure was going to be in charge for the next five days or so: sunshine, good times, and the damp cold days of April were behind us. Now this morning we awaken to window shaking gusts, low clouds, and thirty-five degrees. God grant me the serenity to accept the things I cannot change....

We are working our butts off to find strength and silver linings and keep the smiles rolling. In truth, the girls don't afford us much room to whine.

Erin's Fireballs kept smiling and laughing through a 4–1 beat down in a driving rainstorm. That was how our Saturday began. The only whining came from the coaches. The good news is that pictures were postponed and our next four games don't start until 10:00 A.M.!!!

The other good news is that Shannon and Grandma and Papa made no attempt to spectate. Instead they enjoyed breakfast and Wi-Fi at McDonald's. Shannon's appetite continues to be off the charts. Her Egg McMuffin "tradition" with Grandma on Fireball game days just might carry us all the way through healing season.

After a hot shower it was Erin's turn with Grandma and Papa; they loaded up the Mustang and headed for Shakopee where E was able to separate and enjoy some Harkins cousin-time. Erin and her cousin

Laurynn Harkins have a serious connection (OK, not serious … in fact mostly super silly). But a sister-from-another-mother kind of relationship that we are truly grateful for.

That freed up me and Jen to visit with friends while Shannon played hockey. Shannon's teammates continue to go out of their way to set her up in these spring games. She lit the lamp twice Saturday; tried not to celebrate like Ovechkin, but her smile was clearly visible from the top row of Graham Arena's rink four. Olivia, Allison, and Maddie seem like they are having fun spreading the puck around, and Shannon is quite comfortable camping in front of the net looking for cheesy deflections and juicy rebounds. Fun stuff. As for Shannon's back-checking … we won't go there … the kid has a brain tumor … cut her some slack.

After the game we ate slices at Mr. Pizza with the Pankows, Grafstroms, and Leqves, families that have been along for so many of Shannon's happiest moments over the past several years. Shannon always loved sports, but when she started playing hockey three years ago she blossomed as a person and a personality.

Our challenge continues to be enjoying life without getting sucked into a vacuum of what is to come. The happier the moments are, the harder it gets to stay in them. At the Anglin farm down by Spring Valley we hiked, rode mini-bikes, chowed down on soup and hot dogs, burned a fire, and laughed a lot. We have been introduced to a highly efficient, s'more hybrid that I think is the future. You place your roasted marshmallow between two Keebler Fudge Stripes. Change is possible.

By the end of the night Shannon struggled to stay comfortable. She was exhausted but never wanted any of us to see it. Jen and I can tell. So the ride home was kind of a downer because the kid was just cashed and telling us about tightness in her lungs and rib cage. That's how it goes. Shannon's challenge will be finding acceptance that her body can't rock like her mind thinks it should. We're ten days into the forty-two days of healing.

Today Erin comes home (YEAH) and we are going to see Grandma and Grandpa O'Hara at brother Mike's. More family time … it's all good!

POSTED BY DAN

DC RACE FOR HOPE

Just a quick Monday morning shout out to Shannon's D.C.-based family: Cousin Kevin and his fiancée, Meaghan; Cousin Brendan and his girlfriend, Hannah; and Cousin Charlie and Aunt Bridgid (who flew in from Minnesota). This gang took part in The Race for Hope yesterday to raise money and awareness for brain tumor research. They were "Sprinting for Shannon." Very cool.

Dan and his brother Tim plan to run the Med City half marathon here in Rochester Memorial Day weekend with a similar mission. (Anyone else out there planning to run Med City, let us know, and we'll include you in a potential shirt order ... still investigating ...)

We are hoping to get some help/relief from Dr. Laack or the nurse practitioner, Denise, today as Shannon's side effects have started to make her more uncomfortable. She really is focused on feeling good enough to play in the golf meet tomorrow, so that's our goal this first part of the week.

Anger reared its ugly head last night around here, from all four of us and in different ways. We're mad as hell. But, we're in the midst of the daily grind of fighting, and we need to fire up and find the strength to continue. More later ...

POSTED BY JEN

MONDAY, MAY 2, 2011

Well, so much for the "new normal." Today was anything but ... Shannon did go off to school, although she was still feeling uncomfortable with an ache in her lungs and some other issues which she prefers I not discuss here (think prune juice). We called radiation oncology to find out what we should do, and our nurse practitioner, Denise, fit us in for an 11:45 appointment. After hearing Shannon's symptoms, a CT scan of the lungs was required. We learned today that Shannon's tumor type will sometimes throw off blood clots that can settle in the lungs, heart, or brain. News that we might have a new problem to deal with was a bit hard to take. Denise comforted us with kind words and told us to stay strong and get through this episode. We would have results this afternoon and, if necessary, add a blood thinner to Shannon's drug regimen to alleviate the clots.

Shannon had her daily healing and then it was off to St. Mary's to have the CT scan. An IV was placed in her arm so that contrast dye could be used. The nurse explained that when the contrast dye goes in, it feels like a hot flash and then you have the sensation that you peed yourself. What a bonus! Shannon made it through just fine, and Dan and I only cried a little bit.

Denise called us just a couple of hours later to let us know that the scan was negative—no blood clot. Shannon's aches are most likely the result of fatigue and the medications taking their toll. Just a bump in the road and we should expect those along the way. Listening to her body and recognizing when she's tired is a new skill that Shannon must acquire quickly.

By the time we reached after-school hours, we were all too exhausted to complete what should have been the rest of our day. No work for me, no golf or hockey for Shannon, and no Fireball practice for Dan and Erin. We opted for staying at home and enjoying a Mexican feast that was delivered by our friend Shelly. Grandma Gwen joined us and so did Uncle Mike and Aunt Connie. We were teasing Mike that he seems to be so willing to spend time with us now, especially on Mondays, Wednesdays, and Fridays when meals are delivered!

Dan and I discussed today that we have moved from the shocked phase to the angry phase. Anger might not be productive, but it's real. We're mad that Shannon's not feeling well; mad that she has to curb her activity level; mad that we had a bump in the road today; mad that Erin feels like she's second fiddle; mad that the sun won't shine ...

This journey is so all consuming for us right now that we are out of touch with the events happening around the world. I can't discuss what Kate's dress looked like or talk about the intel that brought down Bin Laden, but I can tell you about the side effects of Temodar and Decadron, or direct you to the most convenient spots in the Mayo patient parking ramps! We have to laugh a little or we'd cry all the time.

So, we'll get up tomorrow and start again, hoping for smooth sailing, no bumps in the road, and a little sunshine ...

POSTED BY JEN

Community

Dan and I met when I was in college studying broadcast journalism, and he was the sports director at the local TV station here in my hometown. I needed an internship for some experience and inquired if they could use my help. The rest, as they say, is history. Dan likes to jokingly tell people I was his Monica Lewinsky. Trust me, it was less tawdry than that. And I don't wear dresses.

So Rochester, Minnesota, has been home for us. We knew that we knew people, but we had no idea how intertwined we had become with this town. I taught school and tennis to thousands of kids and adults over the years, and Dan was a recognizable face to anyone who kept up on the local sports scene.

Rochester, Minnesota, is dominated by the Mayo Clinic. It is a world-class medical facility, and in our town of 100,000 people, 30,000 are employed there. Needless to say, with daily visits to the downtown campus, we inevitably ran into someone we knew, almost on a daily basis.

As we carried on through the radiation phase with Shannon, people provided us with meals three days a week and emotional support more often than that. Cards and emails were coming in, and everywhere we went, people wanted to stop us and wish us well.

Part of it was because we were now sharing our journey so publicly through the blog. Word of mouth was letting more and more people know about our online journal, and people who were more loosely connected to us started to follow along. Encouragement came to keep writing, so we did.

Another part of it was Shannon's attitude of continuing to live life, and laugh and smile her way through it. Everybody wants to help a kid like that. Even the high school golf team that Shannon had been a part of for all of two weeks before she was diagnosed wanted to help. Most of the girls on the team had no idea who Shannon was until she became "the girl with the brain tumor." That may have been Shannon's "in" with the upperclassmen, but they came to love her for her attitude and her determination. She was receiving radiation treatments every day, and still showed up for practice with a smile on her face, willing to work and improve. She just wanted to be a part of the team like everyone else. And they loved her for it.

TUESDAY, MAY 3, 2011

A remarkable day in a remarkable journey. The ups and downs of this deal are just exhausting!

Tonight's exhaustion: the result of a giant up. Shannon was able to compete in a high school golf meet. And she competed like a normal JV player shooting a 65 in her nine-hole match on Eastwood Golf Club's front nine. She finished ninth out of sixteen golfers entered in the JV meet. As a team, Mayo's JV shot a season-best of 206. The Spartan Varsity shot a season-best of 349. Those are really good scores folks! Heck, two girls in the varsity meet carded eighteen-hole scores of 73! So for a kid that loves sports—a family that loves sports—it was just a thrill to be a part of. Jen and I were nervous wrecks, but Shannon continues to amaze and come through in the clutch.

It's difficult to put into words how grateful we are for the opportunity Coach Myhro and an incredibly unselfish roster of Spartan golfers gave this family. Love and thanks. Those two words will have to do.

After a celebratory dinner we returned home to watch Frankie Liriano finish off a no-hitter vs. the hated White Sox. Shannon was so excited about that we could hardly get her to sleep. Us too. It's amazing what a little sunshine can do for ya!

POSTED BY DAN

Chip shot | Taking part in the junior varsity golf meet vs. Mankato West and Rochester Century

One of the gang | Rochester Mayo High School Girls Golf Team 2011 *(Shannon front row, left)*

FRIDAY, MAY 6, 2011

Another busy Thursday is behind us and no news is good news. Shannon's blood counts stayed the same, her neuro exam showed no decline in strength or coordination, and her side effects are being managed. She can continue to do whatever she feels up to doing.

We had a couple of friends who have known Shannon her whole life get a chance to see her this week and they were astounded. If you didn't know her diagnosis, you would never believe it. Sometimes I still can't believe it. She looks "normal." The only noticeable change is the acne on her face caused by all the chemicals being pumped into her body. While acne is new for Shannon, she's not the only seventh grade girl out there with pimples on her face! Shannon has completed the first third of her forty-two-day treatment plan, and we are all impressed with her determination and spirit. We have our moments, but we are doing the best we can each day.

Erin carried on with fifth grade life this week: completing the MCA standardized tests, doing the mile run each morning, and goofing around on the bus with her pals. It was Erin's friend Emily's birthday this week, and we did our best to embarrass Erin by holding up signs at the bus stop and dancing in honor of Emily. Emily thought we were funny. Erin, not so much …

The weekend is here. Fireballs are on the pitch tomorrow at 10:00 A.M.

My iPod is trending toward songs about love this week. Check out: Adele, "Make You Feel My Love"; Adrianne, "10,000 Stones"; and Alexi Murdoch, "Orange Sky."

POSTED BY JEN

SATURDAY, MAY 7, 2011

I'm up early this morning while the rest of the house sleeps. That's good bloggin' time for me. The iPod shuffle function is off. Just straight Bruce this morning. Looking for inspiration from *The Wild, The Innocent, and the E Street Shuffle* album in order, in its entirety. I vividly recall doing this back in high school: listening to this same record over and over on the turntable with headphones plugged into our stereo back in our Bloomington house. *"Hey, Spanish Johnny, you want to make a little easy money tonight?"*

My Friday was lined up to be a good one. Jen and I closed on a home refinance, which is a great thing for our overall financial health. I went for a quick training run. Beautiful day. And then it was off for the Spring Open at our home track, Willow Creek Golf Course, for eighteen holes of tournament fun with my good buds Opie and Cuber. I've played in this event for a bunch of years in a row. The field includes a familiar group of old IBM'ers and random connections to many phases of my life. Traditionally, the Spring Open is one of the favorite events of my golf season.

But Friday I just couldn't flush it all away and leave my troubles behind. I thought I could, but I couldn't. And the boys were great; in fact, there were man-hugs all over the place for me. Mostly guys don't want to talk about real-world stuff, but my guys were in tune with the big stuff going on in my life. And I just sucked. I hate my new driver. I can't pronate and everything is a weak fade right. Concentration is not in my bag at this time. Mostly, I just wanted to be with my girls.

So that's kind of disappointing. I know I am going to need to find happiness in the things I know I like to do. I'm just not there. And my fear is that the invites to do fun stuff will dry up … especially if I suck.

Jen taught tennis at the RAC and came home to report that she too struggled Friday. And she loves to teach tennis and be around the kids. Somehow we need to work through this. We will. Just taking some time to settle into our "new normal."

Grandma helped out again to get Erin off the school bus and Shannon came home from golf practice at about the same time as I got home from the Spring Open. But then I was grumpy. Even the Twins shelling Tim Wakefield and the Red Sox didn't help much.

Erin and I had a talk in the backyard about our new life and it was tough. She has a lot on her mind. I told her that Aunt Suzie and cousin Maggie are coming to see the Fireballs play Saturday. Erin told me she knows they are coming to see Shannon. I told her no; they were coming to see her play soccer, which they are.

On Friday nights, Shannon and E used to always get caught up on DVR'ed shows they had recorded during the week. I told Shannon that Erin would still like doing that with her, and we left the girls to figure it out. Jen was tired. I made a couple phone calls in our office.

I later went down to find the girls had made a bed with sleeping bags on the floor, GLC blaring on the TV (GLC is family code for *Good Luck Charlie*, a very funny Disney series we like to watch together). So that's where they slept. Just like back in the day.

Saturday we have Fireball action. A 10:00 A.M. kick-off gives us some morning time together without having to rush out the door. That's nice. We like to sit around in the mornings together ... cook a big breakfast ... just chill. The smell of coffee and bacon fills the house.

Then Saturday gets busy, as the girls will head north with Grandma up to cousin Laurynn's dance recital. Jen and I will go see my folks in Edina and then we will connect later at Uncle Eric's in Shakopee. I have to be honest, I don't like being away from the girls for very long. Maybe that's my problem on the golf course.

Speaking of golf, I just clicked over to see that Seve Ballesteros finally lost his battle. I knew he was really sick ... I did not know he was fighting a brain tumor ... hits me like a heavy punch to the gut ...

POSTED BY DAN

MOTHER'S DAY

Saturday is a day we can mark down in the good column. It was our first soccer game of the season that didn't require a parka or a raincoat. Erin scored a goal, and the Fireballs soccer squad got their first win of the season.

A group of fans was there to cheer for Erin: Shannon and Grandma H., Aunt Suzie and Cousin Maggie, and even Erin's teacher came by to check in on her. A good day for the E and some reassurance that people are looking out for her too.

We accomplished the rest of what we had planned: the girls and Grandma and Papa attended Cousin Laurynn's dance recital while Dan and I visited with Ed and Tess and watched the Kentucky Derby.

The Fireballs | Erin O takes the field

We finished the night with a cookout at my brother's house and then headed home. Shannon felt good yesterday and enjoyed herself right up until the fatigue set in and she couldn't keep her eyes open.

Not a day goes by that we don't have at least one moment of sadness or fear or anger. Today it was reminiscing with my family about when Shannon was a baby. Any time we start thinking about life milestones, it gets tough. But that's what people do; we mark time by the stages our children go through. It's normal, it's natural, and it's just harder for us to think that way now.

But, we are learning how to just enjoy the good days. One day at a time, right? All that running around yesterday sets us up for a day at home today. Glad for that. Happy Mother's Day, everyone.

POSTED BY JEN

MONDAY, MAY 9, 2011

We are stringing together some really great days. Shannon and Erin continue to amaze us with their energy and overall enthusiasm for life. It helps that Shannon has been feeling strong even though we are working on nearly three weeks of radiation and chemo. Monday marked Shannon's thirteenth radiation healing session and nineteenth straight day rockin' the Temodar. And she played hockey again.

It also helps that we have been experiencing some really cool stuff together and that we continue to be surrounded by family and friends that seem to be enjoying every minute of us. We keep talking about blessings, but certainly the sense of appreciation for the here and now, and for so many people in our lives, has been heightened. This has been a really important adjustment we have had to make in our lives and the way we live. One day at a time.

So on Mother's Day we had a chance to meet Sheryl Crow. Our friend Cris Fischer hooked us up sweet.

Sheryl's tour came through the Mayo Civic Center in Rochester affording the girls a chance to experience their first arena concert. Live music always brings out our emotions but obviously this show had even more impact. We're going to have to plug Sheryl's new record, *100 Miles from Memphis*. A little more of a '70s funk and really soulful music. Sheryl's final set included all her classics that the girls knew; "Soak Up the Sun," "All I Wanna Do," etc. I know we have posted on this blog that so many songs and song lyrics seem to be directed at us right now (and no doubt our eyes are wide open).

Sheryl made an early comment about Rochester in the show, "The Mayo Clinic, I know it well...." Then later expanded to say she spent a lot of time here with her grandma, and Rochester will always have a sweet spot for her because of that experience. Then she closed the show with a stirring, soulful rendition of "I Shall Believe." Yepper...

POSTED BY DAN

Meet and greet with Sheryl Crow

I Shall Believe | Another one of the spiritual events in our journey

WEDNESDAY, MAY 11, 2011

My best pal Teri was here for a visit, which was wonderful. Not the best circumstances that brought her here, but I'm still grateful for the visit. You know that girlfriend in your life who already knows all your crap, so you don't have to pretend that you have everything figured out? Yep. Teri hadn't seen Shannon and Erin since they were little, so it was great to see her getting to know the people that our babies have become. During her visit, Teri and I laughed a lot, and we cried some too …

Shannon continues to feel good and continues to want to go to school, healing, and off to golf practice. While most things this week so far fall in the good column, Erin is struggling. I think she is bummed to be left out of spending time with my friend and me. Shannon has gotten that extra time as we run her to healing, home to rest, and then off to golf practice. Erin is expected to go on as she always has and complete her school day, while the rest of us have adjusted our schedules and are spending more time together. Not fair, I get that.

I know Erin got some extra TLC today from her teacher at Bamber Valley. Much needed. Erin is going to tag along on our busy appointment day tomorrow, which is good. She wants to be "in it" with us too, and if she's along, she won't miss out on a thing …

Another busy Thursday ahead. Good night.

POSTED BY JEN

FRIDAY, MAY 13, 2011

Thursday, Shannon's doctors told us the tumor is responding nicely to the first three weeks of healing. Before we could turn backflips down the halls of the sixteenth floor of the Mayo Building, we were reminded the response was predicted. In fact, about 80 percent of gliomas respond favorably to the first doses of radiation and chemo drugs like Temodar (aka temozolomide). Still, it was another great day!

Erin skipped school to be with us for our Thursday consults, which started with a full neuro work up with Dr. Keating. Dr. Keating and Dr. Kotagal were the pediatric neurologists tasked with breaking the news of our prognosis four weeks ago. Dr. Keating seemed to be enjoying today's exam as Shannon was put through the ringer starting with many of the coordination tests you might see in a roadside sobriety test and then working through reflex, hearing, eyesight, balance, and memory drills. She nailed it.

Dr. Keating shared that, "It is our job to worry, it is your job to prove us wrong and right now, Shannon, you are proving us wrong!"

The temozolomide's effect on Shannon's blood work was also predicted. And, while all her counts remain well within the "normal" range, certain numbers are trending downward. Nothing to freak out about. We knew the drops were likely. But when these white cell counts drop we have to be careful. Even catching a common cold at this time can be a bad deal. So getting solid rest, washing hands often, and practicing good nutrition become really important. Shannon insisted I wash my hands before making breakfast this morning.

Shannon also continues to taper off Decadron, the steroid she's been taking since the tumor was first discovered. From the diagnosis, the dexamethasone was effective in reducing swelling in Shannon's brain. But now the tumor is responding to the healing and the steroid will no longer be necessary. Today she will be down to just 2 mg. In another four days we'll go down to 1 mg. By the end of next week we will hopefully be able to be done with the Decadron. Of course, every action has a reaction. The steroid has clearly been a kicker to Shannon's energy levels. The combination of weaning off the steroid and the cumulative effects of the radiation and chemo could take its toll. But nothing surprises us with this kid ... these kids ... both our girls have been performing way above their pay grade.

Shannon's radiation oncologist, Dr. Laack, also gave us a good amount of time and attention Thursday. That's big stuff considering Dr. Laack's reputation as one of the best. Shannon meanwhile was looking at her watch anxious to be done with a long day at Mayo. "Got it, I'm good!" But, when doctors like Keating and Laack give you extended time ... you take it ... you come up with questions ... you show them pictures of your kids with Sheryl Crow (Dr. Laack was at the show too) ... you share and you learn. But I can tell you with 100 percent certainty that both these doctors are enjoying Shannon and our family. Even in a cramped radiation exam room in the Mayo Clinic's Charlton Building, we can find something to laugh about.

I also have to point out that halfway through our healing, the loving relationships we are forging with our support teams are incredible (Denise, Jacque, Heather, Michelle, Shanan the Scheduler, Janelle, Kelli ... on and on ...). It's hard to believe that we are going to be sad when daily healing ends, but saying goodbye to these people will be hard. It goes back to what I posted a while back: if you like my kid, I like you!

Outside, spring has sprung. Our feeders are bustling with activity. The gold finches have returned to SE Minnesota ... rose-breasted grosbeaks ... orioles ... even an indigo bunting has been spotted.

The other big news here on Willow Lane: Shannon and Erin are the proud owners of a sweet E-Z-Go electric golf cart that can shuttle them around the neighborhood. The cart's majority stockholders are Grandma and Papa Harkins, Uncle Eric, and the Shannon Fund. Jen and I get to use it too.

POSTED BY DAN

New wheels | The girls and Sunny cruising the neighborhood in our new golf cart

Eyes Wide Open

When you are faced with adversity, you become so acutely aware of the world around you. The blinders are off and you see the world and its harsh realities. But, awareness can also bring gratitude for the things that are good. And even during the radiation phase, things were pretty dang good for us. Awareness and gratitude became a theme for us, for sure.

Spending part of each afternoon at the WFMC (World Famous Mayo Clinic) was less tedious than I thought it would be. It just became routine. Shannon would finish her school day at 12:35 P.M. We would pick her up, head downtown, and make it there just in time for her 1:00 P.M. appointment. She'd be done by 1:20 P.M. and we'd be on our way home to rest. We had a keen awareness and gratitude for the fact that our lives could be so "normal" during this time. All we had to do was look around the waiting room to realize that people were coming from all over the world to receive this treatment; we were getting it right here in our own backyard.

We were, of course, aware that Shannon was going to radiation, lying on a table and having her brain tumor zapped. Some days I would feel so sad and defeated that my little girl had to go through this. Some days Dan and I would just sit there and stare at each other. Some days we still couldn't believe this was happening.

But Shannon would come bouncing out of there with a smile and say, "See you tomorrow!" as we left. Desk R employees and patients alike couldn't help but smile at this beautiful twelve-year-old girl, taking it all in stride. So, most days, we left feeling grateful. We were fighting. Those radiation beams were killing the tumor. And we were continuing to live a mostly normal life. We had gratitude for that.

We've now learned that some kids with this type of tumor don't have as good a response to radiation. For some kids with a brain stem glioma, the tumor grows aggressively even during the radiation therapy phase. Some kids lose function within the first month or two and never regain it.

Hard to believe, but Shannon was one of the lucky ones. Awareness and gratitude.

SUNDAY, MAY 15, 2011

I find myself wondering why we don't live this way all the time? Being open to people's generosity, allowing people into our lives, people sharing what they can, and making the extra effort to let someone know that you care? I know it sounds corny, but this world would be a happier place. Instead, we usually put our heads down, avert our eyes, and mind our own business.

It struck me yesterday as the Fireballs played a game in the rain in forty-five-degree temperatures. Terrible conditions, yet the sidelines were packed with people who wanted to show Erin that they care: grandparents, an aunt and uncle, old friends, basketball teammates and coaches, even kindergarten teachers who haven't had Erin as a student since 2007! None of these people were required to be there, but there they were to say "I care," and specifically, "I care about Erin." People have been following our story and they were there to show Erin some extra love. (By the way, we won 1–0 ... not that whether we win or lose is important ...)

Last night the girls hung out with their first best friends, our old neighbors Abby and Tessa. Things were the same as they ever were ... except they're not. Seeing Shannon and Erin hang with their pals made Dan and me sad. They were happy and having a great time as usual, but we felt sad. I can't completely explain it, but when we have a good day, it's bittersweet. I guess it's part of learning to appreciate each good day because the future is unknown. I've heard it said before, but the words have real meaning and evoke real emotion now that we are living it.

Today we have another opportunity to do something fun. Off to the Twins game with some sweet seats courtesy of one of my brother's co-workers, eleven rows up behind home plate. More generosity toward us. Humbling. Hopefully the sun will shine and the Twins can find a way to win.

My favorite song on my morning music mix comes from Mat Kearney, "Won't Back Down":

> I won't back down,
> I won't turn around and around,
> And I won't back down,
> Doesn't matter what comes crashing down,
> I'm still gonna stand my solid ground ...

POSTED BY JEN

MONDAY, MAY 16, 2011

Breaking down the early season challenges of our Minnesota Twins comes down to the most elementary of baseball concepts: balls and strikes. Our pitchers are throwing too many balls. Our hitters are swinging at too many balls. Twins starter Brian Duensing walked the first two batters to open the game Sunday. The game ended with Jason Kubel watching strike three cross the plate with the bases loaded. It was the third backwards K of the game for the Twins. It's all about strike-zone command and discipline. And right now our Twins have neither.

I came to that conclusion yesterday from the padded seats of the Champions Club section at Target Field. The Champions Club is basically a yacht club right behind home plate at the ballpark. The sun shined. All elements were in place for this family to have another memorable experience together. However, José Bautista and the Toronto Blue Jays spoiled the competitive aspect of the outing. Still it's really hard to get too upset about our Twins' bad start.

Sweet seats | At the Minnesota Twins baseball game

Shannon and Erin really enjoyed just relaxing together for a few hours. During batting practice we were down goofing around by the dugout and Joe Mauer smiled at the girls as he walked by. I said, "Hey Joe, what up?" Shannon elbowed me in the ribs for being a dork.

The combination of warm sunshine and really comfortable seating was just what we needed because Shannon started showing signs of fatigue from three weeks of radiation and chemotherapy.

The girls have to grind out two more solid weeks of school before the end-of-year field trips and really fun stuff kicks in. Do you remember how great that was? Remember cleaning out your desk? Erin is about to do that for the final time at Bamber Valley Elementary. What a great place that school has been for this family.

POSTED BY DAN

TUESDAY, MAY 17, 2011

This alternate reality we are living in is making it hard to be the kind of parents we're used to being. We've tried to teach our kids that when they want something, they have to work hard, be patient, and earn it. We try not to give in to instant gratification. I'm certain that we've used the line "money doesn't just grow on trees" at least once or twice.

But now when we want something, we get it. Live for today, right? This change in how we operate almost brought Shannon to tears yesterday. She's wanted a whole set of golf clubs, an upgrade from the mix and match kids set that she has been using. Before the golf season started we said, "Let's wait and see if you enjoy it, and then we'll talk." Now we run out and get them. Shannon notices the change. She looks us straight in the eye and says, "We're only getting them now because I have a brain tumor." She's right. Normally we would say "wait for your birthday" or "let's see how much you grow this year," but right now it seems ridiculous to make her wait. Shannon felt good enough to play five holes with Dan and me yesterday and another ten holes with Papa today. So of course she should have clubs that fit her and she should have them right now.

Yet, Dan and I don't want "living in the moment" to send the wrong message. There is a foreboding undertone. We need to keep remembering that living in the moment doesn't mean Shannon doesn't have a future. What the future holds for her is the great unknown. We have to keep believing, keep the faith. I hope we spend a really long time perfecting our "live for today" philosophy.

So, I find myself struggling because my most important job for the last thirteen years has been to care for my kids, teach them about the world and help them understand it, and plan ahead so we're prepared for what's coming next. What do I do now? One of them is sick and the other feels slighted. I don't know exactly how to help them draw lessons from this thing we are experiencing, and I sure as hell don't know how to prepare for what's next.

Reeling a bit, for sure. And yet, we are having an OK week. Shannon carries on with school, hockey, and golf. She took three tests today and finished a six-page creative writing assignment. She continues to amaze. Erin is doing what needs doing at school and preparing for her piano recital. Dan and I are working a little. Life goes on, albeit with a new set of golf clubs ...

POSTED BY JEN

THURSDAY, MAY 19, 2011

Some days are better than others.

Thursday started the fifth week of Shannon's healing. For me this was a tough one. And Shannon showed some signs of stress that—to this point—she has done really well to hide from us.

What bothered me the most was that I was a source of her stress. She scolded me for suggesting to members of her healing team that there was fatigue denial in play. She was pissed. And being the mature adult I am, I pouted. Then I got sad.

For the first time I got an up-close look at Shannon's hair loss as she showed Dr. Laack and our nurse practitioner, Denise. I was completely in denial about this and perhaps did not want to look hard enough to see it. Shannon has been wearing her hair straight down some days and some days—like today—pulled back in a really cute little pony with a wide headband that does a great job of covering the scorched areas around her ears. That's where for four weeks they've been pumping the highest concentrations of radiation into her perfect little skull.

And today when she pulled off her headband to show her radiation team I just lost it. And I never recovered. In the van on the way home my crying got Shannon crying. I told her I was so sorry. I was sorry that she had to go through this. I was sorry that I couldn't do anything to help her. I was sorry I couldn't keep it together all the time. I felt so helpless.

And what did Shannon do? She comforted me by telling me it's impossible to go through something like this without crying sometimes. She made it OK again. And then we went home and napped together in front of the Twins game. Kicked Oakland 11–1 ... hello, Justin Morneau!

Really, Thursday's meetings with her doctors went well. Their message is consistent: get your rest. Take it where you can get it. It's OK to nap. In fact, Shannon must nap. Especially if she wants to keep her activities going, which she does because Dr. Laack told her activity is good. And Shannon is doing anything they ask of her. Anything that helps her fight.

This week's blood work was still within the normal ranges, so Shannon gets to keep playing hockey. This weekend she's been invited to play in a tournament with a Rochester-based summer hockey team, the Ice Bucks. Our friend and the Ice Bucks coach, Bob Montrose, had given Shannon an open invite to come play this weekend. So, we'll maybe give that a shot Saturday afternoon after the Fireballs make it three-in-a-row. It's good to have goals.

Friday, Shannon has her last golf practice of the season; the Mayo High School girls will play a little nine-hole intrasquad scramble to mark the end of the JV and B-squad seasons. The varsity girls will keep playing. Watch out for the Spartans in sections!

And you know what? Everything is going to be OK. Tomorrow I will do better!

Paolo Nutini is playing now ... *"Why can't we just rewind ...?"*
POSTED BY DAN

SUNDAY, MAY 22, 2011
We all survived the Rapture yesterday, but, with the way our day started, I was having my doubts.

Here's a quick summary of Saturday morning.

While sitting at a red light on our way to the Fireballs game, we were rear-ended by a lady who was either dialing or texting on her phone. Everyone was all right, but the hatch and bumper of my van are smashed.

The Fireballs game took place on yet another rainy day. Rain started as we kicked off and continued and intensified throughout our seventy-five-minute game. At least it was a warm rain this time. The girls played hard and never complained. We tied 4–4.

Soaking wet, we hustled to the car, and the kids changed into dry clothes on the fly as we headed to Mankato for Shannon's opportunity to play hockey. We had to really hustle to get her there on time. Not exactly the kind of entrance you want to make when someone is being generous and offering you an opportunity like this. Plus, have you ever tried to get a giant hockey equipment bag out of a minivan without opening the hatch? No small feat.

After that, the day improved. The Ice Bucks played a good game against a quality opponent and lost 1–0. Shannon played hard and did just fine out there. She really pushed herself to play at this level and was tired at the end, but she did it and she enjoyed it. The girls on the team and the parents of those girls were very kind to our family and were genuinely happy for Shannon to have this opportunity. They included us in the post-game laser tag event and socializing. Even Erin got to play laser tag and hang out with some friends who are a part of this team as well.

Yet again, I found myself with this ache of sadness after a fun event. All those girls love playing hockey, and all those parents love watching their girls play hockey. Same for us. Being on the ice competing with a team might be Shannon's favorite place in the world. But, as parents chatted about who would coach what team next year, and where all these girls will go to high school, I had that queasy feeling in my stomach, and I got a little angry that we don't get to think that way anymore. Sometimes "one day at a time" pisses me off.

Despite the bumps in the road, it was a good day. The things that went wrong were really the small things: our van will get repaired, and we can't do anything about the weather. But the things that really mattered went right. Erin played hard and had fun with the Fireballs. Shannon played hard and had fun with the Ice Bucks. Our kids got to socialize and just be kids for the afternoon. As Dan and I lay down last night and recounted the events of the day, we were able to put this one in the good column ...

POSTED BY JEN

MONDAY, MAY 23, 2011

The pressure seems to be mounting as the school year and the forty-two days of healing come to a close—pretty much at the exact same time. Sandwiched in the middle of these next two weeks is a really big, busy Memorial weekend where there will be many family and friends gathering in Rochester.

I am up early Monday morning because I can feel it. I am trying to be cool about it because the kids key off my moods and attitude. Like most moms, Jen is our steady family leader: careful, cautious, organized as she hustles around Sunday nights packing lunches and backpacks, folding laundry, making sure we are good to go each and every Monday morning. I don't know about all dads, but in our house I am the emotional straw that stirs the drink. For better or for worse.

Typically, my Sunday nights and Mondays are spent organizing and attacking my work week. So that routine has always been pretty healthy around here. I manage me, Jen manages everyone else. (Come to think of it, moms are way underrated.) Like most kids, Shannon and Erin thrive on that routine, predictability and consistency. All of which has been blown out of the water over the last month.

So we tried to restore some of that as we met Sunday night as a family to talk about some goals and expectations for the upcoming week. Another "new normal" activity that we are trying out. Staying focused on the final few weeks of school is high on the list of goals. Down the stretch they come ...

Jen and I both struggled with our emotions Sunday at Erin's spring piano recital as she played a duet with her teacher Ms. Glenna; they teamed to perform Randy Newman's "You've Got a Friend in Me." The duet was supposed to be Shannon and Erin playing together. But when the tumor was discovered Shannon decided to let piano lessons go. Erin later revealed to us that she felt Shannon's piano skills were diminishing as they practiced this piece together. We now know why. Erin did great in the recital. She is about as cute as a ten-year-old can get.

Ms. Glenna honored one of her twelve-year students at the recital, a brilliant kid who will go to California to study computer science and music. We're watching him perform this amazing original piece and thinking ...

Those milestone events are just so hard for us now. And with graduation and wedding season upon us, we need to figure out a way to enjoy and celebrate these milestones as here-and-now events without reflecting.

On Thursday, Dr. Laack was talking to Shannon about recognizing her limitations and not pushing it too hard to get through finals. There are laws on the books to protect kids like Shannon and to allow her to complete finals whenever she can. Shannon, of course, is most determined to finish the school year with every other seventh grader ... taking finals ... walking out of school June 9 with hands high in the air!

Dr. Laack realized she was talking to a brick wall and conceded, "Shannon if anyone can do it, it will be you." So we're going with that. Let's go get 'em girls!

POSTED BY DAN

TUESDAY, MAY 24, 2011

How to possibly describe what has happened today ... I dealt with insurance companies and rental car companies to make some progress toward getting my van repaired. I filled out a ream of paperwork for the county and state as we cover our bases on the cost of Shannon's care. After all that, we had a bit of a cluster f*#! and, while I'll spare you the gory details, let's just say my mom had a mini public meltdown that involved sobbing. Seeing her cry made me break down. Then, seeing me cry made her snap out of it and get it together because she's my mom and that's what moms do when their kids are hurting—they suck it up and stay strong for their children. Through all this crying, believe it or not, Dan was the emotionally stable one. Steady, Eddie ... it's a brave new world everyone!

In all seriousness, all of our emotions are very close to the surface. Little "things" can seem like big things and every "thing" seems like just one more thing. Seeing my mom cry was OK for me. She's human and she's hurting, just like the rest of us.

On a more positive note, Shannon continues to power through

her days at school; just eleven days left. Dan, my mom, and I picked Shannon up today and she was full of energy and ready to tackle day number twenty-four of thirty-one at Radiation Desk R. Only seven healing sessions and eight doses of chemo to go. Jacque and Janelle were there to check in on us and had a new headband they had picked out for Shannon. She took an afternoon nap, which has become part of the daily routine, and then finished off some homework.

Erin had a good day too. It was hat day at Bamber Valley, and Erin chose the giant stovepipe hat in the green, orange, and white of the Irish flag, drawing a little attention for just being a crazy fifth grader today. Plus, no homework tonight meant a chance to tool around on the golf cart after school. She ended the day with her last piano lesson of the spring with Ms. Glenna.

Dinner tonight involved a visit from my five college tennis teammates. They all live in the Twin Cities area, and we've kept in contact in the (gulp) twenty years since I graduated from St. Thomas. (Holy crap, when did I get this old?) After the events of the day, I wasn't sure I had the energy to prop myself up for them, but here are five moms with twenty-one kids between them, finding the time and energy to deliver dinner all the way to Roch. If they could pull it off, I could too. I'm glad they came.

I found a good mix on the iPod this afternoon as I mowed the lawn and listened to some music. Today's song suggestion comes from surfer dude Donavon Frankenreiter. Check out "All Around Us." *"One day we'll all be taught, love is all we got."*

May tomorrow bring us less paperwork and fewer tears …

POSTED BY JEN

FRIDAY, MAY 27, 2011

With today's fortune cookie at lunch we unwrapped this nugget: *"Courage conquers all things; it even gives strength to the body."*

We have completed five weeks of radiation and chemotherapy in our battle against the brain stem glioma that was diagnosed on April 15. "We" is just a figure of speech, much the way the caddy of a major champion would tell the story of how "we" played a great round at the

Masters or US Open. "We" is Shannon who is showing "us" the courage to conquer all things.

Thursday's blood work looked good again. White cell counts continue to drop but have stayed within the margins of the "normal" range, which means another week of activity for Shannon without restriction. So Thursday night—of course—she played hockey.

Shannon was having a good day. Her spirit and tolerance for appointments were boosted by the chance to share lunch downtown with a school friend. She was even able to take Anna in to see where she is radiated deep in the bowels of Mayo's Charlton building. Her meeting with our social worker, Kelli, was of the hurry-up variety, "I'm not sad today, I'm not mad today … I just want to have lunch with my friend." A change in her Thursday routine made things move along nicely.

One more week of healing. Hang on, baby. I have to say that I am stunned at how well Shannon has tolerated the drugs and beams of radiation that are coursing through her body. The doctors tell us that even two weeks after treatment concludes, the Temodar and radiation are still working their magic. But it's possible that fatigue and other side effects could still impact Shannon's energy levels well into June even though our final healing session is June 3.

One thing that has changed … Shannon has accepted the advice of everyone on her medical team and started taking naps. Serious two-hour power naps. We get home from healing right around 1:30 and for the past three days she has slept from about 2–4:00. Perfect. And now she has enough energy to stay up to catch the end of the Twins or NHL playoff games. Last night she stayed up late enough to finish reading and homework that was tied to a science final grade. Determined to finish seventh grade like everyone else.

So this weekend, 155 of us will gather together in support and wear "I Love Shannon" shirts in the Med City Kids Run, 5K, Half Marathon, and Marathon. The forecast for Saturday is for warmer temps … high seventy-three … a thunderstorm somewhere … we pray just not on our parade!

POSTED BY DAN

Family Ties

Shannon had the best of both worlds: plenty of attention on one side of the family and plenty of examples on the other. She was the first on my side of the family: first great-grandchild, first grandchild, and first niece to my only brother. My parents, Grandma and Grandpa Harkins, were young grandparents with the time, energy, and wherewithal to spoil this little girl. They lived here in Rochester when Shannon was born, and they were our first and best babysitters. Shannon would do sleepovers and craft projects and just about anything she wanted when Grandma was in charge! What happens at Grandma's house stays at Grandma's house …

On the O'Hara side of things, Shannon was one of many. She was the new baby for all the cousins to gush over, and grandchild number eighteen for Dan's parents. Baby sister Erin would make the final count nineteen just three years later. We have plenty of examples of fun, love, and friendship that take place with such large family gatherings. There was a cousin in just about every age bracket to look up to. The O'Haras are a loud and loving bunch, and you better be able to take some ribbing to hang in this crowd. No doubt, this is why Shannon learned how to be funny and engaging at an early age!

We were a close family, but busy lives kept us all running in different directions in recent years. Everyone gets busy with their own kids, their own stuff. Sometimes we made the effort to see each other, and sometimes we just felt like it didn't fit into our schedules. "We'll catch you next time."

With Shannon's diagnosis, everything changed. Priorities changed. We were changed. Our families surrounded us when we needed them most, and they would continue to do so over and over and over.

SATURDAY, MAY 28, 2011—MED CITY 5K
POSTED BY DAN

I love Shannon | Family and friends gather at the Med City races to show their support

MEMORIAL WEEKEND IN REVIEW

Our holiday weekend was a busy one. Most events centered around the Med City races here in Rochester. The festivities kicked off Saturday morning with the Kids Run, which Erin, her three pals Emily, Katie, and Lindsey, her cousin Laurynn, and several hundred other elementary and middle schoolers took part in. As the 1.2-mile race approached, Shannon looked at Dan and me and said, "I want to run." She went from spectator to participant. Instead of watching these girls

Kids Run | Determined to finish in the lead

Taking it to the streets | Family and friends at the 5K walk

run for her in shirts bearing her name, Shannon ran with them. OK, not exactly with them. She wasn't about to let Erin or her fifth grade friends beat her! Crossing the finish line, she was smiling from ear to ear.

The afternoon was spent picnicking in the park behind the Mayo Civic Arena. Fifty or so friends and family showed up and donned "I Love Shannon" shirts. Both sets of Shannon and Erin's grandparents, nine aunts and uncles, ten cousins, two great uncles, Dan's friends from high school, our maid of honor ... while Shannon doesn't mind the attention, and she certainly understands why we are all gathering, she doesn't necessarily want or need to talk about it. She just wants to laugh and smile and enjoy people's company. So we did. And at 3:00, on a gorgeous spring day, we all hit the street in our Shannon shirts for the Med City 5K.

Sunday brought more Med City events. Dan and his brother Tim ran the half marathon. There were people wearing "Shannon" shirts everywhere! Some we knew, some we didn't: co-workers, church friends, school friends, old babysitters, even a golf teammate's boyfriend wore one. The idea for the shirts was to allow us to show support for Shannon but also to raise awareness for Brains Together for a Cure, a local non-profit that funds Mayo Clinic research. Maybe we can all wear these shirts again in October for BTFC's 5th Annual Brain Tumor Walk. Last year their grant money went to Dr. Nadia Laack, Shannon's radiation oncologist.

Shannon and Erin and cousin Laurynn cheered on Dan and Tim in the half marathon with signs and loud cheers at the six-mile, eight-mile, and ten-mile marks. As we were waiting at each spot, several Shannon shirts would pass, and we would give them an extra loud cheer. We watched Dan and Tim cross the finish line, hand in hand, arms held high.

Dan must have trained well for this race and seemed no worse for the wear. By the afternoon, he was even up for a little golf. So, Dan, my brother Eric, my dad, and I played eighteen holes. And guess who joined us? After thirty-nine days of chemo and twenty-seven radiation treatments, Shannon played the first eighteen-hole round of her life. Did I mention she's determined?

So a successful gathering for family and friends is behind us, and now we look ahead. But not too far. The final four days of healing are this week. I'm struck by how fast this has gone and how much ground we have covered. The knowledge we've gained, the relationships we've developed or rekindled, the awareness about who we are and who we mean to be. The longest six weeks of my life have flown by.

Making the most of each day leaves little idle time ...

POSTED BY JEN

WEDNESDAY, JUNE 1, 2011

Tossin' and turnin' at o'dark 30, so it's back to the blog for some confessin' ...

I was quite disturbed by yet another Twins one-run loss. How many ways? How many different kinds of ways can they lose ballgames? A simple mind might think it's almost like the same dark cloud that is hovering over this Rochester, Minnesota, O'Hara family is also following the Twins through their 2011 journey. But I'm certain that isn't what has my mind working hard in the middle of this night.

A friend sent me this verse from James 1:2–4,

> Dear brothers and sisters, when troubles come your way, consider it an opportunity for great joy. For you know that when your faith is tested, your endurance has a chance to grow. So let it grow, for when your endurance is fully developed, you will be perfect and complete, needing nothing.

His point of support was that we can grow through challenging times and events if we don't let them consume us.

Bible verses, prayers, music lyrics ... they are all around us everyday. In most cases they just need an application, and an open mind to apply them. Can you tell I have my iPod going? Currently playing new Sheryl Crow, "Long Road Home." *"Bring me sweet relief, rid me of human grief, I am free from every hurt ..."*

I feel the need to address the issue of control. It is an issue that probably creates the most stress around our home. Probably not unique to us. But in a time of crisis or inexplicable circumstance, controlling behavior can be a toxin. For someone in a program of recovery, it's a huge red-flag wavin' in the wind. Let go, let God, right?

Jen and I addressed this with our Mayo Clinic case worker today. Great stuff to get out on the table. It's so easy for me to point fingers all around me as to the reasons for this or that. It's meeting other people's needs ... it's trying to be everything to everybody ... it's my family ... it's the weather ... it's the Twins bullpen ... the list keeps growing. And really all I need to do is look in the mirror.

The painful truth is that none of us have any control. And what is going to happen next, who knows? That is certainly the hardest part. I make light of Jen's planning instinct more than I should. But this lack of control is really hard on her as she—like most moms—attempts to lay out summer plans: enrolling the girls in camps, locking down trips to the cabin, scheduling stuff that needs to happen like it has every other summer.

It's like Jen said in her post yesterday: the longest six weeks of my life have flown by. Hell, these six weeks may have been the easy part! The doctors set that up for us in April; forty-two days of chemo and radiation treatments that will end Friday. Then you go away and enjoy life for four weeks. Then come back and we will scan Shannon's brain and will know more. You kidding me? Enjoy life? I suppose this is where our endurance is supposed to grow?

So perhaps that's why I'm awake this morning. I suppose this is where I would open the floor to comments. But this is something Jen, Shannon, Erin, and I will need to figure out, because if we are lucky—and God is willing—it could go on like this for a while. How about for about five years while they master proton beam therapy or the next technology that will shrivel this growth in Shannon's brain?

Staying 100 percent in the present becomes the real challenge. Yet, that is the only thing we can control. Erin graduates from Bamber Valley Elementary Thursday. Friday she has a field trip to the DNR trout hatchery in Lanesboro. Shannon will take seventh grade finals and then ring the bell at Desk R, a ceremony for patients completing radiation treatment. Saturday we have Fireballs and hockey and more family ... and life goes on ...

It's likely Twins manager, Ron Gardenhire, is also tossin' and turnin' this morning.

Must own music: Tristan Prettyman, "Madly." All better now.

POSTED BY DAN

FRIDAY, JUNE 3, 2011

It's a sunny and windy Friday morning here in Roch, and I am finding a few minutes to relax. Starting my day with coffee and live tennis from Paris—the French Open men's semifinals. Going to root hard for Roger Federer today, but it's a long shot ...

Thursday was eventful as Erin graduated from fifth grade at Bamber Valley. It's the only elementary school our kids ever attended, and since Shannon started kindergarten there in the fall of 2003, it's been a big part of our lives. There were plenty of tears shed during the ceremony. Some were shed for Erin reaching this milestone, but emotions got the best of us when one of the fifth grade speakers, a neighbor of ours, talked about Shannon and her fight. Many of these families are connected to us one way or another, and there was a round of applause from the parents and students who acknowledged our battle. Erin's classmates surrounded her for support as she cried. My first instinct was to feel badly for Erin; this was her day and the celebration was supposed to be about her. But, the reality is that when Erin or any of us looks back on this stage of our lives, it will always be intertwined with Shannon's health. We cannot pretend it isn't so ...

The rest of the celebration was more light-hearted as we ate lunch outside with Erin and her pals and their families. Nothing more needed to be said about what had transpired. Erin has good friends and her friends have good families.

We didn't have our normal Thursday of appointments as we had adjusted our schedule to accommodate the graduation and Shannon's finals schedule. We did manage to do blood work and see all of our doctors over the course of a couple of afternoons this week. Nothing but positive reports: blood work looks good and, by all accounts, Shannon has tolerated the treatment incredibly well.

So now we've reached a milestone day—the last healing session.

Radiation will end today at about 1:20 P.M. when Shannon rings the bell at Desk R to signal the completion of treatment. I find myself feeling conflicted. Proud that she has been so strong and hardly ever complained about this hand she's been dealt. She just battled through it every day, usually with a smile on her face.

But, I also feel sad and scared. Scared about the unknown. At least for the last six weeks we felt like we were doing something, taking action, talking daily with Jacque and Janelle and working our way through it. I'm sad that we won't have that daily support. After today,

The bell tolls | Shannon signals the end of six weeks of radiation therapy

we will return for a set of follow up appointments next week, and then take three weeks off from appointments and doctors as Shannon rests and recovers, and the chemo and radiation continue to work on the tumor. We will return the first week of July for a follow-up MRI and get our first look at how effective the treatment was at shrinking the tumor. The first week of July will also begin the maintenance phase of chemotherapy: strong doses of Temodar daily for five days, then twenty-three days off. That's the plan going forward to try and keep the tumor at bay.

So, wherever you are at 1:20 P.M. today, have a good thought for our girl. The bell will be ringing, and my guess is, Shannon will be smiling ...
POSTED BY JEN

HEALING SESSIONS ARE COMPLETE
POSTED BY JEN

Desk R | Saying goodbye to the radiation team

Smiling | of course

MONDAY, JUNE 6, 2011

A final push to summer vacation for the O'Haras.

Erin told me last week after her fifth grade graduation that ceremonies are for parents "but field trips are for kids!" Her fifth grade class departs this morning for the Eagle Bluff Environmental Learning Center. Three days and two nights deep into the bluffs of SE Minnesota near Lanesboro. She's so dang excited. We're excited for her too, but it might be kind of warm in those dorms at Eagle Bluff. Record highs are predicted for Monday and Tuesday. I think E will be just fine.

Shannon's seventh grade class heads to Oxbow Zoo Monday. Field trips and fun activities mark the final days of school. On Thursday cue the Alice Cooper classic "School's Out for Summer!" (No, I do not have that one loaded in the iPod.)

So with Erin away on a road trip, Jen and I will take Shannon to our Mayo Clinic appointments Tuesday. A final blood draw to check platelet counts, another thorough neurological exam with Dr. Keating, and a final rundown with radiation oncologist Dr. Laack, who was kind enough to make an appearance and hand out hugs for us at Shannon's bell ringing last Thursday.

Even though the acute healing phase is complete, the radiation and chemo are still working their magic for the next couple weeks inside Shannon's brain. But we expect mostly positive reports as Shannon has been feeling strong and her energy levels have been setting the tone for the family.

We hope the heat holds for our trip to Lake Hubert next weekend. Either way, the kids are ready to rock!

POSTED BY DAN

TUESDAY, JUNE 7, 2011

I am writing from the comfort of our air-conditioned house as it is crazy hot here today—ninety-nine degrees this afternoon! I find myself thinking about Erin and the hundred other fifth graders spending two nights down in the dorm style rooms at Eagle Bluff. Not ideal conditions, to say the least! I'm anxious to have her return tomorrow and share her stories with us.

The last couple of days have been strange without our daily routine of heading to Desk R for healing sessions. Dan and I even found time to play a round of golf together today. Something we did and enjoyed often before everything changed. Today we hit good shots, we hit bad shots, we made birdies, and we made bogeys, just like the good ol' days. Sometimes we let our minds wander to where we've been and where we're headed, but we did our best to enjoy a good walk together ...

Today's appointments brought some closure to the treatment phase and provided a game plan for what's ahead. First off, Shannon, Dan, and I had a chance to chat with our social worker. She continues to provide support and strategies for us as we try to balance what we want and need with the wants and needs of our family and friends.

The support continues to be amazing and we never want to discount how important that is to us. But, sometimes the timing just isn't right. Sometimes we are just mad or sad or tired or don't want to talk and nothing anyone could say or do makes it better. Yet people try, because they care. We strive to be as graceful as we can on this journey, but sometimes we fail.

While Shannon met with the social worker, Dan and I spoke briefly with Dr. Khan in hematology and clarified that the maintenance dose of chemotherapy will begin in early July. The exact date is yet to be determined, but the guideline is six weeks after the last dose of Temodar was taken, which puts us around July 13. Dr. Kahn also explained that Shannon won't have to do another infusion treatment, but instead will begin taking an oral medication, Bactrim, each weekend once she starts taking the Temodar again. This will provide the protection her lungs need when her immune system is depleted by taking the chemo.

Shannon's second appointment today was a follow up with Dr. Laack in radiation. We learned that the hair loss will end in the next week or so and that the timeline for it growing back is around three months. She also confirmed that the follow up MRI will take place exactly four weeks after radiation: July 1. So, that day, Shannon will have a scan and then an appointment with Dr. Laack to see the results. It goes without saying that we will be anxious to see how effective the treatment was.

The last appointment of our day was with our neurologist, Dr. Keating. She loves to chat, and while Shannon was eager to move things along, Dan and I enjoyed sharing stories back and forth with her. A complete neuro exam showed all positive signs and Dr. Keating told Shannon she looks great. She also complimented Shannon on her strategic placement of her headband! We will next meet with Dr. Keating in August to check all the neurological markers again.

All that's left on Shannon's Mayo Clinic schedule this week is a blood draw on Friday. One more check of the counts before they free us for three weeks. After that, we have no return appointments scheduled until the MRI on July 1.

So the next five days: two more days of school, one golf team party, one blood draw, one last soccer game, one hockey camp, one cousin's graduation open house and then we are free to go and travel and enjoy the first part of our summer and try not to think about the tumor …

I updated my iPod today and the song that struck me was Cold-play's "Everything's Not Lost."

When I counted up my demons
Saw there was one for every day
With the good ones on my shoulders
I drove the other ones away …

POSTED BY JEN

FRIDAY, JUNE 10, 2011

I had a chance to catch some of Oprah's final show. Say what you want about Oprah, but she has been an incredible inspiration to the masses. On this day I was caught up by her ability to articulate her values and the confidence she has in those beliefs. She reminded me that in God's universe "there are no coincidences, only a divine order."

She also stated that the ability to make a difference, to be a difference maker is right there in all of us. You just need to go take it … assert it … be it. Oprah's confidence makes it sound so easy.

Around our home the only person with that kind of certainty is Shannon. Our "going-into-eighth" grader has the most confidence in exactly what her role is. And she's seized the opportunity to be a difference maker.

For me, Jen, and Erin there seems to be less certainty in what we should be, how we should act, and where to focus our energy. I was a little out of sorts this week without the structure of daily radiation, which provided us an order, a certainty to each day.

With the kids focused on the field trips and the final days of school, I tried to work on my golf game, but on the golf course my lack of certainty is completely exposed.

Thursday night, at the Rochester Mayo High School girls golf banquet, Coach Myhro reminded us how critical confidence is to golfers, and the girls should work on that as they practice and play this summer. Shannon always handles herself well on the golf course because she has always had so much confidence, and a commitment to what she is doing. So I'm going to try that now. I know I can do it. I've been good before. I'm going to be good again. And—darn it—people like me! (Stuart Smalley's voice echoes ... that's not helping ...)

Shannon took home the "Spartan Award" given to the player that displayed courage and spirit through the course of the season. Shannon's buddy Courtney was "Newcomer of the Year." It was a good night. Again, a challenge to keep emotions in check. But this night was about the golf team. Good luck at state, Katrina.

I want to use this forum to express tremendous gratitude to the families of the thirty-two players out for Mayo High School golf this spring. You played a really key role in keeping our spirits high in some really tough times. Shannon loves being part of a team. Just loves it. Thanks for making a difference.

Now if there is divine order, and no coincidences, Erin will get Mr. Myhro as one of her teachers next year when she is a newcomer at Willow Creek Middle School.

Thursday, Erin said a tearful goodbye to Bamber Valley Elementary. Thank you Mrs. Hammel. Erin will never forget you. Aloha means goodbye.

I have some solid song recommendations this morning: Ray LaMontagne, "You Are the Best Thing"; Donavon Frankenreiter, "Bend in the Road"; and an oldie but goodie from Joni Mitchell, "Big Yellow Taxi" (but the version I really like is from Counting Crows). *"Don't it always seem to go, that you don't know what you got 'til it's gone."*

So now we plow forward into a summer of unknowns. We will do so with confidence and gratitude for the many blessings we have in our lives.

POSTED BY DAN

GRATITUDE

I am feeling a little self-conscious about this blog today. It feels a little presumptuous. Everybody has stuff going on in their lives. Everybody. Anyone reading this could blog about their lives and it would give us a chance to know them better. We've chosen to write this blog as a mea-

A shoulder to lean on | Dan and Shannon, two peas in a pod

sure of self-preservation, so we didn't struggle to communicate individually with the family and friends that we wanted to keep in the loop. But, while what we are going through is all consuming and seems to be all we can focus on sometimes, we want to be mindful that other people have stories to tell too.

Spending time on the Mayo 16 E pediatric unit always helps with perspective. We were there yesterday for Shannon's blood draw and a quick look around at the children who are disabled and the looks on their parents' faces helps me find gratitude quickly. For now, Shannon is a smiling, soon-to-be teenager ready to do her best to enjoy a summer of fun.

The blood counts were good. Better than good. Nine days after ending chemo and one week after finishing radiation, all of her important numbers—platelets, hemoglobin, leukocytes—have begun trending back up. No appointments necessary from now until July 1.

We finished soccer season today with a matchup against Erin's first best friend, our old neighbor Tessa. Fun stuff. The Fireballs have been a great team to coach. So now with no more school, no more soccer, and no more appointments, we are off and running with our June travels: a trip to Lake Hubert, followed by a trip to Lake Michigan, followed by a trip to the Wisconsin Dells.

There's a little detail about this summer travel we're planning that I feel compelled to mention. The freedom to do all this without stressing about it is due directly to the generosity of others. So, thank you.

POSTED BY JEN

Sisterhood Rules

Sisterly love | Shannon, age 3½, Erin, age 9 months

Baby sister Erin Irene joined the family when Shannon was almost three. Shannon loved "her baby" and loved being the big sister. Shannon thought she was born to be in charge, so being the boss of Erin was a role she took seriously!

Luckily, Erin was born with a calm and gentle personality. We called her "The Little Observer." We have the home videos to prove that while Shannon was a ball of energy and emotion, Erin was there taking it all in. She had the same big, brown eyes as her big sister, but there was less fire in them.

As they grew, they became playmates, best friends, and best enemies. They played games like restaurant and school for hours on end. Shannon was always the cook or the teacher, and Erin was always relegated to the role of waitress and student. These games would go along smoothly until Erin got fed up with playing second fiddle, and then Shannon would have to go into sales mode to convince her little sister to keep playing. A daughter after her father's heart! Sometimes it worked, and sometimes it didn't.

Shannon was not one to swallow her frustration, which is evident in this second grade journal entry she wrote:

10-26-06
What I Really can't stand

What I really can't Stand is when
my sister bugs me! Somtimes when I
am sleeping and it is like 6:45° She
comes in to my room with are dog
and then are dog Sunshine jumps up
on my bed and liks my face! Then
She says I got up eraly and Sunshine
keep buging me. I say well don't wake
me up! And if you wake up and it
is 6:30am go back to bed! And
anoter reason my sister bugs me.
is sometimes my sister trys to
anoy me and I say Quit it then she
says Quit what? And then she keeps
doing it then I lighty push her
and she fakes crying and then
my mom and dad put me in my
room. And when I pay back by
annoying her and she gets really
mad and that makes me happy.
And that is all the reasons
my sister annoys me Well there
is a copie more.

Shannon's school journal entry | Second grade, 2006

As Erin grew older, she wanted more say in the matter, which led to the creation of a document that Shannon and Erin called "The Sisterhood Rules."

Sisterhood Rules

1. We have equal power (except when Shannon babysits)
2. We both have to agree (if one person does not get their way they do not get mad)
3. We both have to listen to each other's comments with an open mind
4. One person must ask if she would like to borrow the other sister's item/s or property
5. When one sister is talking the other may not interrupt them
6. No one takes credit of something that's not their idea (except when the other person says it's okay

If one person breaks the Sisterhood rules she must say sorry and they must also say it sincerely. The other person must also say it is okay and they will be happy.

_____
Signature

_____
Signature

_____
Initial

_____
Initial

The infamous, self-created "Sisterhood Rules" | A binding contract for Shannon and Erin!

Typical loving, fighting sisters. We couldn't have imagined that eventually Erin would be an only. Who knew that before she was a teenager herself, Erin would be forced to find her own way? She would lose her boss and her best friend.

TUESDAY, JUNE 14, 2011—LAKE HUBERT
POSTED BY JEN

Our favorite spot on earth | The O'Hara family cabin on Lake Hubert, Nisswa, MN

THURSDAY, JUNE 16, 2011

Our summer whirlwind is just getting started, and we are already exhausted!

Not really, but sort of. I think we are just discovering that this hyper-speed pace we are choosing "is what it is." I kind of hate that expression, but in this case it "is what it is." The good news is that there is very little time to pout or over-think because we unpack from one event and start organizing and sorting laundry for the next event.

Our trip to Lake Hubert worked out well with the girls getting some extended time with Grandma and Papa O'Hara and also their "quirky" Aunt Molly and Uncle Norv! Games of Five Crowns and Quirkle were interspersed with chill time on the beach, boat rides, and trips to Nisswa and to Shannon and Erin's favorite shopping destination: The Chocolate Ox. The laughs and happy times are a constant.

The weather was better in Nisswa than almost anywhere else in Minnesota. The south winds kept the water calm in our bay, and the loon pairings were active and fishing close to our dock. The water was a cool sixty-eight degrees but as usual, crystal clear.

The clouds broke Tuesday afternoon and we had several sunny hours on the beach with temps around seventy-five … really nice. Good time to throw the football off the dock, float on a raft, sit in the sand, and read. Our neighbors, the Gustafsons, gave us access to their boats. Each day we went for a ride around the lake. The girls love being out on the water. On one of our boat rides we saw a grouping of around thirty immature loons gathered together in the middle of Lake Hubert.

On Wednesday it rained and made it the perfect time to pack up and head back to the Roch. I was able to manage some work at the cabin with internet access wherever my Sprint AirCard can find a cell signal. With Jen driving, answering emails on the drive was also a solid use of my time. I still have some good opportunities for new business in my pipeline that I need to keep in the air. So far, so good. I enjoy my work and my company and most of my customers, so I do not mind checking in and replying even on vacation days.

Shannon and Erin are such troopers—great travelers.

So we were home Wednesday night … Shannon played hockey. We watched the Bruins hoist the Stanley Cup and a Twins win over the

White Sox. Thursday, the girls overnight with their BFF's, the Gushu-laks, in Pine Island, and Saturday we leave for Milwaukee. Our ferry across Lake Michigan departs Sunday, and then we will experience the eastern shores of Lake Michigan for a few days.

South Haven forecast is calling for hot temps, maybe some summer thunder boomers. In Michigan, no one knows our name or our story and that might be—literally—just what the doctor ordered.

POSTED BY DAN

MONDAY, JUNE 20, 2011

Our commute across the Upper Midwest took us by auto from Rochester to Milwaukee on Saturday. Then with the auto (and Sunny) on the bottom deck, we spent Father's Day on the Lakes Express ferry into the Port of Muskegon, Michigan. Now we are sixty miles south on the sandy beaches of Lake Michigan. Warm and muggy ... storms predicted. The adventure continues ...

POSTED BY DAN

TUESDAY, JUNE 21, 2011

Just as the doctors ordered, we are enjoying our "time off" from appointments and medications. Enjoying it, but I still feel like we are living in an alternate reality. When you are on a perpetual vacation, is it really a vacation?

Don't get me wrong, this is a beautiful place and a part of our country that the girls have never seen. They do love an adventure. We are renting a house, exploring new towns like Saugatuck and South Haven, and building sand castles on the shores of Lake Michigan.

Erin is our little fish. If there's swimming to be had, she's in. Even in fifty-eight-degree water! Shannon loves walking up and down the beach, but she has not been quite herself. A little more quiet, a little more sassy ... maybe she's just acting like an almost thirteen-year-old on vacation with her family! So, we try to call her on her attitude just like we would if everything was normal ...

One more full day ahead of us here. Lots of beach time and hope-

A new adventure | The beach at South Haven, MI

fully a walk to town for lunch. The forecast is for hot and humid weather with a chance for a thunderstorm to blow in across the lake. Works for me...

POSTED BY JEN

WEDNESDAY, JUNE 22, 2011

Today was get away day. We were up early packing the van and headed sixty miles north to Muskegon to catch the 10:15 A.M. ferry back to Milwaukee. Shannon had a bit of an upset stomach and didn't eat much breakfast. That turned out to be a good thing. The water was pretty rough on our ride and Shannon ended up getting sick. Six weeks of radiation and chemotherapy couldn't make her puke, but Lake Michigan got the best of her.

It feels like each day there is at least one instance that brings my emotions to the surface. Today this was it: Shannon was embarrassed and had a moment of fear about being sick and asked me point blank, "I don't think this is anything to worry about, right? It's just the rough water, right?" Of course it was, but she still had to ask. Just our daily reminder that we are always waiting for the other shoe to drop. Seeing the fear in her face made me cry, and I struggled during the rest of our ride to gain my composure. I knew intellectually that this almost certainly had nothing to do with the tumor, but seeing her get sick got to me. I put the iPod on to settle by mind. David Gray and his track "My Oh My":

> *My oh my, you know it just don't stop*
> *It's in my mind, I wanna tear it up*
> *And tryin' to fight it, tryin' to turn it off*
> *But it's not enough …*

One rough boat ride aside, we had a great vacation in Michigan that included not only the four of us and our dog, Sunny, but also my friend Teri and her dog as well. Having Teri drive the three hours from her Ann Arbor home to join us for our adventure was wonderful. Walking and talking on the beach with T was good for my soul. I miss her already.

Yesterday was made to order: hot and humid all day, with the temp reaching ninety-three degrees. It was so hot even I went swimming! (I take an endless amount of grief from my water-loving family for being such a wimp.)

The five of us took a midday walk down the beach a mile and a half into the town of South Haven. By the time we got there, we realized that all of us walking back home was going to be asking a lot of Shannon and Erin. (Probably of me and Teri too!) So, Dan ran back down the beach, in the hottest part of the day, to the house and drove the car into town to meet us and shuttle us home. Women's lib be damned, the four of us girls appreciated his chivalry.

Last night we had one of those experiences that we will always remember. While the girls enjoyed some down time relaxing and watching TV, Teri, Dan, and I enjoyed some conversation while looking out over Lake Michigan. On the summer solstice, the pink sky of the setting sun gave way to ominous storm clouds rolling in across the water. Lightning strikes were constant out across the horizon, and we watched the storm cells approach from miles away. Amazing. As we sat and tried to figure out the meaning of life, Mother Nature reminded us that some things in this universe are just simply out of our control ...

POSTED BY JEN

SATURDAY, JUNE 25, 2011

This weekend we are in the Wisconsin Dells celebrating the forty-fifth wedding anniversary for Grandma and Papa Harkins. The ten of us are sharing a condo at Kalahari. Today was spent time enjoying the outdoor waterpark and indoor amusement park. Shannon and Erin and cousins Laurynn and Jack are daring the adults to keep up with them. We are doing our best!

POSTED BY JEN

MONDAY, JUNE 27, 2011

Our Dells vacation got a little messy. Sunday while Jen, Eric, Papa, and I were hacking it around Trappers Turn Golf Club, Shannon got sick back at Kalahari. More vomiting and we cut short our golf to take her to the ER in Baraboo. Grandma's texts and voicemails alerted us as we found a cell signal at the turn. The cell coverage in the Dells is not strong.

Dr. Rodriguez from Mayo Neurology was on call and advised us to head in to the nearest ER so Shannon could get checked out. She wanted to rule out an anaphylactic shock to the Bactrim she began taking Saturday.

The Bactrim was prescribed to help Shannon's immune system for the next round of chemo, set to start here in the next week or two. Shannon was to take two doses on Saturday and two on Sunday. She made it through the Saturday dosage, but she puked up Sunday's pill shortly after taking it.

Logic would tell you the introduction of Bactrim coupled with some overexertion from a couple exciting days at Kalahari should explain the reaction. But the panic on Shannon's face told us she was worried it was tumor related. She asked us as we rushed out to the car to head for Baraboo, "Is there a chance I will die today?" Oh, Sweetie.

Cousins at Kalahari | Enjoying the Wisconsin Dells with Laurynn and Jack

After examining Shannon and listening to the twelve-year-old explain her journey as an oncology patient at Mayo Clinic, the ER doc in Baraboo called Dr. Rodriguez in Rochester to consult. He told us Dr. Rodriguez was the expert on tumors, but he knew his anaphylactic shock and said definitively this was not it. And we were discharged.

Shannon is well aware that Friday she will undergo an MRI that will determine her immediate future. There's no doubt she's processing. There's no doubt she's scared. We are all scared. So separating daily twelve-year-old ailments like water in the ear or some nausea relating to sea sickness or overexertion is impossible to discount as the stand alone symptoms of a summer packed with activity.

We feel so badly for Gwen and Chuck, Eric and Jen, and Jack and Laurynn who did not sign up for this either. And for sister Erin who quietly goes about her business of being a happy and fun loving ten-year-old. Just like our journey across Lake Michigan, 95 percent of the trip to the Dells was really great, but that 5 percent was the ass kicker.

Bruce Springsteen's "Long Walk Home" comes up just at the moment I am trying to find the words for this blog entry. *"Hey pretty darling ... gonna be a long walk home ..."*

POSTED BY DAN

UPDATE

Just a quick update on Shannon. She did vomit again overnight and that prompted us to follow up with neurology and oncology today. After speaking with doctors and nurse practitioners this morning, there are a few possible explanations:

One, it could be just a flu-type bug, which is obviously hard to prove.

Two, it still could be a reaction to the Bactrim, which is designed to be a long-acting drug. Shannon was relieved to hear from hematology today that she will not have to take her scheduled doses this coming weekend. We will wait until our hematology appointment next Tuesday, and then make a new plan for the necessary antibiotics to accompany the maintenance chemo.

A third potential explanation was offered today by Dr. Laack. If the tumor is "dying" (her word, not mine) then the tissue in the brain around the tumor could be swelling in response to the tumor change. Swelling could cause nausea, vomiting, headaches. This would be discovered at the Friday MRI, and steroids would be ordered again to help relieve this, just as they were at the beginning of Shannon's treatment.

The response of our medical team to our questions was very prompt and has helped ease our minds a bit. We're feeling grateful for the Mayo Clinic today. The doctors have said they would be surprised if these symptoms were from tumor growth. It should be too soon for that. Still, as any parent knows, it's hard to see your child sick and weak. Even harder knowing what we know.

So, for now, Shannon needs to lay low. Her day has consisted of TV, movies, naps, Tylenol, Zofran, Saltines, and her new favorite Gatorade flavor, Rain Lime. Maybe the Twins will even give us something worth watching tonight ... it doesn't hurt to dream, right?

POSTED BY JEN

Fear Factor

When someone you love is living with cancer, you live with a little bit of fear inside you all the time. Waiting for the other shoe to drop. Even when things are going well, you know what could be lurking. You are hypersensitive to every ache and pain and complaint. And there is always a date marked on the calendar for the next time you will get a look at the tumor. The next MRI scan may be weeks or even months away, but you still know it's coming.

Fortunately, or unfortunately, we only had to do this a few times during our journey. Some people battle cancer for years or even decades, and yet they still experience this feeling of uncertainty each and every time.

As the time approaches for the next scan, the anxiety can be all consuming. You can't sleep, you can't eat, you can't even think straight. It is hard to avoid thinking about the "what if?" We would go about our days as best we could, all the while feeling something in the pit of our stomachs.

You can rationalize all you want, but your emotional self just gets the best of you. Staying in the present was a real challenge during scan week.

WEDNESDAY, JUNE 29, 2011—MRI MOVED TO TODAY
Shannon has continued with the nausea, vomiting, and headaches and also has begun experiencing some tingling in her lip and tongue on the same side of her face that she is having the ear pain and head pressure.

So, they moved the MRI from Friday to today at 12:55 P.M. We will see Dr. Laack late this afternoon and then we will know more. Trying to narrow down what is going on.

Lots of anxiety for Shannon. She's worried about making it through the claustrophobic feeling in the MRI tube. Hard enough when you are feeling good, let alone on an upset tummy.

So, all those good thoughts you've been saving for us for Friday, we'll take them today …

POSTED BY JEN

MRI UPDATE

Shannon made it through her MRI, but Dr. Laack couldn't access the results of the scan for our meeting. She was told by a radiologist that there was some shrinkage, but Dr. Laack is the expert at reading brain scans and was not going to tell us anything definitive until she saw the scan.

In the meantime, Shannon underwent a thorough exam to help pinpoint the cause of the nausea. It may just be the flu. It may be a reaction to Bactrim. It may be radiation and chemo on the attack.

So we're trying to keep Shannon hydrated. Forcing blue Gatorade tonight. Watching *The Voice* together on Jen's birthday. Trying to turn the corner.

Dr. Laack will call us in the morning when she gets a closer look at the scan. Then we will post.

POSTED BY DAN

THURSDAY, JUNE 30, 2011

Wow, are we on a rollercoaster ride this week. First, the good news: today's follow-up call from Dr. Laack provided a more positive take on the MRI results. She feels that the radiologist was being very cautious when he told her yesterday that there was "some" shrinking of the tumor. After seeing the MRI scan for herself, Dr. Laack said she was "very, very pleased with the response of the tumor." The contrast dye that was used during the MRI showed that it is "leaking" into the tumor, which means that there is "significant change" in the cells from the treatment. So, Dr. Laack was upbeat and offered hope that the treatment is having the intended effect. The next MRI in two months will hopefully show continued shrinking of the tumor. But, as we discussed with Dr. Laack yesterday, there is no magic bullet, no overnight miracle. Shannon beating the odds will have to play out over time.

Now for the bad news: Shannon has continued with the nausea and vomiting and was on a different anti-nausea pill today that really wiped her out. She was unable to even keep fluids down, so we ended up at St. Mary's late this afternoon for a liter of IV fluids to help with the dehydration. Poor girl. Still no definitive answer on what's causing her to feel so sick. Could be the flu. Could be cells being released from the tumor and touching a nausea center in the brain. Hard not knowing and hard seeing her down and out.

Hopefully Shannon can rest a little easier tonight. She is perking up a bit as the anti-nausea meds wear off and the fluids take effect. She even managed to eat a piece of toast! We are headed back to St. Mary's tomorrow morning so Shannon can receive a second liter of fluids. Hopefully that will get her headed in the right direction.

POSTED BY JEN

FRIDAY, JULY 1, 2011

Shannon had another infusion of fluids this morning. That's two liters of the saline that has been pumped in to her body in the last eighteen hours. We are back home and Shannon is just wiped out and throwing up anything we try to get her to eat. We've been on the phone with our team in radiation oncology, and we're treating this like the flu since the vomit is now accompanied by diarrhea. Lovely. Diarrhea would not likely be a symptom consistent with tumor swelling around or near the nausea center in her brain. Probably TMI.

We are desperate to get some nutrients in her. But even four bites of a milk shake with instant breakfast mix in it came right back up. We are armed with a couple different anti-nausea drugs and just sitting and watching and hoping she can find some stability.

We had to bail on the Twins game tonight with cousins Joe and Leila and Pat and Mame. Shannon wanted us to go without her. That

82

wasn't going to happen. She has been such a warrior for us—so hard to see her so weak and feeble.

POSTED BY DAN

SATURDAY, JULY 2, 2011

First of all, if Jen kicks the bucket we are so screwed.

Managing the meds alone would push me to the edge: the new Zofran, the old Zofran, the Phenergan, the Decadron, the pill cutter, etc. Then there is the managing of the rest of us; the pills are kid stuff compared to managing the kid stuff. And then there's me ... let's just say it's a good thing I can cook.

Shannon continues to struggle finding any adrenal chemical to drive thirst or hunger or generate any energy to spark a rally. Maybe we are making slow progress, but it is really slow. And it's really putting a strain on all of us because it is so frustrating to put a finger on the cause or find any relief.

Over the past four days, we have demanded much consultation with our Mayo radiation/oncology team and they are just as confounded. We have added a 1 mg dose of the steroid Decadron to see if that will help tame any possible swelling or add some spunk.

This morning started with promise as Shannon asked for and ate half of a banana. And later a small portion of a bagel and a trip to the backyard to watch Erin and Jen tie-dye shirts. But after settling back onto the sofa she threw up again. Mainly what came up was liquid but certainly there was not enough nutritional substance processed to fuel a Shannon comeback. Still, she found some joy in watching the USA Women's World Cup win over Colombia. There was sparkle in her eyes. Progress.

But then the sofa monster got her again, and she never really rallied for the rest of the day. Back to the sleepy eyes, lethargic, unresponsive Shannon struggling to find enough energy to even call for help. Grandma came over for a few hours of relief work and got her to take in some chicken soup and more Gatorade. (I'm not sure the poor kid will ever be able to drink Gatorade again after this week.)

Tonight we made another call to the on-call radiation/oncology resident, and we will meet him at St. Mary's in the morning for another IV infusion to keep us current on fluids.

Maybe tomorrow will bring more promise and less frustration. Maybe we will get more sparkle and fewer snarls. Maybe tomorrow we will all stay happy and Shannon will get hungry. And maybe Matt Capps will be able to close out a win for the Twins ...

POSTED BY DAN

SUNDAY, JULY 3, 2011

We are back at St. Mary's this morning at PITC (Pediatric Infusion Therapy Center). This is a good thing. It means Shannon is getting more fluids, and she's not having to do it in the ER.

We met Dr. Barney at Desk R for a quick exam. Dr. Barney is the radiation/oncology on-call physician, and he needed to see Shannon before he could order up the IV treatment. And he pulled the strings to get us in here at PITC. In fact, he ordered up one for Sunday and Monday, and we just worked it out that we will be back Fourth of July morning as well, as we try to stay ahead and keep Shannon hydrated.

Dr. Barney's exam found that her resting heart rate was fine, but after forcing Shannon to take a short walk it spiked again, indicating some dehydration.

The nausea has subsided slightly, but not completely. In fact, Shannon threw up again when we got up here for the infusion. But her eyes are brighter. She is moving a little faster. Still requesting a wheel chair to get around the hospital.

So we are watching Rafa vs. The Joker in the Wimbledon men's final, reading the Sunday paper, and taking on some fluids that will hopefully lead to a better day. Baby steps.

POSTED BY DAN

FOURTH OF JULY

If I messed with our karma by complaining about our "perpetual vaca-tion" awhile back, I sincerely apologize. This blog is much more fun to write when we're giving vacation updates instead of health updates!

Today is a better day than yesterday, and yesterday was better than the day before, but progress is slow. Shannon had her fourth liter of IV fluids this morning and that helps her to perk up. We'll see how long it lasts today.

Thank goodness for the kindness and caring of the nurses we've come in contact with over these past five days in the PITC. Here it is, a beautiful sunny, holiday weekend and nurses Shelly, Tall Tammy, and Short Tammy all acted like they didn't want to be any place else. Just here to help us help our kid feel better.

Erin has been along for these infusions this week, at her request. She likes to be "in the know." She gathered information from nurse Short Tammy during the first infusion about how the pump works and how fast they can infuse the fluids; 600 mL per hour was the pace that worked best for Shannon. So, the next day, with nurse Tall Tammy in charge, the pump was set at a slower speed, and Erin politely explained that Shannon could tolerate it at a faster pace. So Erin suggested, "Let's crank it up so we can get outta here sooner!" By the time we arrived today, Erin's reputation preceded her. Nurse Shelly had a note left by Tall Tammy suggesting she check with Shannon's little sister to make sure everything was going as it should!

So, we're trying to laugh in between our tears. Tomorrow brings another step in the journey. Our four week "rest period" has ended and we head back to Mayo 16 for a blood draw and a hematology appointment to make plans for the maintenance dose of chemo that is scheduled to start this week. We'll see if they delay it a few days as Shannon works to regain her strength.

Hopefully today is the day the vomiting will stop and the sparkle will return to Shannon's eyes. We miss our sassy Shan. She's been a shell of herself, and that has been so hard for all of us to see. The crux of all our emotions this week is this: Shannon has looked like a cancer patient. Imagine that. How could it catch us by surprise? Time to step back and remind ourselves that each good day is a good day …

Happy Independence Day, everyone.

POSTED BY JEN

TUESDAY, JULY 5, 2011

My whiteboard calendar is mocking me. You know the color coded one that I keep on the kitchen wall to track the activities for the four of us? My family loves to tease me because I'm a little obsessive about it. But now, I think I need a one day calendar. I could wake up in the morning and say, "What are we going to try to do today?" I really shouldn't plan any farther ahead than that. Because, I thought we were moving forward—there had been no vomiting for a day and a half—but then tonight, after having a relatively good day, Shannon vomited up her dinner. Now she's horizontal on the couch and so angry and frustrated. This is as down in the dumps as she's ever been. Damn.

At our hematology appointment today, Dr. Rodriguez listened to all of Shannon's symptoms and told us she feels this is most likely tumor and treatment related. The cells dying in the tumor are wreaking havoc in the adjoining healthy brain tissue. Shannon has lost eleven pounds. So, we will wait a week on starting the maintenance dose of chemo and try to give Shannon's body time to recover. A follow-up appointment is scheduled for next Monday to check Shannon's weight and see if she's ready to start the Temodar again.

After hearing from Dr. Rodriguez, Dr. Laack called this afternoon and upped the steroid dose to try to curb the nausea and any brain swelling there may be, and to hopefully spark Shannon's appetite. Shannon is under doctor's orders to stay home, stay out of the heat, rest, drink lots of fluid, and eat lots of calories.

So that stuff that I wrote on the color coded calendar for this week—hockey, golf, St. John's Block Party, shopping at IKEA—never mind. We'll get up tomorrow and see what we can do …

POSTED BY JEN

FRIDAY, JULY 8, 2011

The steroids are kicking in. The appetite is back. The food is staying down. The sass is back. And the Twins continue to own the White Sox. All is right again on Willow Lane!

We're rebounding nicely but not completely out of the woods as

Shannon still has vomit paranoia and is not moving around too much. As usual, she's following doctor's orders to the letter; she was prescribed rest and calorie ingestion.

Shannon had a good eating day Tuesday, but threw it all up that night. Her confidence was really jolted. Not to mention her abdominal muscles are really sore. Wednesday she ate small portions but kept it down. And Thursday she started craving foods and eating with more and more confidence. Reese's puffs, ham and cheese omelet with an english muffin, carnation instant breakfast milk shake, mac and cheese, pizza rolls, banana, shredded pork and jo-jo's from John Hardy's, a snack size McFlurry ... do not try this at home. The challenge for the rest of us in the house is watching and not participating.

The forced-rest forced us to open a Netflix account, and now we are streaming movies in bulk. Cousins Jack and Laurynn were in town and joined us for a movie Wednesday. Thursday it was *The Devil Wears Prada* with cousin Gracie and Aunt Megan.

The brightest side is that Shannon is once again interested in socializing. For several days there she did not have any interest in interacting with any of us. But now she's got her text back on. Friday she has a buddy coming over to hang out, maybe go to a movie if Shannon is up to it.

The only downside is that Erin is becoming increasingly annoyed at her big sister. With Shannon sick, Erin was forced to tiptoe around like the rest of us. But now that Shannon has carte blanche to order us around and sit on her butt, Erin's eye rolls are increasing in frequency. Hey, that's just like the old normal!

A couple musical observations to share: the youthful English singer-songwriter Adele has it goin' on. Man, she sings some soulful tunes. Highly recommend. Saturday, Jen and I are excited to see Eric Hutchinson at the St. John's Block Party; we are so proud that our home parish is producing such a cool summer music festival, and Saturday we will get away for a few hours to take in the music of this young American singer-songwriter.

Deep breaths.

POSTED BY DAN

SUNDAY, JULY 10, 2011

Grandma took a turn hanging out with the girls last night so Dan and I could take in some live music at the St. John's Block Party. We enjoyed local Twin Cities favorite Jeremy Messersmith whose style is self-deprecating and quirky, but the highlight was definitely the energetic and engaging Eric Hutchinson. He's charismatic, young, and talented, what's not to like? My personal favorite is his song "Oh!" *"We get lost in the back of our minds ... everybody's got the love, but they keep it inside ..."*

I can't sing a lick and can barely hunt and peck out a tune on the piano, so I'm envious of those who can stand up on a stage and make beautiful music. I joked with Dan that I want to be a bass guitar player in a band. I think it's the perfect role for me: learn a few chords, stay in the background, and keep the beat. One of our friends heard us joking and tried to call my bluff. He's got a bass guitar and amp cluttering up his basement that he'd be glad to donate to my musical fantasy!

Speaking of friends, Dan and I were a little apprehensive about being out and socializing. It had been a rough week, and we didn't want to be a black cloud when people were just hoping to go out and have a good time. But, as we've learned before, people are kind. I can't count the number of friends from different segments of our lives who genuinely wanted to hear how we were doing and gave us a chance to talk. Somehow, we were able to talk about Shannon just enough, and yet listening to the music provided an escape. Very nice.

Meanwhile, back at the ranch, Shannon has been feeling better and eating better, but she's frustrated by the things she's missing out on. While Erin has been off socializing, swimming, and sleeping over with friends, Shannon has been mostly confined to Willow Lane, following doctor's orders to eat and rest. She really wants to be golfing and playing hockey with her peeps. Luckily, her best buddies rescued her for a couple of low-key outings to the movies, and that lifted her spirits a bit. I can't blame her for being a little pissed off ... what (almost) thirteen-year-old wants to spend every minute of every day with her mom and dad?

Shannon has been a trooper about the meds being ramped up again. Managing the nausea has required round the clock Zofran and twice daily doses of steroids and antacids. In addition, this weekend meant trying the antibiotic Bactrim again to protect her lungs from the immune system suppression that's coming with the next round of chemo. This time around—knock on wood—she's tolerating the Bactrim. It's a lot for a young lady to manage. I can't dwell on it or it makes me sad, but it's her reality now. I told her today that I'm proud of her. She gave me a half smile ...

So the weekend is drawing to a close and tomorrow we will be back at Mayo to follow up with Dr. Rodriguez. A check of Shannon's weight will determine if she's strong enough to start a little more activity this week. If she's strong enough, then she will start the five-day maintenance cycle of chemo as well. Take the bad with the good, I suppose.

This week will be a little different around here as it's just us girls. Dan is traveling this week. I won't go into details because it's his story to tell, but here's a little teaser: it involves one of his customers, a private plane, and several golf courses ...

POSTED BY JEN

MONDAY, JULY 11, 2011—APPOINTMENT UPDATE

Shannon had her return visit to hematology today and, by following her doctor's orders to eat and rest, she put on seven pounds in six days! Dr. Rodriguez was happy to see Shannon bouncing back and looking more like her old self.

So, Shannon was pleased that Dr. Rodriguez gave her a little more freedom to enjoy these summer days. Shannon needs to take it slow, meaning no strenuous activity yet. Unfortunately that means no hockey camp or Speed, Agility, Quickness class this week. But, she can take the dog for a walk or hang out with her friends, and hopefully be ready to play in her golf league by next Monday.

The other news out of today's appointment is that Shannon was given the go ahead to start the maintenance dose of chemotherapy tonight. As we've mentioned before, the protocol is five days on Temodar (chemo) and Kytril (anti-nausea), then twenty-three days off for ten cycles.

Shannon will also continue taking the steroids as they have helped with the headaches and head pressure she was experiencing. Dr. Rodriguez wants to be very cautious. So, even though Shannon doesn't like the restless feeling the Decadron gives her, tapering off the steroids will have to wait until at least this weekend, and then it will be a slow process.

All in all, a positive report today and our spirits are good. Tonight Shannon and I made a list of the pills she needs to take this week. We're off and running with the next phase of treatment ...

POSTED BY JEN

WEDNESDAY, JULY 13, 2011

This week is moving along just as we had hoped it would. Both girls have been spending time with their friends, and Shannon and I have also taken on a project: redecorating her room. I was covered in paint from head to toe today. Tomorrow we shop for accessories!

The maintenance dose of chemo is going fine. We wouldn't necessarily expect any side effects this soon, so we'll keep our fingers crossed. We have an appointment on Friday to check Shannon's weight again and hopefully get clearance for more activity next week. Today she and her buddies watched the Women's World Cup and then walked to Kwik Trip for ice cream. That was the most activity she's had in two and a half weeks, and it definitely tired her out a bit. It's going to take time to get her strength back.

Now that we are home for a few weeks, we are having meals delivered again. It's such a kind gesture and it frees us up to enjoy our days since we're not spending time preparing meals. (If you know me, that last sentence made you laugh because I never spend time preparing meals. Never. Seriously. Thank goodness I have a husband that can cook!)

So today we: entertained friends, painted a bedroom, assembled and installed a closet organizing system, mowed the lawn, and ate a turkey dinner complete with stuffing, mashed potatoes, and gravy! An all around good day.

POSTED BY JEN

SATURDAY, JULY 16, 2011

The Shannon room remodel turned into quite a big project and had an offshoot project break out in Erin's room as well. It's consumed the last few days, but it's been really fun. We're hoping to put the finishing touches on them today.

Some good news, some bad for Shannon yesterday. First the good: the first round of maintenance chemo finished last night and Shannon's excited to have a few less pills to take. We'll see if the Temodar catches up with her next week, but so far, so good. The bad news: her weight dropped four pounds this week. Now she's got until her Tuesday weight re-check to put a few pounds back on, or they will start her on another drug to stimulate her appetite. She does not want that and told Dr. Rodriguez, "I know I can eat more!" I feel a little responsible since I was a single parent while Dan was away last week. It seemed like we were eating plenty, but apparently I wasn't as diligent as I needed to be. Shannon's appetite is a tricky thing right now; she needs to eat even when she's not hungry. Basically, she needs to graze all day long.

So as I write, she and Dan are at the grocery store loading up on food. Shannon's energy and attitude are good, so I'm hopeful that she'll put her mind to it and gain the weight back.

POSTED BY JEN

SUNDAY, JULY 17, 2011

I hate to admit it but me being away again on "business" has helped to steady the ship.

For most of Shannon and Erin's lives I have traveled for work, usually a couple of nights out of most weeks. The girls grew accustomed to my trips. Jen also settled into a routine with me on the road. Our household would invariably benefit as Mom always found it easier to complete "work at home" projects and activities with me gone. There was a certain balance to that routine that has been missing since Shannon's diagnosis April 15.

Business travel can be brutal. Some weeks you wonder what the heck you are doing. If you are an outside sales representative of some company your office is often a Hampton Inn in Duluth, Minnesota, or a Courtyard by Marriott in Normal, Illinois. But if this is what you do and you are good at it (and you enjoy making deals and growing business), you endure the travel because that's what earns you the medium-sized bucks.

However, the best part of going on business trips is coming home. The kids are excited to see you. The wife can't keep her hands off you (OK, that was a stretch). Overall, there is freshness each and every week. Absence always makes the heart grow fonder.

When I returned from my trip late Thursday it was there again. That feeling that you are home again and all is right in the world. And, my goodness, had they been productive. A trip to IKEA gave Jen many assembly projects to piece together, and the girls got to play "Design on a Dime" with their rooms. And the upgrades turned out great. The girls were excited!

So it was a good week. And Shannon looked great. All you have to do is take one look at her big brown eyes to see how she is feeling. That was noted on Friday when we were in to check Shannon's weight, which was down marginally. But, Dr. Rodriguez said all you have to do is look at her to know that Shannon is back.

Still, we were ordered to rest up, stay out of the heat, and continue to build Shannon's strength.

So this weekend that gave us license to sit around, eat, and watch some great sports drama together. The highlights included another Irish win in a major, Darren Clarke's triumph in the British Open; the Twins taking three-of-four from Kansas City to pull within five games of first; and the event all of us were most excited to watch, the US Women's World Cup soccer loss to Japan in penalty kicks. Shannon watched over at her friend Megan's. Jen, Erin, and I watched together at home and couldn't help but smile at the joy on the faces of the Japanese players. Truly, that country needed the pick me up that the World Cup title provided them.

The perfect song for the mood is now playing; from Norah Jones' album *Feels Like Home* ... "What Am I to You?"

POSTED BY DAN

TUESDAY, JULY 19, 2011

We have been experiencing some unprecedented heat and humidity here in Minnesota, with a record-setting dewpoint and heat index yesterday. It's the kind where your glasses fog up when you go from inside to out. On top of that, Shannon was still under doctor's orders to take it easy. Yet Monday, we couldn't help but loosen the reigns a little. We let Shannon play in her nine-hole golf league with her friends early in the morning. It's something she's wanted to do, and this was the first Monday that we've been home and she's been healthy enough, so we said OK. Then, we had the opportunity to go see the Twins play from a suite at Target Field, thanks to one of Dan's customers. So we thought, what the heck, there's AC in the suite, let's do it. But after the game, walking to the car and starting the drive home, Shannon's cheeks were bright red, and it made us wonder if we had made a mistake. She can't afford to lose weight or get dehydrated. We made it home and laid low the rest of the evening, all of us a little nervous for today's weight re-check.

But, the weight check was good. Shannon put back on the weight she'd lost last week. All that forcing herself to eat has been working. Shannon's been dealing with the reality that all the drugs she needs to take have affected how she feels, but she still needs to eat. She's not "sick," but she doesn't feel quite right. Her stomach feels unsettled and her energy isn't what she'd like it to be. She's tired early at night, but can't sleep in late. This is just how it is now, and while it bums her out, she's coming to terms with it. When she's tired, she goes to bed. When she wakes up early, she has cereal and watches SportsCenter while she waits for the rest of the house to awaken. She tries to snack all day and keeps track of when it's time to take her meds. She's taking ownership and control because she does not want to be babied.

I, of course, want to baby her in the worst way. The maternal instincts are strong. I wish I could take it all away and make her be a happy-go-lucky teen, enjoying a summer of late nights, sleeping in, playing hockey, and sunning at the pool with friends. The truth is, we all have to accept and try to enjoy what she can do right now and not lament the things she can't.

Some good news on that front today as Dr. Rodriguez was pleased with Shannon's check-up and gave her the go ahead to increase her exercise a bit. So tomorrow we're off to the Athletic Club to give Shannon's Speed, Agility, Quickness class a try. This is another activity that has been on Shannon's wish list, so being cleared to give it a go feels like progress. I hope Shannon can enjoy the opportunity to be out there and not be frustrated by her limitations. It's all part of learning to live with her disease. For all of us …

POSTED BY JEN

FRIDAY, JULY 22, 2011

I have been struggling a bit this week. I have been irritable and intolerant and just overall lacking confidence.

The Bloomington Lincoln class of 1981 is gathering tonight in Minneapolis, and I chose not to attend. Based on the events of the last three months, I just don't feel up to it. I had a ton of fun in high school; no doubt it was a great phase of my life. I graduated with a class of over five hundred and have remained in consistent contact with only a handful of my classmates. I would certainly like to see many of these people. I just don't have the energy to tell our story over and over. I know there are plenty of my classmates who have been through challenging situations and could lend support. Like we've noted many times, people everywhere face really big stuff all the time and come out on the other side.

Maybe that's gnawing at me. Shannon told me, "You can't please everyone." That remains a constant challenge in this current phase of our lives.

Another possible explanation for my irritability is that my physical fitness has been slowed by the extreme heat. I suppose I could be out there at 6:00 A.M., but even then the humidity has been so aggressive that it doesn't feel very good. It's better today. I got a walk in this morning and then just took a bike ride with Erin.

No doubt, my physicality is tied to my serenity. It's true for all of us in our house. In fact, Shannon is starting to sound out her plan to get back in shape. Today, she is back at the Rochester Athletic Club for her Speed, Agility, and Quickness class. She wants to shoot pucks, she wants to hit golf shots, and she wants to get stronger. Next week Shannon turns thirteen, which means she can work out on the fitness floor without restriction at the RAC. So she's talking about that and getting her head wrapped around getting ready to play sports, which is great. That makes her happy. We just have to temper her enthusiasm and keep the pounds on. More breakfast shakes.

So let's pray for more moderate weather so we can all get back outdoors!

POSTED BY DAN

Stubborn Streak

When Shannon was an infant turning toddler, we would rock her to sleep and attempt to very carefully place her in her crib. If she awoke, there would be hell to pay. Shannon was none too happy to be put to bed. I can vividly remember the sound of her pacifier hitting the door as she threw it at me while I was trying to leave the room!

She continued this pattern even when we moved her to a "big girl" bed. Every night she would get out of her bed and come stand next to our bed wanting to sleep with Dan and me. Certainly we made some rookie mistakes as first time parents and gave in to her demands too often. Live and learn. But when little sister joined the family, Dan and I knew we needed some control. We tried to say no to Shannon. We were changing the rules, and she was not very happy about it! She would stomp down the stairs, give it a few minutes, and then return to our bedside crying. Then we tried closing her door to keep her in her room. That did not produce the desired effect. We've got the hole in the door to prove it.

Stubbornness caused Shannon problems in those younger years, but as she battled to live the life she wanted to live, it served her well. She had plans, and she didn't want her disease to stop her. As Shannon carried on through her summer battling the tumor and the drugs and the fatigue, she put her mind to the things she wanted to do. And when her body allowed, she did them.

SUNDAY, JULY 24, 2011

A busy week is almost behind us, and an eventful week is ahead. This past one was filled with more appointments than we'd like, but the results were mostly good, so positive overall. Shannon's energy is bouncing back now nine days after the first round of maintenance chemo. She fit in some time with friends, some golf, and even a little open skating. Erin has had some summer fun too. In fact, I am watching her and her friend swim as I write.

In addition to our hematology appointment, the girls had their dental check-ups as well. No cavities and the only change is a new toothpaste prescribed for Shannon since radiation can affect the enamel on your teeth. Our dentist was well aware of Shannon's fight and even requested one of the Shannon the Cannon bracelets that she'd seen on several of her patients.

Added to those two appointments was a hearing test and consult to check on Shannon's left ear which has been bugging her. No sign of any infection or obvious problem and her hearing is excellent, so it's most likely just another side effect of tumor related changes in her head. The doctor was able to put Shannon's mind at ease that there is no reason not to swim—or to fly.

Speaking of flying, this Friday, July 29, Shannon will turn thirteen. A milestone. Over a year ago, Grandma and Papa Harkins proposed an idea they had for their four grandchildren: each grandchild gets to plan a special birthday trip to take when they turn thirteen. Just the grandchild, Grandma, and Papa to a destination of the child's choosing—within reason. (Funny side note: cousin Jack may need some explanation of "within reason." He's only eight, but he's thinking that for his thirteenth, Grandma and Papa will take him to Spain to see a bullfight!)

Shannon is the oldest, so she gets to go first. Shannon decided back in February that she'd like to see the Twins play an away game and it just so happens they are out in Oakland on July 29. Oakland isn't a great destination, but the city across the bay certainly is. So, a trip to San Francisco was planned. Mind you, this plan was hatched before Shannon got sick. There have been many sleepless nights for me, Dan,

Grandma, and Papa as we tried to figure out how best to carry out this birthday wish. Should we all go? Should we postpone? Would Shannon be healthy enough to travel? Why did something that was suppose to be a great gift now become something that was causing great stress? We've spent weeks avoiding talking about it, so unsure if it would even happen.

In the end, Shannon decided for all of us. She doesn't want our entire family to come; she wants her trip, just like she had planned. Her own special trip. She wants to tour Alcatraz, see the Golden Gate Bridge, shop on Fisherman's Wharf, and watch the Twins play on the road. Shannon knows she may tire easily, but she's planning for down time when she needs it, and early bedtimes if necessary. Papa assured her that an early bedtime is not a problem for him! And, knock on wood, Shannon's health is good enough right now to go and enjoy it. So grateful for that. So, today she began preparing by painting her nails, updating her iPod, and going over the list of meds she'll need to take on the road.

Monday we see Dr. Rodriguez for a blood-check and weight-check. Barring any changes, on Wednesday, Shannon, Grandma, and Papa will be off on their adventure. When she returns on Saturday, Shannon will be a teenager ...

POSTED BY JEN

GOOD TO GO

Quick update: Shannon's weight-check was good. She's almost back to her original weight, and blood counts were well inside the normal range. Operation Birthday Trip is a go!

POSTED BY JEN

THURSDAY, JULY 28, 2011

All is well on the birthday trip. The flight went smoothly: no issues with nausea for Shannon, and she enjoyed the complimentary hot dog and chips on the Sun Country flight. She is keeping Dan and me informed of their whereabouts via text. Dan and I were chuckling last night

Shannon's thirteenth birthday trip to San Francisco | Fisherman's Wharf with Grandma and Papa Harkins

because Shannon was sitting on the wharf enjoying some pasta with Grandma and Papa, but she kept texting us for updates of the Twins score in Texas! I told her to quit texting and enjoy the view.

We passed our day away quite nicely as Erin and I tagged along with Dan on a business trip, and that gave us a chance to take in the Minnesota Zoo. Erin liked showing her dad around the place on his first time there. The dolphin show and bird show were highlights. Erin enjoyed some one-on-one time with us, and we laughed a lot.

Our anxiety regarding Shannon's trip has been replaced by contentment and joy, especially as we see pictures of Shannon in San Fran. The smile on her face says it all. Today Erin, Dan, and I will stay busy again with some shopping to put the finishing touches on Erin's room redesign while Grandma, Papa, and Shannon head to Alcatraz.

POSTED BY JEN

Big, brown eyes and the ever-present pacifier

FRIDAY, JULY 29, 2011— BIRTHDAY GIRL

Shannon is thirteen today. As we've written before, milestones are tough. Reaching one makes you think about the next one, and that's something we just shouldn't do. So, celebrate today and stay in the present.

Shannon is loving her adventure, and with all she's been through these past four months, she deserves some joy. From the sounds of it, Grandma and Papa are loving it too. Yesterday took them to Alcatraz, Market Street, and across the Golden Gate Bridge for dinner in Sausalito. Today they've scheduled a cable

Sightseeing on her birthday trip | On the boat to Alcatraz

car tour of the city, then off to Oakland to see the Twins play. They'll be home tomorrow. Can't wait ...

POSTED BY JEN

SUNDAY, JULY 31, 2011

Jen and I just closed out a July for a lifetime watching *Apollo 13* with Shannon and Erin. The house is quiet again. Everyone is asleep but me as I sort through so many thoughts and feelings from a month that began with so much fear and turmoil but closes with such gratitude and hope.

Shannon's birthday weekend culminated with a blowout backyard brat bash that was full of laughter and joy!

A month that started with IV infusions ended with cake, cousins, aunts, uncles, and both sets of grandparents gathered together in celebration of a milestone and a remarkable turnaround. Our support

O'Hara cousins | Tessie, Nora, Maggie, and Grace pay a visit to celebrate with the new teenager

teams—the Harkins and O'Hara families—continue to rally around us. That has remained a constant, and we are so grateful.

Shannon's thirteenth birthday trip to San Fran (she returned to Rochester Saturday evening), our time together with Erin, and our weekend reunion and birthday party have us all feeling fortunate to have so much love in our lives.

At St. John's Sunday morning, we felt the love as well with close friends in pews all around us. The girls giggled their way through the worship. There was a day when we would have given them dirty looks for squirrely behavior during mass, but that's all changed. Giggle away.

August starts with blood labs and a check-up with our team in hematology. Shannon's energy levels are always an indication of how her blood counts will read. And right now she is full of steam and intends to participate in both golf league and her conditioning class Monday. We expect that the doctors will recommend a tapering of the steroids that helped stabilize things over these past few weeks.

The steroids work magic to tame things around the tumor. They also do a number on Shannon's complexion. She's ready for a decreased dosage of Decadron.

I suspect August will be a blur, as the school planning, shopping, and sports sign-ups are already underway. We get a week at Lake Hubert. We get to be together. Time … we get time … we have time. We will enjoy. One day at a time.

POSTED BY DAN

TUESDAY, AUGUST 2, 2011

August brings one of those tasks by which us moms mark time: shopping for school supplies. Erasers, pencils, markers, folders, and just the perfect binder. It only took five different stores to almost complete this task. If we could just find the elusive yellow notebook, we'd be set!

Our appointments yesterday went well. Shannon's weight is back to where it was the day she was diagnosed, and her blood work was good. Shannon enjoyed sharing the gifts she had brought back from San Fran with her medical team: some sourdough bread, some Ghirardelli chocolate, and a picture of Shannon behind bars at Alcatraz.

The only part of the appointment that didn't go as we had hoped was the tapering of the steroids. Shannon wants to get off the steroids ASAP, but her medical team is taking it slow, going down just a half a milligram every five to seven days. Shannon is feeling good and not experiencing many headaches, and they don't want her to take any steps backwards. With this cautious approach, it will take about a month to completely taper off the steroids.

Shannon's energy continues to build, and she's gaining steam this week—working on her golf game and her fitness. She's thinking about this year's hockey season and next year's golf season. I have to keep reminding myself, it's OK for her to think that way. She can until she can't, right?

As Shannon is gaining steam, I am lying awake at night. Things are going well, so it must be time to fret! I am thinking about Wednesday's neuro-opthamology appointment and Thursday's neuro exam and next week's chemo and this year's hockey season and next year's golf season … I guess I haven't quite mastered the concept of staying in the present.

But, if practice makes perfect, I'm bound to improve because this is how it is and how it will be; the calendar will be filled with appointments and medications, but that doesn't need to keep us from enjoying today. Today was a good day and tomorrow can be one too …

POSTED BY JEN

FRIDAY, AUGUST 5, 2011

Erin is down and out with an ear infection. Of course, it could have something to do with the countless hours the girl spends in the pool. She can swim for hours. But the last few nights have been tough. We're hoping the Amoxicillin does it's magic soon as Erin has a big sleepover birthday party Saturday that she is looking forward to.

It's pretty cute to watch Shannon shift into nurturing mode for her sister. She made Erin toast and set her up with some ice water next to the bed—and made sure she had the remote. Then Shannon was off to the RAC where she is completely focused on getting stronger. She worked with a personal trainer Thursday to lay out a conditioning strategy for her soccer and hockey seasons. Shannon has a nine-week plan in place. Look out.

Thursday also included another thorough neurological exam with Dr. Keating, our primary pediatric neurologist. Dr. Keating said Shannon completed her best testing since diagnosis. Her eye movements were stellar. Nothing she found would keep Shannon out of competition.

Going forward, the neuro exams will alternate months with our MRI's. At a minimum, someone from pediatric neurology at WFMC (World Famous Mayo Clinic) will be eyeballing Shannon every month. That's a tremendous benefit of being a local patient. If you lived in Wichita, monthly exams would be tough. Again, the care levels we are receiving are phenomenal. We are grateful.

Shannon's rebound has allowed me to return to digging up sales activity for my employer, EFS Transportation Services. In fact, next week I will hit it hard on a trip to Peoria and Quincy, Illinois. Quincy in August … you kidding me? Doesn't get any better than that.

Need to add another one to the Shannon blog playlist: John Hiatt, "Have a Little Faith in Me":

> *When the road gets dark*
> *and you can no longer see*
> *just let my love throw a spark*
> *and have a little faith in me …*

I also have to affirm a song my wife recommended a few blogs ago … caught me again this week on a walk … Jack Johnson, "All At Once." One of these days we will compile and post the Shannon blog playlist. It's pretty solid.

And today I leave you with a prayer that really works for me when I get stuck in the muck:

> Lord, make me a channel of thy peace;
> that where there is hatred, I may bring love;
> that where there is wrong, I may bring the spirit of forgiveness;
> that where there is discord, I may bring harmony;
> that where there is error, I may bring truth;
> that where there is doubt, I may bring faith;
> that where there is despair, I may bring hope;
> that where there are shadows, I may bring light;
> that where there is sadness, I may bring joy.
> Lord, grant that I may seek rather to comfort than to be comforted;
> to understand, than to be understood;
> to love, than to be loved.
> For it is by self-forgetting that one finds.
> It is by forgiving that one is forgiven.
> It is by dying that one awakens to eternal life.
> Amen.

POSTED BY DAN

SUNDAY, AUGUST 7, 2011
Medication List—Week of Aug 8–Aug 14

Monday 8/8
8:00 A.M. Decadron (1 mg), Zantac, and Kytril
4:00 P.M. Decadron (1 mg) and Zantac
8:00 P.M. Kytril
9:00 P.M. Temodar

Tuesday 8/9
8:00 A.M. Decadron (1 mg), Zantac, and Kytril
4:00 P.M. Decadron (1 mg) and Zantac
8:00 P.M. Kytril
9:00 P.M. Temodar

Wednesday 8/10
8:00 A.M. Decadron (1 mg), Zantac, and Kytril
4:00 P.M. Decadron (1 mg) and Zantac
8:00 P.M. Kytril
9:00 P.M. Temodar

Thursday 8/11
8:00 A.M. Decadron (1 mg), Zantac, and Kytril
4:00 P.M. Decadron (1 mg) and Zantac
8:00 P.M. Kytril
9:00 P.M. Temodar

Friday 8/12
8:00 A.M. Decadron (1 mg), Zantac, and Kytril
4:00 P.M. Decadron (1 mg) and Zantac
8:00 P.M. Kytril
9:00 P.M. Temodar

Saturday 8/13
8:00 A.M. Bactrim, Decadron (1 mg), and Zantac
4:00 P.M. Decadron (1 mg) and Zantac
8:00 P.M. Bactrim

Sunday 8/14
8:00 A.M. Bactrim, Decadron (1 mg), and Zantac
4:00 P.M. Decadron (1 mg) and Zantac
8:00 P.M. Bactrim

Dan watched me as I filled the pillbox today for the upcoming week and said, "I think people would find this interesting. You should post that on the blog." So there you go. This is what Shannon's med schedule looks like as we begin round two of the maintenance chemo tomorrow, and continue to taper down the steroids this week. Shannon is so responsible about taking these; when I forget, she remembers.

Shannon continues to feel energetic. She's playing golf again today, and yesterday she took part in the last Saturday morning hockey group as well. Shannon said she felt like one of the weaker ones out there, but she looked pretty good to us. We think everything she can do is just a bonus, but she doesn't see it that way. Good for her.

Erin is feeling better and having a good weekend as well. She went tubing on Lake Zumbro and had a sleepover at her friend's house last night. She was all giggles this morning when I picked her up. Good summer fun.

Tomorrow we head back to Mayo: blood work and weight-check and the go-ahead for the chemo. I am hopeful that this will be our only trip to Mayo this week. One day and be done with it. Please, please, please ...

I continue to catch myself looking too far ahead and worrying. I was rambling on about something or other that may or may not happen, and Dan looked at me and said, "You just can't help yourself, can you?" Nope. But I try. Try to stay in the present and enjoy the good that is happening right now.

I had an inspiring correspondence this week with an acquaintance who is going through his own struggles with cancer. He was given a bad prognosis but continues to live with grace and hope. I strive to live like that, so I wanted to share his words with you:

Fear comes when we focus on the things outside our control. Confidence and courage grow as we focus on the things within our control ... I cannot change the fact that I have cancer. It is out of my control. But I do control my attitude and my determination to never give up. I will live with gratitude, thankful for all the blessings that I have been given. Attitude, effort, persistence, and gratitude are always within my control, and so I focus on them. How long I will live is outside my control, and so I do not worry about it. Each day I have is a wonderful gift.

POSTED BY JEN

It Takes an Army

I never imagined how many people in the medical profession we would consult with over the course of nine months. It takes an army to fight a brain tumor, and we had a good one. Starting at the Mayo Clinic and finishing at St. Jude, the list of doctors, nurses, nurse practitioners, and techs who were an active part of Shannon's treatment could fill up this page. But the core group of doctors—Dr. Laack, Dr. Keating, Dr. Khan, Dr. Rodriguez, Dr. Rao, and Dr. Wetmore—were amazing. It's not lost on me that these doctors were all female. Not a bad example for my girls. We have commented before about the good fortune we had of living just a few miles from a world-class medical facility. And eventually, when our journey took us to Memphis, we found ourselves at another one.

These doctors and nurses manage to get up each day and offer hope, compassion, and support even when they know what the outcome will likely be. A brain stem glioma diagnosis is a death sentence. And yet, they managed to smile, connect, and engage with Shannon even though they knew they would almost certainly lose her. And Shannon wasn't their only patient. How does one get up and go to work knowing that they don't have the means to save their patients? We met so many people who have dedicated their lives to treating children and some, specifically, to treating terminally ill children. It takes a very special person to make this their life's work.

We have written at length about the support we felt from our friends and our community, but the support from the medical team was equally important. When we had a question or needed a consult, these doctors and nurses made us feel like Shannon was their most important patient. They answered our calls and emails. Their ability to look this young lady in the eye and treat her with respect was amazing. They all knew what was going to happen, and yet they helped Shannon stay hopeful and enjoy the time she had left. They encouraged her to play golf and play hockey. They made it possible to go away on trips to Lake Hubert and San Francisco. And in the end, they made it OK to go home, be at peace, and say goodbye.

MONDAY, AUGUST 8, 2011

The good news: we don't have to return to Mayo any more this week, just as we had hoped. One and done. The bad news: a couple of blips today that sent Shannon's mood south.

First, her weight was down a couple of pounds, so she was reminded to keep snacking and keep the weight on. Shannon explained that she has been active and working out and losing a couple of pounds was just fine with her. She wants to feel lean and strong. Losing weight is not an option, though, so a milkshake is in her future tonight.

The second blip was the news that we won't be tapering the steroids during this week because of the Temodar. The doctors don't want to make any medication changes that could muddy the waters during the chemo weeks. We were also told that they might keep Shannon on a small dose of steroids for quite a while. That really bummed her out. Shannon thought the taper would continue every five days, and in her mind, she was going to be off the steroids for ten days before school started. She was hoping that the steroid rash on her face would be cleared up before she hit the halls for eighth grade. It's not bad enough to have a brain tumor; she gets puffy cheeks and acne as a bonus.

So, I did what any reasonable mom would do when her child is down in the dumps; I took her to the store and bought her some stuff. Some new crackle nail polish and a new neon sports bra helped her feel a little bit better. Retail therapy at it's finest!

Despite things not going exactly as she had hoped today, Shannon's still got some spunk. She's currently yelling at the Twins on TV. Same as it ever was …

POSTED BY JEN

THURSDAY, AUGUST 11, 2011

No news is good news this week. Shannon is tolerating the Temodar just fine and staying busy with workouts at the RAC and time on the golf course. Yesterday she played three holes in the morning with her sister and then nine holes by herself in the afternoon. She's got plans to get out there again today with me. The golf cart is being put to good use.

Erin just headed north with Grandma Harkins for a couple of days at Grandma's family's cabin in northern Wisconsin. Erin had been debating whether or not she wanted to go without the rest of us coming along, but Shannon and Erin came to the conclusion last night that some separation would be good for both of them!

Today Dan is completing a thousand-mile road trip for work, drumming up some new business that will require a return visit in a couple of weeks. This is how it used to be back before everything changed.

I find myself thinking about my return to work. I am planning to start teaching some tennis again when the fall session begins right after Labor Day. As we've been frequenting the RAC lately, I've been running into my fellow tennis pros. I miss those guys (and gals).

It's time to get out and enjoy another beautiful day.

POSTED BY JEN

FRIDAY, AUGUST 12, 2011

I asked a friend today, "If you knew all your relationships were temporary, would you go about your business any differently?" That's where I have been living this week, and I have to say, I have had a pretty terrific week.

Of course, all our relationships are temporary. Life is temporary.

Somehow I am at peace with that reality tonight as I write this entry on the eve of my forty-eighth birthday.

Surrender? No chance. Give up hope? No way. But acceptance of our circumstances is bringing me peace at this stage of our journey.

And with Erin in Wisconsin with Grandma and her Harkins cousins, Jen and I have been enjoying our Shannon time. The kid is funny—just a joy to hang out with.

We squeezed in a workout at the RAC, shot some pucks, enjoyed slices at Mr. Pizza, and went skate shopping. We were planning to trade up for another set of used skates but ended up having Shannon fitted for a brand new set of Bauer Vapors, her first pair of new hockey skates. Thanks to our buddy Bob at Shoot-n-Save for making us a deal we couldn't refuse.

After shopping we napped around while watching the PGA Championship. Then we played nine holes together.

Shannon did not play very well but hit the pin on the par-3 seventeenth at Willow Creek, and made the three-footer for her second career birdie. Jen and I were OK on the golf course, but loving our Friday night together and not too concerned about good and bad shots.

Perhaps that is why I am in a grateful mood tonight. Life is good. And Saturday is my birthday, and I get to play golf while Jen and Shannon paint a bathroom.

POSTED BY DAN

TUESDAY, AUGUST 16, 2011

We're going to have a busy final day before vacation. This morning we are going to weigh in at Mayo 16 and check blood counts after Shannon's second round of maintenance chemo. We expect that the counts will be good because Shannon has been feeling good. We will see one of our doctors. We will update later.

Shannon wants to do her own *Myth Busters* experiment with the scale at Mayo 16 and the scale at the RAC. At the RAC last week she was pumped when she hit ninety-two. Today she wants to find out if the scales say the same thing so she can monitor her weight after workouts at the RAC.

Her workout routine has been intense. Monday she walked nine holes with her golf league in the morning. Then she put her soccer gear on and worked on moves, kicked the ball, and ran the hills in our yard until her cheeks were red. Then Monday night we hiked around the reservoir with our friends the Grafstroms.

She was really pumped to see Jim Thome hit his 600th homer. Shortly after, she lay down in our bed and the next thing we knew she was out. Never moved her. The second round of Temodar in her maintenance dosage (260 mg) has tired her out. She has napped more. But she's tolerated it pretty well. Eight more cycles to go (five days on, twenty-three days off).

We are reaching the end of our summer, and we are looking to restore order, normalcy, and routine to our lives. When we return from Lake Hubert, we will have a few days to prepare for the start of school.

Ellen Wente delivered our last meal Monday, and it was fabulous (a secret lasagna family recipe, salad, watermelon, bread, and a mocha ice cream pie that had no chance of survival). Ellen ran the point on our meal program along with Amy Pankow, as they coordinated families and food that have been delivered to our home since May. Every Monday, Wednesday and Friday we had a home cooked meal delivered. I wish I could list off all the families that stepped up for us. Incredible generosity of time and talent. We always seemed to get every family's favorite meal.

But it is time to restore order, normalcy, and routine to our lives. The meal program has meant the world to us. After Shannon's diagnosis, we lost our energy and creativity in the kitchen. I'm a bit of a foodie and love to create ... but I just lost my desire.

Our favorite line over these last months as the clock hit 5:00 P.M. on a Monday, Wednesday, Friday: "The food window is open, look for cars!" So all we can say to that is a giant THANKS! Way to pay it forward people. We wish we could have a giant banquet to say thanks back at ya. Maybe some day.

Time to pack ...

POSTED BY DAN

WEDNESDAY, AUGUST 17, 2011

It is early in the A.M. and I am up prepping for our trip to the lake. The weather looks pretty good, and the girls are very excited to head to one of their favorite places on earth.

Yesterday's check-up went well. The blood counts are good and the weight is holding steady, even up another pound. Shannon's been working out hard, so she feels like if she's gaining weight, it might be from adding muscle. The Temodar has definitely made Shannon feel fatigued. She told me, "I could just sleep all day," which is fine during summer vacation, but may present some challenges once the school year starts.

The approaching school year is causing Shannon some great anxiety. While Erin is quite excited to head back to school, Shannon is feeling apprehensive. The steroids have done a number on her face and the radiation did a number on her hair, and now it's almost time to go walk the halls of eighth grade. No matter how many times Dan and I tell her she's doing great and she looks great, all things considered, it comes down to how she feels about herself. There were tears yesterday as she let it all out.

So, hopefully a trip to Lake Hubert will brighten her spirits and help us all recharge our batteries before we head into the start of the school year.

POSTED BY JEN

FRIDAY, AUGUST 19, 2011

Our first two days at Lake Hubert have been perfect tens. Warm temps, sunny skies, and low winds, which means we've spent endless hours doing this:

Fun and games | The girls (and Sunny the Wonder Dog) spend hours jumping off the dock and playing in the lake

Which usually leads us to an hour or two spent doing this:

Nap time | Dan and Shannon take a break

We have absolutely no complaints about either activity!

POSTED BY JEN

SATURDAY, AUGUST 20, 2011

Nothing eventful happening from the lake. Unless you consider BBQ chicken, pasta, and fresh green beans an event. Actually, a quick little squall line blew through as I grilled. But now the sun is out, the wind is dying, and we are in for a beauty sunset. Might be fire time. Or do we hit the Ox again for cones???

More of the same R & R, which has been terrific for all. Shannon feels great. Erin is great as usual. And Jen and I are doing the best we can to stay in the here and now. That's the best place to live.

Forecast is OK for Sunday but looks like we may see some heat again Monday, Tuesday. Good thing we have a lake. Love to all—we are so grateful for our time together!

POSTED BY DAN

MONDAY, AUGUST 22, 2011

Just another Monday.

Reflection time | Peace and quiet at the lake

We are living life to its fullest up here in Nisswa. It's just the four of us, Sunny the dog, and no agenda.

We spent our Sunday morning worship in Lake Hubert. Calm, crystal clear waters, sunshine, treading in the deep water on noodles, hangin' out on the beach. No doubt, God was smiling down.

Then our friends down the beach at the Gustafson cabin fired up the Glastron and offered the girls their first attempts at water skiing. Shannon and Erin are veteran tubers but have never attempted old-school water skiing.

From skiing we took advantage of free golf at the Garden Course at Grand View where Shannon, Jen, and I hit the ball around while Erin played Annie Leibovitz with her new camera. Lots of laughs ... not funny was that Jen clipped me by a shot while Shannon posted a respectable forty-three.

From golf we drove to find dinner on the opposite side of Gull Lake from Brainerd Int'l Raceway where the annual drag races were pouring out onto Hwy 371. Steer clear. We settled on an early dinner at Bar Harbor with the blue hairs and reloaded on sweets at the Chocolate Ox on the way back to the lake.

The day was topped off watching a kids' choice movie *Soul Surfer* about surfer Brittany Hamilton who lost an arm—and almost her life— in a shark attack. I was not ready to emote, but this story took me there as the family rallied around this determined and stubborn young lady who reminded me of Shannon in so many ways. The family dealt with grief and faced their tragedy together in different ways ... but together. Also, reminded me of our little unit. Some did better than others. In the end, of course, Brittany triumphs, inspires, and leaves you feeling hopeful.

Jen checked in with hematology at Mayo Clinic this morning, and Shannon's steroid dosage was reduced by another 0.5 mg. Getting closer to steroid free. Feeling hopeful today. And two more days in paradise with a forecast that could not be any better. Live high!

POSTED BY DAN

WEDNESDAY, AUGUST 24, 2011

We head home from the lake today, and even though there are two weeks left before school starts, this feels like the symbolic end to our summer. And we've have had a great one. We've been places, seen people, done things, and have a heightened sense of awareness of enjoying every memory we've made. Gratitude.

This week has been no different. Shannon learning to ski has been a highlight, and the last two days she's made runs up and down the bay. We've worked and played around the O'Hara family cabin, and the four of us even managed to put in three new dock sections together. Then there was the debacle last night: We were out of our swimsuits for the first time all day, dressed and ready to head into town for pizza and ice cream. Dan couldn't find his glasses and then realized he had jumped in the lake with them on. Back in the water (OK, everyone except me) to do some diving to locate the missing glasses before the sun went down ... luckily, the glasses were found, and we laughed about it (mostly at Dan's expense) over a pepperoni pizza at our favorite place, Rafferty's in Nisswa.

So, now it's time to turn our attention to the things ahead: fall hockey tonight, school orientation and schedule pick-up tomorrow, and Shannon's next MRI on Friday. It's been easy up here to almost forget about Shannon's illness. She doesn't seem like a cancer patient when she's swimming and skiing and kayaking. But one look at my calendar reminds me otherwise.

I'm not sure how this next phase will be as I've been trying to psych myself up to put my energy toward the regular life stuff that's ahead: school, homework, fall sports, work for me and Dan ... there's a part of me that wants to just stay on this perpetual vacation and spend all of our time together doing whatever we want, but that's not realistic. Shannon wants to be a normal eighth grader. Erin wants to start middle school. They want some structure.

Shannon's health dictated what we did this summer: when she felt good, we were on the move, and when she got sick, we circled the wagons and looked to our families and friends for support. I imagine that things will be the same going forward. As long as she's feeling good, we will forge ahead with normal, everyday activities, same as last fall and every fall before that. And I'll try not to waste energy worrying about the giant "what if" that follows us around. Stay in the present and enjoy today …

POSTED BY JEN

New Normal

Once you learn that your child has a terminal disease, nothing will really ever be normal again. But "new normal" is a term we used over and over during this year as we tried to right the ship every time it veered off course. And the ship went off course a lot. If you're a slightly obsessive compulsive mother who likes to know exactly what you are doing three weeks from Thursday, well, this cancer journey is going to be a struggle for you!

Things are always changing: medications, added appointments, the need to consult with doctors, the need for flexibility from teachers or coaches, making plans and then realizing you are not feeling up to doing what you thought you'd be doing that day, and so on.

I am a planner (my husband may call me an over-planner on occasion), and part of how I cope with life is knowing what's in front of me. So, learning to be flexible was a really hard reality for me to grasp. But for my kid, I can do anything. Each time it was necessary, we would adjust. And every time, Shannon led the way.

FRIDAY, AUGUST 26, 2011

Factoids from the last two days:

School schedules have been picked up; both girls are busy figuring out which friends will be in classes with them. Texting and social networking being put to good use! Shannon and Erin seem happy with their teachers, lockers, and schedules ...

Soccer info: The girls have heard from their coaches and it looks like Shannon and Erin both have some buddies on their teams. Practices will start next week.

Hematology appointment: Weight and blood counts are good. Shannon keeps pushing to decrease the steroids. Dr. Rodriguez has a soft spot for her, I think, and Shannon convinced her to go down another 0.5 mg starting Monday.

MRI: Shannon's third scan was done this morning, and we meet with the doctors next Tuesday to see the results. Shannon was in good spirits this morning—she's an old pro at it by now. She doesn't seem stressed or worried about the results, so Dan and I will try to follow her lead on that ...

This weekend: As I write, Shannon is golfing with Papa, Erin is at a pool party, and tonight we head downtown for the Greek Festival. Dan's playing in the city golf championship this weekend, and Shannon's planning to caddy for him during Sunday's round here at our home course.

That about covers it ...

POSTED BY JEN

LATE NIGHT UPDATE

We have written before about how touched we are by the kindness of others. Today that kindness came from one of our doctors. Dr. Keating saw that Shannon's MRI results had come back so she took a look at the scan. Happy with what she saw, she wondered who had shared the results with us. She pulled up Shannon's record and saw that we weren't due to get results until Tuesday. At 4:40 P.M. on a Friday afternoon, Dr. Keating took the time to pick up the phone and put our minds at ease. She said she wanted to help alleviate our PMS—Post-MRI Syndrome—where patients and their families are filled with anxiety while they wait for the results!

We will have more facts to share after our Tuesday appointments with Dr. Rao and Dr. Laack, but a late afternoon call from Dr. Keating let us know that treatment continues to show good results. And that's making for a happy weekend at the O'Hara household.

POSTED BY JEN

SUNDAY, AUGUST 28, 2011

My golf game was highly suspect, but my looper was sure cute!

A friend shared a prayer with me that lends perspective to three putts and double bogeys: "Don't worry about anything, pray about everything, and thank God for all you have."

POSTED BY DAN

Caddying for Dad | The Rochester City Golf Championship

TUESDAY, AUGUST 30, 2011

We received some great news today. The MRI showed tremendous progress on the tumor in Shannon's brain. It is almost 60 percent smaller than when it was discovered in April.

Our radiation team did as well as they could have expected. Dr. Laack and Dr. Rao felt this was best case scenario coming out of a worst case diagnosis. The radiation delivered the punch the team had hoped for. The cancer is not gone. Chemo continues to try to stymie further tumor growth.

We are too tired to process anymore tonight. More to come … need more time to absorb …

We want to share more about Dr. Laack's efforts. We want to tell you about the meeting we had with the team at Willow Creek Middle School. Very cool, positive stuff.

POSTED BY DAN

THURSDAY, SEPTEMBER 1, 2011

Wow. What happened to summer?

Jen and I have been scuffling with our emotions since our Tuesday consult that showed us amazing progress vs. the pontine brain stem glioma living in Shannon's head. We are really pleased no doubt. The tumor had measured around 3.8 cm in April and today is around 1.8 cm. We saw it with our own untrained eyes.

The Mayo Clinic radiation team really scored. I mean, they told us this kind of a response was possible—could happen—but many times there is no stopping a high grade glioma. Dr. Laack was thrilled … considered it best-case scenario.

Dr. Nadia Laack designed the radiation attack plan, carried out by a physicist and a dosemetrist (our friend Janelle Miller, hockey mom), and then a team of radiation techs that all made Shannon feel like she was their only patient. Pros. All of 'em.

But that phase of our fight ended in June. The radiation still might be having a slight effect today. But for the most part, the radiation was the big dog in our fight.

Closure. We said goodbye to Dr. Laack. She is off on maternity leave any day now.

Shannon has received the maximum amount of radiation with minimal collateral damage. We are so fortunate. Many people have asked us about proton beam therapy as a treatment option. The major benefit of proton therapy is that it limits collateral damage. Our photon beams carried just as much punch as Shannon could have received had proton therapy been used.

Delivering photon beams to the pons region of Shannon's brain and around the brain stem is quite risky. It is possible she could have lost her taste buds, use of her tongue, use of her eyelids, or some other function that could have altered her lifestyle tremendously. The photon beam treatment we underwent was administered with such precision that Shannon has had no cognitive side effects to speak of. Even the hair loss was limited. So we are extremely grateful for that.

But we are not turning back flips. I don't think thrilled is a word Jen and I can throw out there to describe our reaction to the MRI. We are really pleased. But the closure on the radiation phase of our treatment forced us to look ahead and ask what's next? That remains one of the great unknowns.

Shannon will keep taking chemo: five-day cycles every twenty-eight days until April. Temozolomide, or Temodar, is really our last line of defense. Our team has prescribed MRI's every three months now to check out the tumor. That is good news in itself, an indication that perhaps we are dealing with a lower grade tumor. If you recall, we opted to pass on a biopsy that would define the biology of the tumor. We agreed the biopsy was too risky.

So we will keep living in today and work really hard to stay there. That's really a tough way to live.

The same day we went to see the MRI we had a family meeting with the eighth grade counselor and some key people on the team at Willow Creek Middle School. They wanted to lay out a plan for the school year for Shannon. The counselor emailed Shannon's teachers to offer them the chance to sit in. Every one of them showed up. It was the teachers' second day back at work to prepare for the new year, and they all gave us their time and attention and, most importantly, their assurance that Shannon is in good hands.

POSTED BY DAN

SATURDAY, SEPTEMBER 3, 2011

Labor Day weekend, the official end of summer. The girls are hanging on to these last moments. Both managed to sleep in today, and then lamented the fact that in three days they will be on the bus at 6:50 in the morning!

Shannon and Erin have made the most of these late summer days: sleepovers, school clothes shopping, soccer practices, and a mani/pedi with Grandma so they'll be looking sharp for their cousin Kevin's wedding today. Shannon managed to find time to take in the Mayo football game last night as well. Eighth graders going to the Friday night football games ... I love that her life feels so normal.

We've had lots of reminders lately that while we've been so focused on our lives and what we are going through, other people we care about are facing tough times too: a friend whose sister has pancreatic cancer, a friend whose husband was badly injured in a bike accident, and just yesterday I heard from a dear family friend who lost her mother way too young. All these people are supporting us on our journey. Yes, our kid has cancer and the future is unknown, but there are plenty of reminders that life gives no guarantees. Shannon feels good today, so we should try and feel good today right along with her.

We've been so busy running around that we haven't had much time to play the iPod lately. But, on this rainy morning, the four of us have been hanging out with the tunes on in the background: Eric Hutchinson, Matt Nathanson, David Gray, Jack Johnson. My favorite lyric of the day comes from the Irish band The Script and their song "This = Love." *"Time flies, but you're the pilot ..."*

POSTED BY JEN

Wedding day | Celebrating with cousin Kevin and his new bride, Meaghan

KEVIN O'HARA GETS MARRIED

The girls had a great day watching their oldest cousin tie the knot. Lots of laughs, and even some square dancing! Congrats to Kevin and Meaghan.

POSTED BY JEN

FIRST DAY OF SCHOOL, 2011

Yes, this is the obligatory first day of school picture. Two middle schoolers, and you can see from their faces how they feel about it: Erin, a ball of nervous energy, eager to see what sixth grade is really like, and Shannon, a little more subdued, quietly confident about eighth grade.

I am not having my normal first day of school reaction. I was never one of those moms that cried at the bus stop. I was more likely to skip home! (OK, I never really skipped, but you get the idea.) But this year,

I'm a bit subdued myself. Maybe it's because we've had a great summer—yes, I can honestly say that. Maybe it's because Shannon and Erin will be so busy now that the days will really fly by. Maybe it's that my eighth grader is not only managing the first week of school, but managing chemotherapy at the same time.

On the way home from soccer practice last night, Shannon and

First day of school, 2011 | Erin, sixth grade and Shannon, eighth grade

I were talking casually about the end of summer and being ready for school. Shannon said, "This summer went way too fast. It might be because I was sick part of the time, but it felt like it flew by. And that's not good, especially if I don't have that many summers left." Wow. Gutshot. She said it without tears or drama, just matter of fact about her predicament.

So, yet another "new normal" starts today. And while a lot of it is familiar and back to the routine just like the beginning of each school year, I can't help but feel a little differently this time around. Please let time move slowly ...

POSTED BY JEN

WEDNESDAY, SEPTEMBER 7, 2011

I was one with God this morning as I hiked with Sunny around the Willow Creek Reservoir near our home in Rochester. The sun was bright, the water a glassy calm reflecting a cloudless, deep blue sky. Nature was alive all around. Jason Mraz and Eric Hutchinson playlists on the iPod with the dog, her tail high, weaving in out of the tall grasses, flushing various birds, bugs, and creatures. My senses sharp in the cool, clean fall air.

It was just one of those moments when all felt right. The kids were off at school on day two. Jen was off walking with a friend. I had just finalized a proposal that I will present tomorrow in Morton, Illinois—a promising business opportunity for sure. Everyone with a bounce in their step around here this week.

Then I returned home and Jen delivered the news that Shannon had called in from school to report a headache. She didn't want to come home—just wanted us to document the incident as requested from our medical team at WFMC. Damn. Shannon's disease is omnipresent. Acceptance remains the key.

I am not going to allow a headache to take the bounce out of my step. Still have so much to be grateful for! More music ... more exercise ... more work ... more activity ... keep going ...

Gratitude and acceptance. Stay in the moment.

POSTED BY DAN

FRIDAY, SEPTEMBER 9, 2011

It has been a smooth first week of school for the girls. Getting to know their teachers and getting back into the routine. The early rising necessary to make the bus hasn't been too painful ... yet ...

Shannon has been able to tolerate the Temodar again this month, and hopefully next week we can combat the fatigue by making time in the after school hours to fit in some resting/napping.

This week has gone relatively smoothly for me too. It's amazing how productive I can be around our house when everybody leaves me alone! I also taught my first tennis class since April yesterday. It felt good to be out there again.

So the first week of our fall schedule is coming to a close. Homework, soccer, and hockey have filled up the girls' free time and kept us hopping. This weekend will be no different; we have a double-double header with both girls having soccer games on Saturday and Sunday. Time to load up the minivan and hit the road. We wouldn't have it any other way ...

POSTED BY JEN

SATURDAY, SEPTEMBER 10, 2011

Today Jen and I celebrate seventeen years of marriage. I think it's been a pretty good deal for both of us.

It's game day. Both girls with road soccer games and we are off and running.

Happy weekend everyone!

POSTED BY DAN

SUNDAY, SEPTEMBER 11, 2011

My Pandora Radio is playing Gary Jules, "Mad World." Seems appropriate today.

Ten years ago on this day, I was home with toddler Shannon and infant Erin. Dan had just left for a trip to Iowa. I had been a stay-at-home mom for about five months, since the previous April when Erin was born. I often turned on the morning talk shows to keep me company, so I was watching the *Today Show* when the 9/11 attacks took place. But, every time Shannon started to pay attention to what I was watching, I would turn the channel. I didn't want my three-year-old asking me questions I couldn't answer. Trying to protect our little girls from the big, bad world.

Our weekend flew by, just like we knew it would. The girls played soccer under some extreme conditions with temps in the upper eighties both days. They played hard, and we had fun watching them compete. I find myself not really caring about the outcome, and that's a new concept for me! I'm usually about as competitive as they come, but this weekend losing really didn't bother me. Whether it was Shannon or Erin or the Vikings or even Roger Federer, I just can't seem to get too riled up about it. A little perspective at work, I suppose.

Dan and I have a running joke: "Whose day did you ruin today?" or, "Who did you make cry today?" Just a little gallows humor when referring to sharing Shannon's story. Suffice it to say, I'm winning this contest this week. (Ah, there's that competitiveness!) As I went back to work, I crossed paths with many familiar faces, including a lot of the ladies I teach on Friday mornings. I got a lot of hugs and kind words and prayers being sent our way. Same thing with the soccer parents who we haven't seen since last year. People want us to know that they care and they're rooting for Shannon. They want to listen if we want to share. And some people just need to shed a tear with us, and that's OK. Sharing Shannon's battle with others does lighten the load, but at the same time, it's exhausting.

This week will be a test to see how much activity Shannon can handle on a post-chemo week. She wants to practice soccer and play hockey back to back on both Monday and Wednesday. I wouldn't put it past her to pull it off. We will see the hematology people on Tuesday for a weight check and blood counts. The plan is to hopefully taper the steroids to every other day, but we need to discuss that she's had a few headaches and this lingering ear pain.

Shannon was really tired tonight and she accepted my invitation to lay her head on my lap and let me rub her back for comfort. I could have done that for hours.

And now Pandora gives me Coldplay's "The Scientist." *"Nobody said it was easy, no one ever said it would be this hard, take me back to the start..."*

POSTED BY JEN

WEDNESDAY, SEPTEMBER 14, 2011

Yesterday was one of those days ... Shannon was so excited in the morning because it was the first time since April that she wasn't going to have to take any pills. The girls both went off to school happy. But, by the time we picked Shannon up from school to head downtown for her appointments, her mood had changed. She experienced a bad headache during the day, and she was anticipating what that meant. She was right. Dr. Rao would like to keep her on a low dose of steroids for another week and then we will try again to taper every other day. If the taper doesn't work without headaches, Shannon will just have to continue taking the steroids for a while.

In the grand scheme of things, everything is going well. Blood counts are good, Shannon's weight is holding, and her neuro exam was good. But, to a thirteen-year-old girl, all she can see is puffy cheeks and steroid acne and the fact that she has to wear her hair the same style every day to cover up the radiation hair loss. Add to that the fatigue she's feeling this week that kept her from playing hockey on Monday, and it's easy to see why she's feeling down. It's hard enough to be thirteen without all that extra baggage. Damn.

But, today is a new day and we will hope it's a better one ...

POSTED BY JEN

THURSDAY, SEPTEMBER 15, 2011

For our out-of-state and international blog followers, it's a crisp and clear thirty-three degrees this morning with a coating of frost on the ground. Now that's a little early in the season for a hard frost but that's what we're looking at here in Rochester, Minnesota, this morning.

As I write, Jen and the girls are pulling out of the driveway ... a little extra sleep this morning ... an extra half hour with a ride to school instead of a bus ride. We've been doing more of that this week. Post-chemo weeks require extra rest. The second week of school always seems to be tougher than the first week. The novelty of the new school year is replaced by the reality of routine.

Tuesday we struggled with our emotions, but Wednesday was much better. Acceptance that a small dose of the steroid Decadron is necessary to keep Shannon's headaches at bay seemed to have taken hold. Shannon's attempts at tapering off the steroid will take time. Patience. The headaches she experienced Tuesday are not tumor related, just a part of the slow taper.

Amazing to realize how far we've come. After our diagnosis in April, Shannon was taking 6 mg of the Decadron daily. Today we are down to just 0.25 mg per day. Hardly enough for side effects. Baby steps.

(Did you know: steroids were developed at Mayo Clinic and earned Edward Calvin Kendall a Nobel Prize in 1950.)

We had a great night together Wednesday as we shuttled kids around to soccer practices. Shannon chose to skip a late hockey skate. On the way home we stopped for Scoopie Meals at Culver's. We were in a goofy mood and laughing at each other loudly. The tables around us were giving us dirty looks, but we did not care. We got going on a near pee-in-your-pants laugh together that felt really good. Frozen custard always has a positive effect on this family.

Music du jour: "Love is Free" by Sheryl Crow, "Home Again" by Carole King, "Any Major Dude Will Tell You" by Steely Dan:

> Any major dude with half-a-heart surely will tell you my friend
> Any minor world that breaks apart falls together again
> When the demon is at your door
> In the morning it won't be there no more
> Any major dude will tell you ...

POSTED BY DAN

The Sound of Music

I have always found inspiration in music. I can remember my junior high days when I would sit next to my stereo on New Year's Eve and tape record the top 100 songs of the year, staying close by so I could hit pause when the local radio station went to commercial. Then I would spend the next year wearing out those cassette tapes in my Sony Walkman.

In this day of iTunes and iPods, music is so easily accessible to anyone with a computer and a little bit of tech savvy. Dan and I fall into that category, and we found that music helped us immensely on our journey. Sometimes a song would be uplifting and we would play it loudly over the speaker in the kitchen for us all to sing and dance to. Sometimes the girls would take a turn with their musical selections and we'd be cranking up Ke$ha or Lady Gaga or whoever had the latest song on top of the pop charts.

Sometimes we would use music to help us find solitude, to help us think, or to help us write. Sometimes a song would be poignant and meaningful, and then we would reach for the headphones, enjoying the lyrics, the memories, and the tears in private.

We shared our musical selections on the blog, and we'd hear back from people who were glad to be introduced to different artists or songs that were unfamiliar to them. Some friends even followed along by making a blog playlist; each time we referenced a song, they would add it to their playlist. In the end, they had a musical timeline of our journey.

O'HARA BLOG PLAYLIST

Ingrid Michaelson	Maybe
Jason Mraz	A Beautiful Mess
Cat Stevens	Can't Keep It In
Van Morrison	Days Like This
Jack Johnson	All At Once
Van Morrison	Golden Autumn Day
Jason Mraz	Live High
Adele	Make You Feel My Love
Adrianne	10,000 Stones
Alexi Murdoch	Orange Sky
Sheryl Crow	I Shall Believe
Mat Kearney	Won't Back Down
Paolo Nutini	Rewind
Donavon Frankenreiter	All Around Us
Sheryl Crow	Long Road Home
Tristan Prettyman	Madly
Coldplay	Everything's Not Lost
Ray LaMontagne	You Are the Best Thing
Donavon Frankenreiter	Bend in the Road
Counting Crows	Big Yellow Taxi
David Gray	My Oh My
Bruce Springsteen	Long Walk Home
Eric Hutchinson	Oh!
Norah Jones	What Am I to You?
John Hiatt	Have a Little Faith
The Script	This = Love
Gary Jules	Mad World
Coldplay	The Scientist
Sheryl Crow	Love Is Free
Carole King	Home Again
Steely Dan	Any Major Dude Will Tell You
George Michael	Waiting for That Day
Jack Johnson	Never Know
Keane	Hamburg Song

Annie Lennox	Why?
Ben Sollee	A Few Honest Words
Mumford & Sons	After the Storm
Marvin Gaye & Tami Terrell	What You Gave Me
Memphis the Musical Company	Memphis Lives in Me
Crosby, Stills, Nash & Young	Feel Your Love
The Proclaimers	If There's a God
Steely Dan	Only a Fool Should Say That
Bill Withers	Lovely Day
Wicked, the musical	For Good
John Mayer	Dreaming With a Broken Heart

TUESDAY, SEPTEMBER 20, 2011

We've had a great response from people wanting to join us at the Brains Together For A Cure walk on October 8. We've ordered t-shirts and will sell them on a first come, first served basis and donate the proceeds. More details to follow on that, but we will be looking good out there in our lime green "Shannon the Cannon" t-shirts!

It has been a perfect storm of stressful situations lately. In the grand scheme of things, all small potatoes: Shannon and Erin home sick with the season's first head colds, work stresses for Dan and me, winter sports tryouts for the girls, blah, blah, blah ... Each thing individually is not a big deal, but the cumulative effect is wearing on us. As a friend of mine said, it's hard to prop your kids up and even harder when your own tank is on empty. It seems so silly to worry about the small stuff; my family is trying to learn to live with childhood cancer, so why exactly am I worried about what team my kids will be on? Am I insane? Or, maybe that's exactly why I am stressing about the little things. If you don't want to look at the big picture, obsess about all the little pictures ...

Shannon is feeling good this week. The post-chemo fatigue is over, and her energy has bounced back. Her Monday consisted of a full day at school, homework, French horn practice, soccer pictures, soccer practice, and finally an hour on the ice at hockey camp. Today after school she spent her time hanging out with a friend and shooting hockey pucks. She has plans to double up again tomorrow with soccer and hockey. We are also going to try again tomorrow to taper off the steroids. Dr. Rao gave us the go ahead to try every other day for a week and if Shannon can tolerate that with no headaches, then she can try to taper off completely. It's a hurdle that Shannon wants to clear, so cross your fingers ...

POSTED BY JEN

WEDNESDAY, SEPTEMBER 21, 2011

It's not easy being Erin right now. She came home early from school today feeling sick. She can't quite shake this head cold. But no matter how bad she feels, she never has it as bad as her sister does, right? She may feel lousy, but her sister has a brain tumor. That's a tough act to follow. People worry about Shannon and ask Erin how her sister is doing. What is a ten-year-old supposed to feel? How can she process all of this?

It's a parenting dilemma for us, for sure. How can we tell Shannon to let her homework slide if she needs to rest and then tell Erin no resting until your homework is done? How can we listen intently to every ache and pain that Shannon has, and then tell Erin to suck it up and tough it out when she feels crummy? (I guess the Mother of the Year Award will have to go to someone else this year ... again!)

Shannon made it through the school day, soccer, and hockey without a headache, so we will try to continue the every other day taper this week. For today, Shannon is fine. For today, have a good thought for Erin ...

POSTED BY JEN

SATURDAY, SEPTEMBER 24, 2011

It's a foggy but lovely Saturday morning. The house is quiet. We were out late with the kids at a bonfire. Fun for all ages at the Lang home following the Mayo High School football game.

A rare chance to sleep in for everyone (including Mom). We do not have an activity on the docket until a 2:00 P.M. soccer game in Owatonna, Minnesota. We cherish these days. We can leisure around, drink coffee, read, and surf the web, and then we will power up with pancakes and bacon whenever.

The fog should burn away. Looking like an ideal fall Saturday for the Upper Midwest: sunny skies and highs in the sixties. The leaves are starting to change. The nights are crisp and clear. Football weather.

Needless to say I am feeling really grateful this morning. We're doing better around here the last couple of days by staying in the present. Man, does that approach make it easier. We have so many things out of our control right now. Just wildly out of our control. It's probably easier for my simple mind to stay in the present. But I can get ahead of the day really quickly ... I do it ... it's not pretty ... my fingernails take a beating.

Our circumstances have afforded us the chance to forge so many relationships. People have stepped up to help or offer support and taken the time to get to know us. That has been really terrific. I am so proud of Jen who is/was mostly pretty guarded, but when you get to know her she is such a solid, fun person. I have always been pretty much in your face, for better and for worse. But more people have gotten to know Jen because of Shannon's cancer, and that has been a gift.

Change is inevitable. Growth is optional. So, thanks to all the people in our lives who have helped us grow.

Momentum is picking up on the Brains Together for a Cure walk.

Have a great weekend everyone!

POSTED BY DAN

MONDAY, SEPTEMBER 26, 2011

Team O'Hara is hoping for a busy, normal week this week. It is Spirit Week at the middle school, a lead up to the Mayo High School homecoming festivities. Hat day, pajama day, etc. All events are culminating with the homecoming parade and football game on Friday. Both girls are looking forward to the fun.

Shannon is feeling good, and tomorrow we try again to go steroid free. Hoping this very slow taper has done the trick. Erin is feeling better too. She's finally kicking her cold, and over the weekend she had some time with her pals, which brightened her spirits. Dan is traveling. I am working. Just like the good ol' days.

Grandma and Papa Harkins returned to Rochester last night after spending two and a half weeks at their home outside Vegas. It's good to see them again and have them be a part of our activities this week. Two soccer practices and three hockey skates are on the schedule.

Thursday we will return to Mayo 16 for blood counts and weight check in preparation for the fourth round of maintenance chemo next week. Amazing how quickly that cycle comes around again. Time marches on ...

POSTED BY JEN

THURSDAY, SEPTEMBER 29, 2011

Shannon has tapered off the steroids. No drugs for the last three days, and no headaches. Hooray! She got to share that good news during our appointments at Mayo today. This afternoon Grandma and I picked the girls up from school, and we headed downtown for blood work, social worker appointments, and a check-up with Dr. Rodriguez. We did all that, plus stopped at the gift shop and picked up Diet Coke and Mentos for Erin's science experiment, and still made it home in time to eat dinner and get to hockey practice! World-class treatment without really disrupting our lives. I'm grateful for that.

Shannon's check-up was good. Her weight is holding steady. (Unfortunately, so is her height!) Her white cell counts were down a bit, but this is to be expected. The cumulative effect of monthly chemo will cause those counts to drop. Not a huge concern at this point, but Shannon will need to continue having them checked twice a month—right before each round of Temodar and then a week or so after completing the chemo cycle. Best-case scenario is that they stay on the low side of the normal range.

Shannon doesn't grumble about having these appointments. They're just a part of her (our) life now, and she seems to have come to terms with that. In fact, she is quite at ease on the pediatric floor.

Watching her interact, you can almost forget the reason we're there in the first place. Shannon—and Erin—brought lots of smiles and laughs to the nurses and unit secretaries today. For better or worse, the girls' humor tends toward sarcasm. (Now, where would they have learned that?) Luckily, sarcasm plays well with the staff at Mayo 16. I'm grateful for that too!

POSTED BY JEN

MONDAY, OCTOBER 3, 2011

The Vikings are 0-and-4, and I really don't care. How about that? In the pecking order of clutter occupying my mind, the Vikings no longer make the cut. Yes, I know the Lynx are playing for the WNBA title. Again, in the pecking order of clutter occupying my mind ...

It's a Temodar week. Shannon starts another cycle of chemo tonight. The timing is not great. It's a big week for her. At dinner last night we were going over upcoming activities: a couple tests, final week of soccer practices, hockey tryouts, and then the Brains Together walk and soccer games Saturday. To use the words of Jesse Ventura's character from the 1987 non-classic *Predator*, "We ain't got time to bleed!"

We were in Faribault, Minnesota, for a Davies family celebration this weekend. Shannon and Erin's "Grandma-Great" Jeanne Davies turned eighty-five. We're having a fun gathering of Jen's closest rellies on the Davies side. Jen's mom, Gwen, is the oldest of nine; she has eight younger brothers, many of whom were in attendance and yucking it up with all of us on Saturday.

Jen's uncle Scott is Chief of Medicine at HCMC and was chatting it up with Shannon. Scott to Shannon: "So you are off the Prednisone?" Shannon to Scott: "Decadron." OK then! Welcome to our world Dr. Davies. We continue to be amazed at Shannon who remains quite confident in herself. Her fight with cancer is just part of her persona.

We are hopeful the weather holds for Saturday's Brains Together for a Cure walk.

Enjoy the fall weather and colors. Enjoy life. Enjoy today.

POSTED BY DAN

WEDNESDAY, OCTOBER 5, 2011

Shannon has gone a week without the need for steroids. Keep your fingers crossed that the taper is complete, for now. Her adrenal glands must be doing their job because she has not reported any headaches or problems.

We are blessed with so many kind and wise people in our lives. You listen to us, share wisdom, and offer hope and support. In your own way, every one of you helps us "keep it real."

That's a good thing because there seems to be an inordinate amount of uncertainty that has accumulated: work stuff, school stuff, sports stuff, cancer stuff … stuff that can jolt you awake at night. What if …? What if …? What if …?

A friend recommended on oldie but goodie for dealing with uncertain times: Jot down the things that are keeping you up … one at a time … on little sheets of paper … fold them up and toss them in a "God box." Like a mini time capsule. After some time passes, check back on your "God box." Chances are pretty good that each of these items will magically be resolved. Let go, let God, right?

Two nights in a row this week Jen and I held the girls as they cried themselves to sleep. On Monday night Erin let it all out as I tucked her in for bed. Tuesday night, it was Shannon's turn. The pressures in each of their lives just needed a release. Truthfully, comforting a sobbing child is one of the greatest privileges of being a parent. Holding them tightly until all the air returns to their lungs … probably good for all of us. Another reminder that our emotions are living real close to the surface around here. That ain't all bad.

I was fired up to download some new music this week. Then Jen informed me that Bob Seger's iTunes release of 1970s songs does not qualify as new music. I don't care … *"I remember standing on the corner at midnight, trying to get my courage up …"*

Our thoughts and prayers are with the family of Eleanor Mondale Poling this week. Eleanor was treated at Mayo Clinic and pledged her memorials to Rochester-based Brains Together for a Cure.

POSTED BY DAN

FRIDAY, OCTOBER 7, 2011—EARLY A.M.

Sleep is escaping me tonight. Having two emotional girls this evening has kept my mind working into the wee hours. Hockey tryouts have raised the tension level around here. So stressful for Shannon, and having the three-day tryouts coming at the end of a chemo week is a lot to ask of her. It's difficult to wrap your mind around the fact that this drug that makes her lose her appetite and feel fatigued is really working it's magic on that tumor. She'd seem perfectly healthy right now if she wasn't taking this medicine that makes her sick! Shannon felt like she tried her hardest tonight, but didn't perform. Hard for me not to see it as her body failing her just a bit.

But, in the grand scheme of things, it's amazing that she's out there playing hockey. When I think back six months to diagnosis, we didn't know what Shannon would be capable of, come October. Yet here she is, pushing herself and expecting her best. We will get through this try-out phase and she will play hockey this winter, and hockey brings her joy.

We returned home from tryouts, and I helped Shannon review for the four tests she has today. She wasn't in the best state of mind to retain the material, but we muddled through. One more study session over breakfast, and she'll give it a go.

Erin had a mostly good day, including starting piano lessons again. She's really been looking forward to it. This year, Shannon is not taking lessons so it will be Erin's own thing, which is a good thing.

Erin's frustration that it's "all about Shannon" boiled up again tonight. We returned home from tryouts and after briefly chatting with Erin about piano, I headed straight to helping Shannon with her studying. Erin wanted more of my attention. Maybe I coddled Shannon tonight, but I couldn't help myself. So, tonight Dan returned home just in time to walk into that hornet's nest. "Welcome home, honey. I know you've had a long day. Which crying kid would you like to manage?!"

Some days that's how it goes. Some of it is just life stuff. Some of it is just parenting stuff. Some of it is cancer stuff. Sometimes it is such a struggle to make any sense out of what we are feeling. Why do I feel sad tonight? Am I just worried about the day-to-day life stuff, or am really worried about the cancer? Is it possible to separate one from the other? It's like everything is viewed through a different lens now.

The good news is tomorrow is coming and it's a fresh start and another chance …

POSTED BY JEN

SUNDAY, OCTOBER 9, 2011

It has been an emotional roller coaster of a week. We knew we were headed for some delicate territory with the Brains Together For A Cure walk coinciding with hockey tryouts. Hopes and fears and wants and needs. It's hard to sort them all out sometimes …

The walk was an amazing, emotional experience. So many people, so many families, dealing with this terrible diagnosis. Shannon was well represented by eighty or so of us wearing our lime green "Shannon the Cannon" t-shirts. (I'll share a group photo when I get ahold of it.) The weather was beautiful—almost hot—for a fall day. Seeing the family and friends who gathered to support us and our kid: Dan's customer and his family coming from hours away, a high school friend, Shannon's former teacher, RAC tennis ladies and their families, aunts, uncles, cousins, brothers, sisters … I don't have the words to describe it. And then you look next to you, and there's another family doing the same thing. And you exchange a knowing glance with them, and all of a sudden you are bonded together.

Shannon came to the walk directly from hockey tryouts, and she smiled and socialized with the people who wanted a minute of her time. She met some people who knew her story and she handled herself with grace. She introduced one of her doctors to the O'Hara clan. She met other brain tumor patients. At the end of the event, Shannon made a donation from her fund to the board members. So proud of her. Later Saturday, Erin thanked us for organizing such a fun event for our friends and family. So proud of her too.

Today brought us to the final day of hockey tryouts. (Thank goodness!) So much pressure and anxiety for Shannon and all her hockey buddies. Shannon's goal since hockey season ended last year was to be good enough to make the 12A team this year, but it became apparent that this wasn't realistic. Whether she could have gotten there had she not gotten sick, who knows? Her sadness about that was hard to see. But, the kid loves hockey and loves being on a team, and as it turns out, some of her buddies ended up right with her on the 12B team. So, the text messages were flying, and they were all pumping each other up about what a fun team they are going to have this year. By the time we tucked Shannon into bed tonight, the sadness had been replaced with excitement that was making it hard for her to fall asleep!

Man, have we covered some ground athletically in the last eight days or so: we finished two soccer seasons, we survived basketball and hockey tryouts, and in the end, our girls are truly right where they want to be heading into their winter sports seasons—on a team with their friends. Time for a deep breath.

All this activity, all these emotions, yet one of the best parts of

Backyard leaves | Fall has arrived in Minnesota

the weekend was this morning when we just hung around as a family, doing the necessary homework, piano, French horn, laundry, etc. The girls found time to just be pals. Playing in the backyard with the dog as we enjoyed our morning coffee. One of those moments where I forgot, just for a second ...

POSTED BY JEN

BTFAC—TEAM SHANNON THE CANNON
POSTED BY JEN

Team Shannon the Cannon | The Brains Together For a Cure fundraiser

WEDNESDAY, OCTOBER 12, 2011

It's on like Donkey Kong! Hockey season starts tonight. Shannon has been assigned to the Rochester Girls U12 B team—right where she needs to be—playing for our buddy Coach Bart Grafstrom and playing with many of her closest friends. She even gave me the nod to be on Bart's staff as an assistant coach. And, of course, Jen is the team's manager. (No worries—the team website and calendar are current!) Our first practice is tonight at 8:00. We start playing games in early November.

I know many of you may be thinking this is nuts. But this is what we like to do. Once the tryout process is behind you, it's all good. Even Erin seems excited about Shannon's team situation. She knows everyone; many on Shannon's team are sixth grade friends of E's. And many of the parents we will be spending much of this winter with have been some of our strongest supporters since Shannon's diagnosis in April.

In a post last week, I wrote about placing all our frets and uncertainties in the "God box." Well, after much hand wringing, Shannon's hockey season is lined up to be a winner. And that has nothing to do with wins and losses.

Erin's basketball practices will get going next week. We know she's in good hands playing for Team Olson and with the Mayo sixth grade traveling team. Our winter is going to be crazy! But there is nothing else we would rather be doing then chasing our kids in and out of Minnesota's finest gyms and rinks.

One minor detail to work through and we can get on with the fun ... my career. My employer, EFS Transportation Services, is merging with a competitor. It's a joint venture with a new management team in place to manage the JV. I'm reasonably confident I'm going to be on the "A" team but until they give me the formal nod ... where's that "God box?" The merger will take another several weeks to close, maybe longer. Until I hear otherwise, we will keep sellin'.

Years ago, my wife introduced me to one of her favorite songs, a George Michael ditty, "Waiting for That Day." It's now one of my favorites, especially today.

So every day I see you in some other face
They crack a smile, talk a while
Try to take your place
My memory serves me far too well ...
POSTED BY DAN

145

FRIDAY, OCTOBER 14, 2011

I've been meaning to write an update for the last few days, but time just keeps flying by. We've made it to the weekend now, and there's not a lot on our agenda this weekend. Looking forward to some down time around our house.

Thursday was a non-stop day of school, work, and our bimonthly Mayo Clinic visit. Add a piano lesson and some school conferences in there, and you've got a full day. Shannon's check-up was good. She was fatigued this week—post-Temodar, of course—but she managed it well, coming home Wednesday early from school to allow herself some extra rest. Her blood counts and weight are holding steady. Shannon's only concern has been some trouble catching her breath toward the end of hockey practice. She was hoping for a solution to come from Dr. Khan as they discussed it on Thursday. Dr. Khan explained to Shannon that her body has been through a lot, and she should maybe take it easy out there and not push herself too hard. I wish you could have seen the look on Shannon's face—take it easy when she is out on the ice? What? That is not a part of Shannon's plan! Gotta love her spirit. Dr. Khan did say we would keep an eye on it as we get a few more hockey practices under our belts. We will return to Mayo in two weeks for a pre-Temodar blood draw and check-up.

School conferences provided a nice pick me up at the end of a long Thursday. Both girls are doing well academically, but more importantly, both girls are doing well socially and emotionally. Erin came with me to conferences and her teachers all shared how much they enjoy having her in class and what a mature kid she is. Pretty good for a ten-year-old. A couple of her teachers were surprised to find out that Erin was grade accelerated and therefore is very young for a sixth grader. You wouldn't know it.

Shannon's conferences had a similar tone. She's a conscientious student and a joy to have in class. On Wednesday when she needed to come home to rest, she made a point to see each of her teachers, turn in all the work that was due that day, and gather the necessary homework before she headed home. One of Shannon's teachers told me, "I think I will learn more from Shannon this year than she will learn from me."

I share all this with you not to brag about our children, but to let you know that life goes on and we continue to function and sometimes even thrive. We often write here about the struggles we are having, but we get up every morning and try to do what needs doing. For the girls, that means going to school, doing the work, being with friends, being a good student, and a good person. Cancer or not, you can still be a good human. On that front, Shannon and Erin are succeeding.

POSTED BY JEN

MONDAY, OCTOBER 17, 2011

We passed another milestone this weekend. Saturday was six months since Shannon's diagnosis. April 15, 2011, the day the music changed.

Sunday at St. John the Evangelist an unbelievable set of circumstances came together that can only add to the Mystery of Faith. Friends, families, and some of our strongest supporters surrounded us in our section of the church Sunday. I told Jen last night I could feel the love, like a warm blanket. I made reference to that same feeling months ago in this blog. It was in the early days post-diagnosis when the four of us lay together in Erin's bed chatting about life.

When we walked in before 9:30 mass on Sunday, one of the ushers approached to ask us if we would present the gifts: deliver the bread, wine, and holy water to the alter just after intentions. We've done this before, and we were honored to be asked again (even the girls recognize it as a privilege). So we said sure.

One of the intentions was a "Lord, hear our prayer" for the family of parishioner David Van Houten who this week lost a ten-year battle with brain cancer. As Jen, Erin, Shannon, and I stood holding the bread, wine, and holy water in the back of the church, Fr. Mahon pointed out the Van Houten family, who were seated up near the front. The funeral is Monday.

Fr. Mahon recalled performing the Sacrament of the Sick for Mr. Van Houten at 9:30 mass ten years ago when we were celebrating mass over in the St. John School gym while they were remodeling our church space. David stood in front of the parish—he had just undergone surgery and bore a six-inch scar on his skull—as we all held our hands high and prayed over him on that Sunday ten years ago.

At that same mass, Erin O'Hara was baptized. Our eyes are wide open and our faith remains strong.

POSTED BY DAN

Sports

It is possible that Dan and I are a little over enthusiastic about sports. We love them. Love to play, love to watch, love to attend, even love to coach.

When we got married, we took a sports themed honeymoon; we planned to go wherever the Monday Night Football game was that week. So, it was the Chicago Bears at the Philadelphia Eagles on Monday night. This was followed by a round of golf at the famed Merion Country Club on Tuesday morning, then off to Baltimore to catch the Yankees and Orioles at Camden Yards. Now, when you think of romance, you don't necessarily think of Philadelphia or Baltimore, but it was perfect for us!

So, our girls were born into it. A fair number of the home videos we shot during their childhoods have a sporting event on the TV in the background.

Erin is maybe too smart to get so involved. She can't quite understand how we get so worked up about it, because it's only a game and there will be another one tomorrow or next week or next season.

But Shannon, she bought into it hook, line, and sinker. By age ten, she had decided she was a sports fan, and there was someone to root for each and every season. Shannon was loyal to her Minnesota teams, be it Vikings, Wild, Twins, or Gophers. She could name the players, and she would live and die with each victory and defeat. Shannon had felt the highs and lows that only competition can bring, and she loved it.

WEDNESDAY, OCTOBER 19, 2011

Yesterday was quite a day. We've remarked often here about people's kindness and generosity, and Tuesday was one of those days. Such a good day that Shannon, in her teenage exuberance, posted on her Facebook page last night, "Best Day Ever!"

We played hooky and spent the day with Shjon Podein for a behind-the-scenes look with the Minnesota Wild. Shjon is a Rochester native who is well known as a Stanley Cup winning hockey player, but also for all the charitable work he does through his children's foundation, Team 25. His foundation's mission: To improve the quality of life and create an environment of caring and community support for children facing extraordinary difficulties in their lives.

We attended the morning skate where Shannon blushed as Colton Gilles winked at her, then she and Erin smiled from ear to ear when goalie Josh Harding handed them a goalie stick. We heard some choice locker room language as the players ribbed each other, which added to the whole experience!

After the practice we watched the players clear out of the locker room. Nice guy awards go to Nick Shultz, Josh Harding, and Matt Cullen who stopped to meet the girls and shake their hands. Shannon's favorite Wild player, Mikko Koivu, is now my favorite as well. He emerged from the locker room wearing a Roger Federer baseball cap.

Once the locker room was clear, the Wild's assistant athletic trainer, John Worley, gave us a tour. Worley and Shjon are good buddies from the five years they spent together with the Philadelphia Flyers. The girls were wide-eyed checking out the stick room and sitting on the bench at the Xcel Energy Center.

The afternoon highlight was watching the Pittsburgh players come and go and having a chat with Pittsburgh Penguins coach Dan Bylsma. We were staying at the same hotel as the Penguins and using the same Starbucks as well. We said hello to the coach as he came in for a cup of coffee, and he stopped to ask the girls how the Wild looked at the morning skate. We talked about Sidney Crosby and when he might return. He told the girls to have fun at the game, but not too much fun.

While the game was a bit of a dud (the Wild looked really average),

Minnesota Wild locker room tour | Shannon by the locker of her favorite player, #9 Mikko Koivu

it really didn't matter. For a sports-loving, hockey-playing thirteen-year-old, it qualified as the best day ever ...

POSTED BY JEN

SATURDAY, OCTOBER 22, 2011

Jen is away with her friend Teri this weekend. They are getting some R & R at a B & B near Madison.

Shannon, Erin, and I have been having fun visiting friends, taking in a movie, just chillin' like villains. We took in *Dolphin Tales* in 3D Friday afternoon, and I was a puddle with my girls on each side of me. Of course, I cry at previews, so anytime there is a storyline with kids and good music I am a mess. The girls rip me for it, of course.

Our friends from Jacksonville, Florida, Jack and Colleen Jones and kids Mikaela and Jack III, landed at Rochester International last night at 7:45. They are visiting family in LaCrosse this weekend. So we picked them up at the airport, and then we went out for dinner and came back here for dessert. Ended up staying up and chatting until almost midnight.

The Jones' have been our friends since forever. Jack and I did the TV program at St. Cloud State together and they were married a year before Jen and me. They keep moving around the country, and we keep getting together at various stages of life.

They were amazed at how great Shannon looked. And how comfortable the girls seem to be with accepting their place in this world. That part makes me most proud because rolling with it is the only thing we can do until we can't do it anymore.

Off to hockey practice. The Rebels are coming together nicely. We start playing real games somewhere around November 5. Erin starts basketball Monday.

Looks like a beautiful fall day!

POSTED BY DAN

SUNDAY, OCTOBER 23, 2011

I'm home tonight after my getaway weekend. A little change of scenery was nice. Teri and I spent our time walking, talking, and checking out Madison one day, and a local art tour in the tiny Wisconsin towns of Cambridge, Lake Mills, and Fort Atkinson the next.

Girlfriends are good for the soul. They oftentimes help you hear yourself and make some sense of your thoughts. Plus, we laughed a lot. That's good for the soul too.

I returned home to find that the house was clean, homework was done, and as I walked in the door, Shannon was folding the last load of laundry. Nothing left for me to do. My family wanted my getaway to be completely hassle-free. And it was.

Ready for the week ahead.

POSTED BY JEN

WEDNESDAY, OCTOBER 26, 2011

Authoring this damn blog comes with a decent amount of obligation. I am not sure if I am grateful for that or annoyed by it. Having one of those nights. But I think I am grateful for this forum because tonight I need to get some stuff off my chest.

Just heard about a Bloomington Lincoln High School alum—roughly my age—that lost a shockingly short battle with bile duct cancer. Her name was Lynne (Engfer) Sater. Two years from diagnosis 'til death. And in the process of sharing a connection to her death with a friend in the TV industry (Lynne's husband is a TV anchor in Milwaukee), I was forced to break the news of Shannon's illness to said friend who is also a TV anchor in Milwaukee.

The Sater's have three young daughters. I am not surprised to hear she was a great mom, wife, and school volunteer.

Tonight, Jen attended a district team manager's meeting to set up our game schedule for Shannon's hockey team, the Rochester Rebels. (Of course, Jen is the team manager … the Rebels love and need her OCD!) I stayed home with the girls and we did our own obsessing on some good books all three of us are into. Jen returned from the meeting all pumped about our game schedule (thirty-one games including scrimmages), and Shannon went from nearly asleep in her chair to completely jacked about her upcoming hockey season.

One of the things we were waiting on with the schedule was to see if it worked out to take a trip to Florida or somewhere warm around the holidays. Since we no longer make decisions based on what makes sense financially (which is completely whacked) we were just going to go for it.

But the week we would have gone—between Christmas and New Year's—the Rebels have a game at Northfield. When I asked Shannon if she'd rather go to Florida or Northfield on December 28, she looked at me like I was an idiot. Needless to say, we will go somewhere warm at a later date. God willing.

Also, this week I spent some time in the field making sales calls in Iowa and connecting with some really good folks I hadn't called on in a while. They are reading this blog too. They knew what was going on in my life, which was a little jarring. Sometimes I think we lay stuff out here on this blog with no return on the investment. But it's not really about an investment; it's just about sharing a journey. A good reminder that what we do must be about what is good for us and nothing external.

So what does it all mean? I sure as hell don't know. I just know that I can't believe how much I love my family, and I need to stay focused on all the good out there. Because there is a ton of it.

POSTED BY DAN

FRIDAY, OCTOBER 28, 2011

Yesterday was the pre-chemo week check-up for Shannon, and for the first time in six months, the people at Mayo 16 were having a bad day. Computers were acting up, physicians were behind schedule, and they were all stressed out. It stuck with me because as I thought about it, it's amazing that it hadn't happened before. I mean, who doesn't have a bad day at work at least once every six months? Just another testament to the high quality of care we are receiving.

Shannon's counts are holding. She's doing great—for a cancer patient. I only mention this because it's easy to forget that she is in treatment. You wouldn't know it by looking at her. Shannon asked our nurse practitioner, Donna, "Are my counts normal?" The answer is yes and no: for a non-cancer patient, no; for someone who is about to start her fifth round of maintenance chemo, her counts are great. But, what Shannon is really asking is, "Are my counts normal enough that I can continue to play hockey?" And we are grateful that the answer to that is yes.

We discussed what appointments are ahead this month. Shannon will have her bimonthly complete neuro exam with Dr. Keating in two weeks and we will do the post-chemo blood work then as well. At the end of November, Shannon will have an MRI to check the tumor.

We continue to try not to be overwhelmed by the big picture because the little picture looks good. The girls are going to school, going to practices, hanging with friends, laughing, and smiling. We had a few tears this week, but they were algebra related, not cancer related!

Even that makes me smile, because it's a normal struggle that has nothing to do with Shannon's illness. I've come to appreciate those.

We're headed into a fun weekend. Grandma Harkins returns to Minnesota for a visit, we've got a late hockey practice tonight, and an early hockey scrimmage in Apple Valley tomorrow. Then we'll have a quick visit with the Harkins cousins before finally heading to Grandpa Ed's eighty-eighth birthday party in Edina. We will be on the go … and trying to remember to cherish every minute of it.

Currently listening to Jack Johnson's "Never Know." *"We're just human, amusing but confusing and we're trying, but where is this all leading? We'll never know."*

POSTED BY JEN

TUESDAY, NOVEMBER 1, 2011

We have been enjoying an extended stabilization period. Shannon and Erin are just clickin' off the school days and it seems as though each day after school is a whirlwind of activities.

Halloween was strange as the eighth grader decided she was too cool for a costume and handed out candy at home while the sixth grader dressed as a clown. All day. Wore her costume to school loud and proud.

Grandma Gwen and Grandpa Chuck are back in Rochester for a few days to help caddy kids around, hang out with us, and connect with some of their Roch friends. We had a nice meal together between practices. We'll do it again tomorrow.

Overall, nothing too eventful relating to Shannon's health. Our Mayo doctors have ordered our family to get flu shots, and we passed on the request to Shannon's hockey team. An ounce of prevention …

Tonight she took her 260 mg capsule of Temodar before hockey. Watching her skate through drills you would have no idea. That's a tough little girl. Stubborn to a fault. Thank God.

POSTED BY DAN

FRIDAY, NOVEMBER 4, 2011

Keane's "Hamburg Song" brought me to tears this morning on my hike around the Willow Creek Reservoir with Sunny the Wonder Dog. Just caught me in a moment. It's a beautiful song:

> I don't wanna be adored
> Don't wanna be first in line or make myself heard
> I'd like to bring a little light
> To shine a light on your life to make you feel loved.

There was some serious autumn splendor out there with frost lifting and the sun coming over the horizon creating so many interesting patterns of shadow. Wildlife all around. Sunny chased a raccoon up a tree. Sights, smells, and then a really good song—I was vulnerable.

On the way home from hockey practice last night Shannon was quiet, and when probed, she admitted she was worried about the next MRI which will be administered later this month. She has been feeling pressure in her head. She talked about needing to make some balance adjustments recently to keep from stumbling. This was the first we had heard about this in weeks. Caught me off guard and when I tried to offer support or possible explanation she pretty much discounted my efforts and said, "We don't know, we've never been through anything like this before." Nope, we haven't.

The fact remains that we have no idea when the other shoe will drop. To steal from a bit used over and over by our favorite radio personality, The Common Man, when discussing his radio career, "Is this the beginning of the end? The middle of the end? Or the end of the end?" We just don't know. Not to make light of our situation, but it's impossible not to occasionally acknowledge the large shadow we have cast over our lives.

There are so many possible explanations for change taking place that could cause some new head pressure, new balance changes, different feelings. And some of the explanations could be extremely positive. The tumor could be responding exactly as desired. Is the fact that this is happening after four straight days of chemo, five cycles into this stage of the protocol a coincidence? Let's pray on that.

It's a big stretch for Shannon's hockey team, the Rebels. We face Apple Valley Saturday morning and Hastings Sunday night. We have lots of games coming up. Competing on the ice brings Shannon much joy. Let's hope she's out there for all of it.

POSTED BY DAN

Passion Found

Shannon's love affair with hockey started relatively late. Here in Minnesota, many kids are learning to skate and playing hockey by the age of four or five. Shannon had dabbled in a lot of sports and soccer had become a favorite, but nothing else had stuck. In the fifth grade, she heard her soccer teammates talking about hockey tryouts and was interested, so she gave it a go.

Her hockey career got off to a bit of a rocky start because we signed up late, were given incorrect information about when to show up for the first practice, and ended up with the wrong group. Shannon's first hockey experience was on the ice with the older, skilled skaters instead of with the new players. She admitted later that the whole time she was out there, she was thinking this was a really bad idea!

But true to form, she persevered, and we found the right group for her and, as they say, the rest is history.

There is another element to this story, though. A life-changing event had taken place in our house the previous spring, and having Shannon find a passion she could share so closely with her father was a godsend.

When Shannon decided to play hockey, Dan was six months sober. After years of alcohol use that had turned to abuse, he had gone to treatment and was diligently working with his Alcoholics Anonymous program.

One of the scariest things about getting sober is giving up the usual patterns and habits. Dan needed an outlet, somewhere to put his energy. Hockey, like all youth sports, is always looking for qualified coaches to help out. Dan was a hockey player growing up, and he had the skills and personality to make playing hockey really fun for a group of ten-year-old girls.

Dan, now sober and willing and eager, spent countless hours each winter during the last four years of Shannon's life being present and enjoying watching Shannon make friends, become a leader, and play the game she loved. Dan was there on the ice at practice and on the bench during the games to watch Shannon blossom and grow.

Was the timing of these events a coincidence? It couldn't be. Shannon choosing hockey, a game Dan knows and loves, just as Dan needs a positive outlet? Some things happen for a reason. We choose to think of it as a gift from the universe.

MONDAY, NOVEMBER 7, 2011

The sun is shining brightly this morning, and it was nice to drive the girls to school in the daylight, thanks to setting our clocks back yesterday. Daylight Savings Time also allowed us to get up and moving early enough on Sunday to make it to 9:30 A.M. mass. Erin grumbled a bit about having to get up and get dressed for church. That's typical. But what came next I wasn't prepared for. Erin asked me with tears in her eyes, "Why do we even go to church? I pray to God, but he doesn't answer my prayers. Shannon had a headache this week. She's still sick. Why would God do that?" Dan did his best to reassure Erin that while there is tragedy and sadness in the world, there's a lot of beauty and goodness too. The God question is one I struggle with, always. That hasn't changed. But right now, I'm less concerned about answering the God question and more concerned about validating Erin's feelings and letting her express them. Her emotions are very close to the surface. She saw Shannon struggle with some side effects this week and there were physical signs that Shannon is sick. We cannot forget that Erin is seeing, feeling, and processing all of this too.

Shannon was able to play two hockey games this weekend and her squad was looking good. They put the beat down on an over-matched team from Hastings last night. A whole group of friends came to watch Shannon play. She loved it and gave it her all. And while the Rebels looked good, Shannon struggled. Rubbery legs caused by fatigue and some returning side effects meant she was fighting to keep up. Her mind is more than willing, but her body is not quite able. Not while taking her chemo. Not while struggling with pressure in her head and some balance issues. Not with yet another returning symptom as Shannon felt some numbness in her face over the weekend.

We are hopeful that all these side effects are presenting themselves because the Temodar is killing more cells inside that tumor. As a member of our radiation team reminded us, during the last maintenance dose, the steroids would still have been in her system to help counteract any swelling. So, this time around, without the aid of the Decadron, it's possible the swelling and tumor necrosis caused by the chemo is more noticeable to Shannon.

Possible explanation or not, it's still unsettling to have any changes to the status quo. Any different feelings in her body trigger some fear and anxiety for Shannon, and for the rest of us. Tuesday Shannon will have a thorough neuro exam, and the next MRI is looming in a couple of weeks. Until then, we will try to stay positive and tamp down the seeds of doubt.

Maybe this week as the drugs leave her system, we will see Shannon's energy return and her coordination skills sharpen again. Maybe the numbness and the pressure will subside. Maybe Erin can forget for just a while that her sister has cancer. Maybe, maybe …

POSTED BY JEN

TUESDAY, NOVEMBER 8, 2011

Today's appointments brought some relief to the anxiety we have been feeling. Shannon's complete neuro exam showed good, even strength in all her limbs, and good reflexes and control of her eye movement. A slight wobble is present, and the ear pain and some head pressure persists, but Dr. Keating didn't see any changes that alarmed her. She is hopeful that the symptoms Shannon has been feeling are most likely caused by fatigue and the chemotherapy affecting the tumor. And, without steroids, these changes are noticeable to Shannon. We discussed the possibility of needing a small dose of steroids again if these symptoms continue or worsen during the next maintenance dose.

Shannon also did blood work today, and we looked at those results with Dr. Keating as well. The line graphs show the effect that all the treatment and medications have had on Shannon's system. Strange to see the data in picture form that shows how far some of her counts have fallen. Yet, her various counts that are low are still not low enough to cause concern other than to remind us to be vigilant about avoiding illness as best we can. To that end, all four of us got our flu shots today.

So, all things considered, Dr. Keating feels Shannon is doing very well. We will keep an eye on these symptoms during the next cycle of Temodar. We were relieved with how the exam went, but still anxious to see how the tumor has been changing. We will have more definitive answers when Shannon has her fourth MRI next Tuesday.

POSTED BY JEN

FRIDAY, NOVEMBER 11, 2011

It's Friday morning, and the girls are sleeping in. The first quarter ended yesterday, so no school today for students. A little extra sleep and a little down time will be just fine with us.

The weather here has turned cold, and after a beautiful fall, we all know what comes next! Snow had been predicted for us this week, but it skirted by us. Dan was not quite as lucky as he was traveling in Wisconsin and they got the brunt of it. The picture Dan texted to me looked like a winter wonderland.

Erin has been enjoying her school friends and basketball friends this week. One more week before their first tournament, so the coaches added an extra practice this week and next to prepare. Although we are less involved with the basketball team since we are not coaching or managing, we are making every effort we can to show Erin that we are interested in her activities too. This balancing act is not unique to our situation or us. Parents everywhere try to treat their kids equally, but somehow the younger one always thinks they are getting the short straw!

Now that she's a week post-chemo, Shannon feels her energy level is rebounding. She's going to need it. Back-to-back-to-back games for the Rebels this weekend as they kick off play in their district. The regular season begins tonight with a game in Winona.

Happy Veteran's Day, everyone.

POSTED BY JEN

SUNDAY, NOVEMBER 13, 2011

Up early this morning, not exactly sleepless but certainly more restless. It's MRI week. My waking thoughts alternate between Tuesday's brain scan and Saturday's hockey game.

The Rebels' win over Red Wing required an intense three-period effort. Our first year players were given a taste of how quick the pace can be. No time for indecision. The eight Rebel players who were on the team and lost twice to Red Wing last season were especially happy, everyone was. Shannon kept going over specific plays from the game as we dozed off Saturday night. Satisfied and exhausted.

It's seems obvious to Jen and me that Shannon's hockey development has been stunted. The radiation, the steroids, the chemo drugs, the Bactrim, and the anti-nausea meds are keeping her from playing as fast as she once did. Last season, she was one of the Rebels top scorers. This season she is going to have to accept being a solid role player and locker room leader. She just loves being a part of a team.

Tuesday is also seven months to the day since Shannon's tumor was diagnosed. If you would have told us Shannon would be playing hockey and competing in intense games back on those cold, dark days of April we would have traded in all our chips right then and there. We are thrilled and proud and grateful.

How many times when I have been blogging has a poignant song shuffled up exactly when it was needed? Just now ... Annie Lennox, "Why?"

Time to brew some coffee. The Rebels are playing Dodge County at 2:30. Life is good.

POSTED BY DAN

Shannon's passion | Focusing in the locker room while getting instruction from the coaches, and then letting it all out on the ice

MONDAY, NOVEMBER 14, 2011

Have a good thought for this girl on Tuesday as she heads into the tube for her fourth MRI ...

POSTED BY JEN

MRI RESULTS

Unfortunately, not good news to report here tonight. Today's scan showed brightness in the tumor area, which is an indication that the tumor has probably started to grow again. The only other possible explanation is that dead cells have continued to vacate the tumor and that allowed more of the contrast dye to seep in. While Dr. Rao presented that as a possibility, tumor growth is a more likely explanation. She will schedule another scan in six weeks, right around Christmas, to check for further tumor changes.

We are heartbroken, and Shannon is angry. So we enter this next stage of our journey. We will keep a watchful eye for clinical symptom changes in Shannon that would be caused by tumor growth. We will start exploring possible clinical trials around the country that may offer some hope. We will honor Shannon's every wish to the best of our ability. We will lean on you all for love and support.

POSTED BY JEN

WEDNESDAY, NOVEMBER 16, 2011

Today was a day eerily like the one we lived through exactly seven months ago. We were given devastating news that's almost impossible to process. Trying to share this news with family and friends is exhausting, and necessary. Today we knew that each time we picked up the phone we would bring someone to tears.

The difference this time around, though, is there is no definitive course of action for us. What to do next? There is no next treatment plan. If this turns out to be new tumor growth, we will have decisions to make. This next phase of our journey will involve much more personal choice.

We did our best to carry on today. Dan traveled to Illinois, the girls got up and went to school, I did the laundry, life went on … Shannon came home from school and did her homework. She's working on her research paper for English so she will be prepared for ninth grade. She went to the bank to deposit money because she's saving for an iPhone. It's almost surreal to watch her. It is gut wrenching. But, it's not denial on her part. It's her carrying on the life she wants to lead. Both girls were subdued today, but they are functioning.

With the help of the Cancer Education Program at the Mayo Clinic, we are checking into any clinical trials that may be available. We don't know what we will find, but we are going to educate ourselves so we can help Shannon make the best choice. We don't want to grasp at straws and won't chase false hope, but we need to explore our options. The future is more uncertain now than ever, but we will get up tomorrow and do the best we can.

POSTED BY JEN

The Rebels

As kids grow and the calendar turns, there is a new team for every season. Let's be honest, some teams are better than others. Sometimes you like the kids and their parents, and sometimes you just endure and tell your kid to do their best.

The Rochester Rebels Girls U12 hockey team of 2011–2012 was meant to be. I don't know how else to explain it. We were a part of this group of people, this giant support system, at a time in our lives when we needed them most. And they were there with us for some of the best moments and for some of the worst.

The team consisted of sixteen girls, whose parents are all still married to each other, by the way. How often does that happen these days? These girls needed that love and support, because they were on a journey none of them would ever forget. The experience changed them forever. The Rebels bonded together and learned to persevere. They supported Shannon when she was with them. They played in honor of her when she was away receiving treatment, and in memory of her when she was gone.

We continued to follow and root for the Rebels throughout the rest of their season. For us, they will be forever in our memories as Shannon's last team.

FRIDAY, NOVEMBER 18, 2011

Ever since the Rebels' hockey schedule came out in October, we've been looking forward to this weekend: our team's first tournament, a three-day event in the Twin Cities. At the same time in another corner of the metro, Erin's basketball team kicks off the season with a one-day jamboree Saturday in Lakeville.

Certainly, all focus has changed again, but we are coping. A busy weekend with friends, family, and teammates may be just what we need. Some competition might be the perfect outlet for pent-up anger. If only Jen and I could suit up.

Spirits around our house have been lifting with each passing day. I returned from my sales trip to Illinois last night in time for hockey practice. After hockey, Shannon insisted we catch the end of Erin's practice, and then we all enjoyed a Culver's Scoopie Meal together. Then we were home for precious time together organizing for a couple nights in a hotel, two tournaments, and lots of people who want to see us, hug us, offer support, and cheer our girls to happiness.

We are all up for that.

POSTED BY DAN

HOPKINS THANKSGIVING TOURNAMENT CHAMPIONS

This photo doesn't begin to tell the story of the support and love we felt while watching Shannon and her Rebels play their way to a thrilling

Rebels win! | Hopkins Thanksgiving Tournament champions. Shannon's first—and only—tournament victory

tournament victory. So many family and friends from the Twin Cities and Rochester showed up that we filled the stands. Some even took a break from hockey and braved the snowy conditions to drive to Lakeville and watch Erin play basketball. And Shannon's teammates and their families were right in the thick of it, pulling so hard for all of us. They love our kid, and we love them for it. We laughed and cried and cheered our way through two overtime victories. It felt like this was supposed to happen because one of the things on Shannon's bucket list was to win a championship.

But the cold, hard reality of last Tuesday's news was never far from the surface. And by the time we returned home, Shannon was sullen and worrying about her mortality. She said she thinks the tumor is growing. She struggled in the championship game with fatigue and balance. She worries that she will never be able to have that experience again. "It's too bad my first championship came at the end of my life," she told me through her tears.

So today we start trying to buy more time. We broached the subject of clinical trials with Shannon last night. We are headed to Mayo today to sign a release form for Shannon's records and discuss with doctors what options we might have. St. Jude Children's Research Hospital in Memphis, Tenessee, and National Institute of Health in Bethesda, Maryland, have trials going on right now. We have to continue to fight, so we will ...

POSTED BY JEN

TUESDAY, NOVEMBER 22, 2011

We have been all over the map this week with our emotions, but tonight we're feeling pretty good around here. Could be that it's a five day weekend with very little on our agenda. Could be that meeting with our social worker is helping us to process and cope. Could be that a follow-up appointment with Dr. Rao encouraged us to explore our options with clinical trials which will give us a second and third opinion about what the MRI scan shows. She also encouraged us not to give up hope that what we are seeing is treatment effect without the aid of steroids. Could be that Shannon felt up to going to hockey practice tonight. Could be the new iPhones BOTH girls received today!!

I am reluctant to share this news, because it seems quite excessive. To be honest, Dan and I are a little bit embarrassed about it. Erin didn't even have a phone before today! But we had several people offer to do something nice for us, for our girls. And they did.

While what we really want can't be bought—not even from Apple—our girls are grinning from ear to ear. These new toys have brought a little relief from the stress and pain they feel, a little diversion, a little mindless fun, a little joy. So what the hell, new iPhones it is …

POSTED BY JEN

THANKSGIVING

Just looking to string together "A Few Honest Words." OK, I'm already in trouble because I stole that from Ben Sollee, whose song I am listening to this morning as I get my day started with some music and some writing.

Most of my material is not original. I draw inspiration and perspective from people all around me all day. I learn stuff from them and apply it somewhere down the line. Sometimes people say, "Man, is he smart!" And sometimes they say, "Hey, where have I heard that before?"

The truth is on a day like today, Thanksgiving, it is not that hard to string together a few honest words to express how I am feeling. I am scared. I am happy. I am grateful. I am lucky, really lucky. Always have been. I have a heart that lives on flutter and often needs to be swallowed because it is beating in my throat. Summoning up a good cry does not take much. But that's a good thing. It means I am alive and feeling much.

The adversity this family is facing is no different than that of thousands of other families going through really challenging times. And I've stated it many times, embedded in a really bad situation is an amazing journey of support, inspiration, hope, and love. We just needed our eyes opened to it. God keeps putting people in our lives that make it OK.

We are going to celebrate Thanksgiving with the O'Haras today at Doug and Maggie's in St. Paul, a home full of love and laughter. Bring your earplugs! Our thoughts and hearts will be with the Harkins' in Las Vegas also.

Shannon is awake, just walked upstairs with a big ol' smile on her face. Sunny the Wonder Dog is licking her like she's been away for months. Happy Thanksgiving.

POSTED BY DAN

SATURDAY, NOVEMBER 26, 2011

I needed a change of tune from my usual mellow singer/songwriter vibe, so today on the iPod it's Mumford & Sons. While the music is alt rock mixed with bluegrass, the lyrics are still poetry. Songs about fear and grace and love and time ...

Time. It's ever present in our minds right now. How much do we have? How should we spend it? How do we get more of it? The goal is to not waste it worrying about it.

Yesterday, Shannon spent her time watching hockey. That meant she and Dan made a trip to St. Paul for a second day in a row, this time to watch the Minnesota Wild game. After that, they headed to watch her cousin Teddie play a tournament game over in Minnetonka. While taking in Teddie's game made for a really long day, Shannon wanted to see him play. Watching Teddie play five years ago at a tournament here in Rochester is what inspired Shannon to give hockey a try. So, there's always been a connection there.

While Shannon and Dan were on the go, Erin and I had a mellow day. Erin's friend came over to spend the day with her, and then Erin and I finished off our night by watching the movie *Elf*. Erin got some down time in her own home, just what she has been craving.

We have two more days here at home on this holiday weekend. Usually we spend this time getting out the Christmas decorations and getting a tree. The holidays are always a time of reflection on the past year and thoughts toward the new one. That will be a struggle this year. Our goal right now is to fill our time doing the things we want, the things that make us happy, the things that fill us up. It's a strange way to live, not looking back, not looking forward. But, we will try to continue to enjoy the moment we are in as best we can, making the most of our time ...

Well I'm scared of what's behind and what's before ...
And there will come a time, you'll see, with no more tears.
And love will not break your heart, but dismiss your fears.
Get over your hill and see what you find there ...

"After the Storm" by Mumford & Sons
POSTED BY JEN

MONDAY, NOVEMBER 28, 2011

This should be the beginning of a Temodar week, but this course that we were so sure we were going to be on through next March has taken a detour. Shannon has begun presenting some new symptoms, and the first course of action is to start her on the steroids again. Shannon is mad as hell about what she knows this will do to her appearance. Getting off steroids was a great day in this journey and returning to them feels like a step backwards, for sure. But, the slight tremor in Shannon's left side, a little drooping in her lip, and some nausea has forced the doctor's hand on this. The hope is that these symptoms are coming from swelling around the tumor, and the Decadron can have an immediate effect.

Dan and I had each noticed the almost imperceptible change in Shannon's face over the last few days, but neither of us wanted to be an alarmist, so neither of us verbalized it. We each thought, "Maybe I'm being hypersensitive to every little twitch," or "Maybe Shannon's just really fatigued," or "Maybe it's nothing," but Dr. Rao confirmed it during her examination. In the car on the way to school, Shannon was not only mad about steroids, but she was checking her face in the mirror and expressing her anger toward us for not telling her what we thought we saw. I think she only half believed my explanation that we weren't lying to her, just trying not to alarm her. Shannon expects us to be completely honest with her about everything, and the protective instinct we have as parents sometimes backfires in this situation …

So, as for the Temodar, we are waiting at least a couple of days to start this cycle. Shannon's records are being reviewed by two clinical trials right now, and Dr. Rao explained that she would not be eligible for either trial until at least four weeks after her last dose of chemo. So, we will wait to hear from St. Jude Children's Research Hospital and National Institute of Health on whether or not they think we should continue our current course of action and reassess after the next scan, or if they think Shannon is a candidate for a trial and how soon this would happen.

Shannon listened today as Dr. Rao explained the need for the steroids again and also began to discuss the possibility of a clinical trial and what each of them would entail. She listened to all the information and then politely told Dr. Rao, "I need to go now so I can get to school." In the elevator we discussed that if we have to pursue treatment somewhere else, we hope we won't have to go until after the Rebels hockey season is over. Maybe that's a pipe dream, but Shannon is gearing up for practice tonight and an away game in Waseca tomorrow.

It's all so overwhelming right now … to think that these research facilities in Bethesda and Memphis are reviewing our scans today, and Wednesday means we will soon have a second and third opinion to consider. Shannon told Dan and me, "If we have to do something, we should try the St. Jude study [oral meds] first and then if that doesn't work, I would try the brain surgery at NIH." Now, this is putting the cart before the horse a bit, because we don't yet know what their recommendations will be. But, Shannon is trying to process all of the "what ifs" and, truth be told, Dan and I are processing all of this right along with her.

My heart just aches for my little girl. No thirteen-year-old should have to think about how far they will go to try to save their own life. But, if and when the time comes, Shannon the Cannon will lead, and we will follow …

POSTED BY JEN

TUESDAY, NOVEMBER 29, 2011

Not much energy in me to write tonight, but I had a quick score update to post. The Rebels went on the road and skated to a 5–0 victory over Waseca. Shannon scored a goal nineteen seconds into the game. A self-described "cheesy goal" from the side of the net, but we'll take it.

Shannon looked all right out there, fighting her mind and her body a bit, but loving being out on the ice. She even stood her ground at the blue line and got leveled by the biggest girl on the opposing team. No harm, no foul. Shannon bounced back up.

Seeing her skate hard during the game and laugh hard after the game with her teammates was a nice little pick-me-up for all of us ...

POSTED BY JEN

WEDNESDAY, NOVEMBER 30, 2011

We had a good chat with the girls this morning over breakfast. Shannon was receptive to discussing clinical trials. Erin, as always, was an eyes-wide-open listener.

We are in agreement that as long as Shannon can feel productive as a member of the Rochester Rebels 12B's we will keep skating. Watching Shannon and her pals goof and laugh in the locker room and at DQ on the way home from our game in Waseca, it's hard to imagine a treatment plan with more benefit to Shannon's mental health. However, our desires need to be weighed against all possible opportunities to extend Shannon's life.

Dr. Rao told us Monday that the National Institute of Health trial wants Shannon. She's an ideal candidate. But NIH recommended we start immediately while they can treat the whole tumor. NIH Nuerosurgeon Dr. Lonser will tell us all about the procedure. We have his number sitting right here. The NIH procedure would require a surgery: inserting a small plastic tube into the tumor area to apply an experimental toxin directly to the cancer. If we wait too long, we may miss our window of opportunity with NIH. Aggressive tumor growth—even changes in four or five weeks—could make it impossible to treat the entire area. Shannon's next MRI is scheduled for the first week in January.

Enlisting in the NIH trial—post-haste—would mean picking up and heading to Bethesda, Maryland, while Shannon is still feeling good enough to play hockey and go to school. She said to us this morning she usually gets to school and the sadness goes away. Being around her friends is really good medicine. We have so much to consider.

Today we hope to hear from Dr. Wetmore at St. Jude. Will Shannon be a candidate for that clinical trial? That trial involves daily oral meds, a receptor inhibitor to interfere with tumor growth or spread of the cancer. That trial involves a four-week stay in Memphis. So much to consider.

Shannon told us this morning the steroids are working. She feels better. Less pressure in her ear after just three 1 mg doses. But while the steroids help with the symptoms, they are not doing anything to slow tumor growth, they just mask the effects.

Both clinical trials are phase one studies—gathering data. There is no proof that either trial will buy us time. So much to consider.

Today Jen and I are circling the wagons and taking care of business to keep us ready for whatever is ahead.

POSTED BY DAN

DESTINATION MEMPHIS

My oh my, how things have changed quickly. We are headed to Memphis on Monday.

We heard back from St. Jude Children's Research Hospital late Wednesday afternoon, and Shannon was accepted for their clinical trial. The team there feels that what they see on the MRI looks like recurrent tumor. A new round of their receptor inhibitor trial is set to begin and Shannon can take one of the six slots available. Immediately.

The goal of this trial is to test the safety and dosing of this oral medication that is designed to inhibit tumor cell growth and starve the tumor of nutrients by cutting off the blood pathways to the tumor. We will learn more from Dr. Wetmore today, but the protocol is for Shannon to be in Memphis for the first twenty-eight days of the trial for close monitoring. Our hope is that we will get to return home for the

Christmas holiday weekend and then return to St. Jude to finish the first portion of the trial.

So, we have a lot of ground to cover over the next four days. All four of us are going. We gave Erin the option, and she wants to be with us. St. Jude is helping arrange the initial trip to Memphis and housing to get us settled in down there on Monday. Shannon is sad to be leaving school, friends, and hockey. But hopefully we will be moving back by mid-January, and she will feel good enough to enjoy all of those things.

Dan and I can't believe how quickly this is happening, but at least it feels like we're doing something, continuing to fight. We will update with more information as things become clearer to us.

POSTED BY JEN

THURSDAY, DECEMBER 1, 2011

We are completely blown away—again—at the kindness of people in our lives. Word of our Memphis journey has circulated quickly, and the offers are pouring in from everywhere.

Seventeen people have offered to take care of our dog. Six have offered to drive her down to Memphis with clothes and supplies and whatever it is we have requested. Several have offered to dress our home up for Christmas, Griswold style. People are dropping off chili and rice krispie bars, and my mother-in-law has volunteered to do my laundry.

We have Mayo Clinic employees helping us way beyond the call of duty. Erin's basketball team gave her two extra lives in lightning at basketball practice. Shannon's Rebels are planning a going away pizza party.

And then there are the teary-eyed staffers at Willow Creek Middle School who are going to incredible lengths to make sure our kids will keep up with their classmates. Next time there is a bond referendum: shut up and vote yes. These people are heroes.

I just wanted to take a second to recognize these efforts. Everyone wants to help. We are blown out of the water. You are making a difference. You are making it better for us.

I just told a friend that the hardest part is seeing pain in the faces of the people you love. This business of getting to Memphis and fighting the fight is an action plan. That is the easy part. We will be busy and on an adventure together.

The next few days will be hard. And then we are off to Memphis. I will let Jen update everyone on St. Jude tomorrow. I just wanted to say thank you and good night.

POSTED BY DAN

FRIDAY, DECEMBER 2, 2011

Note to the reader: make sure you have a cup of coffee or Diet Coke in hand for this one, you're going to be here a while!

It seems that every time the phone rings, the caller ID comes up Memphis, Tennessee. Over the past three days, we have dealt with people at St. Jude on several different fronts. The research coordinator talked us through the basic logistics of coming to St. Jude. Dr. Wetmore talked us through the logistics of the clinical trial. The travel coordinator helped us arrange our flight, shuttle, and housing. The business office got Shannon registered as a patient and issued her Medical ID number. The business office called back to verify all our information. The research assistant called back to make sure all of these things had been done and that we're ready to come. An email received tonight included an appointment itinerary and confirmed all of the details. We are quickly learning that this is how St. Jude operates. They make sure everything is taken care of. Having a life-threatening childhood illness is bad enough. You don't need to worry about the details ...

Our call from Dr. Wetmore provided a little more clarity about the trial protocol. While we discussed the ins and outs of this trial, we also discussed the fact that twenty-eight days in Memphis would mean being away from home at the holidays. Dr. Wetmore reassured us that she would make every effort to allow us to fly home for the Christmas weekend. We told Dr. Wetmore that high on Shannon's wish list would be a pass to come home for New Year's, that's when the Rebels will be playing in the Stillwater Tournament. Dr. Wetmore gets that. She spent some time on staff here at Mayo, and while she was here, her son played youth hockey.

Dr. Wetmore explained that the twenty-eight-day time frame is at the request of the FDA. This is a drug that is not yet approved, and patients must be closely monitored. But, Dr. Wetmore is obviously very familiar with the care that Mayo provides, and as it turns out, she's also familiar with Dr. Rao. While Dr. Wetmore was at Mayo, Dr. Rao was a fellow. Dr. Rao later worked in Dr. Wetmore's lab. There is a chance that if Shannon is tolerating the drug easily, we may have some latitude to do more of the protocol at Mayo. Not getting our hopes up, but food for thought …

So, here's what we know: We leave Monday morning first thing and when we get to Memphis the shuttle will take us straight to St. Jude Children's Research Hospital. Shannon will have a new patient assessment on Monday afternoon and meet the team, including Dr. Wetmore. Tuesday there will be lab work, consults, and a patient services orientation. Wednesday morning brings a pharmacy consult and then a baseline MRI. If everything goes well, Shannon will start the new drug on Thursday.

We have dotted a lot of i's and crossed a lot of t's, but we are still working out our housing situation. We know that we will be staying right on campus at Grizzlie House (named for the local NBA team) for the first few days. This allows us to be close by while we have lots of appointments and consults. After that, St. Jude will provide housing at the Ronald McDonald House. But, Shannon is apprehensive about this for two reasons. One, Shannon is hoping that somehow, someway, we can find a place to live in Memphis where Sunny the Wonder Dog can join us. Even three weeks away from her sounds like too long to Shannon. Grandma and Grandpa Harkins are ready to bring us our dog and our car if we can find the right situation.

The other reason Shannon is apprehensive about Ronald McDonald is this: she told us, she doesn't think of herself as one of "those" kids … i.e. a kid with cancer. Call it denial, call it coping, but it's been working for her. If we can help this feel more like an adventure and less like a trip to the hospital, we will. But obviously at St. Jude, everywhere you turn, there will be "those" kids and we need to help Shannon and Erin prepare for that too.

We picked the girls up from school today, and they had gifts and cards from teachers and friends. It was a bittersweet day at Willow Creek as they celebrated, yet said goodbye. Goodbye for now. The outpouring of support is uplifting, and people have been coming out of the woodwork to wish us best of luck on our journey. There have been so many offers to help that if we leave tasks behind, or forget something, someone will pick up the slack. I'm 100 percent confident of that, and that's making it easier to get ready to go.

So, all the nuts and bolts are taken care of, and that just leaves us with the feelings and the emotions and the reality of it all. I find myself needing to temper people's enthusiasm about this next step. Yes, we are taking action, and yes, St. Jude is a wonderful place, and yes, we need to be hopeful. Yet the odds are long, and the outlook is bleak. There is no magic elixir, and Shannon will not come home cured. We are only headed to Memphis because the treatment that worked for a while is no longer working. But Shannon is ready to keep fighting. So, we will take a leap of faith and hope for results. Shannon will try this experimental drug and hope that it becomes the next thing that is used to treat brain cancer. We hope for response and deadening of cells. We hope this can prolong Shannon's life. We hope that Shannon can return home to the friends and teammates she is leaving behind and feel good enough to enjoy some more time with all of them. We hope …

Way back in May, local TV station KTTC did a story on Shannon, and in it she said she hopes the doctors will learn something from her case and that her life means something. All the questions that seemed impossible for Dan and me to answer about what is the next right thing to do have gone away. The four of us all believe the next right thing to do is head to Memphis. Shannon wants her life to mean something to someone. It already does, little girl, it already does …

POSTED BY JEN

Memphis on Broadway

Before diagnosis, in our minds, we had it all going on. Perfect little typical middle-class family: go to work, go to school, play some sports, take piano lessons, save some money, take a vacation now and then.

Spring break of 2011 was the one we'd been saving and planning for, New York City and Washington D.C. One of the perks of traveling for work is that Dan racks up hotel rewards points by the boatload. And we put them to good use, staying at the Marriott Marquis in the heart of Times Square, forty-second floor. We had the iconic Times Square view. In D.C., we stayed at the JW Marriott. The address is on Pennsylvania Avenue, and we actually got to see the presidential motorcade leaving the White House right from our hotel room balcony. Perfect.

The girls were at the right ages to keep up with the necessary pace, but also to enjoy it.

On Broadway | Outside the Shubert Theater in New York City, ready to see the musical, *Memphis*

We did it all, from Times Square to the White House, from the Statue of Liberty to Capitol Hill. We have hundreds of photos from that trip, and one of our activities was to take in a Broadway musical, a favorite pasttime of mine. We chose *Memphis*, a story about race and rock and roll. Set in the 1950s, it tells the tale of a white DJ and a black singer who fall in love.

When I look at the photo we took that night, all I can think is that we were blissfully unaware that our lives would be changed forever two weeks later. That's the last photo taken of us as a family B.D.—before diagnosis. I want to be able to remember that as a happy memory. Maybe in time.

The show was amazing, and Shannon and Erin were singing and dancing right along with the music. We downloaded the cast-recording album the next day. Ironically, Memphis, the city, would become a part of our journey.

Leaving Rochester | Headed to Memphis, TN, to take part in a clinical trial at St. Jude Children's Research Hospital

SUNDAY, DECEMBER 4, 2011

The bags are now packed, and we are off on our plane to Memphis first thing tomorrow. This weekend brought us in contact with all the groups of people who have been along for this journey. We saw lots of friends and family who came by to see us, hug us, wish us luck. We attended our regular 9:30 mass and Shannon shared herself with everyone in attendance at St. John's through the sacrament of Anointing of the Sick. Finally, tonight we said goodbye for now to the Rebels. We are as ready as one can be for this next step. If only we could take the good thoughts, well wishes, and prayers that have been sent our way and trade each one in for an extra day on this earth for Shannon. Instead, we will carry your love and support in our hearts, and it will help us to carry on ...

POSTED BY JEN

MONDAY, DECEMBER 5, 2011

We made it to Memphis. It was a really long day, but we are here and admitted, Shannon was examined, and we are cleared for outpatient participation.

Our Minneapolis to Memphis flight took five hours. High winds and low visibility diverted us to Little Rock where we sat on the tarmac for an hour. Shannon's reaction: "Hey, another state I had never been to—Arkansas!"

By the time we got to St Jude Children's Research Hospital it was 5:00 P.M. We made it to our housing here on the campus a little after 6:30 P.M. and we are cashed.

We will meet Dr. Wetmore and her team at the neuro-oncology clinic first thing Tuesday and away we go.

These kids are such troopers. Erin O is a star too. Left our house in Rochester at 6:00 A.M. ... we have no chance of seeing the end of this "Monday Night Football" game.

More details tomorrow. We are safe and sound.

POSTED BY DAN

TUESDAY, DECEMBER 6, 2011

We want to keep you all updated on this new stage of our journey, so we will do our best to write a nightly blog. Things got better here today for us. After a long travel day Monday, and being overwhelmed by our new surroundings last night, today started off rough, but steadily improved.

First on the agenda today were labs for Shannon. A blood draw—something she's done so many times over these past nine months—for the first time ever left her feeling very woozy. An inauspicious start, to say the least! But, some orange juice and some TLC from the nurses at the E clinic (that's the name for the neuro-oncology clinic) helped her to get the color back in her skin and the sass back in her personality. We worked through medical histories, vitals, neuros, etc. By the time we saw the social worker, Shannon was feeling good enough to rip on both Dan and me. Our social worker here is a southern belle named Jennifer. I think the only thing she and I have in common is our name! She didn't quite know what to think of our Yankee dialect or straight-forwardness. She was doing her intake interview, poking around the edges to see how well Shannon, and we as a family, were dealing with things. Shannon told her we lay it all out there. We're honest with our kids and they are honest with us, maybe to a fault. In other words, we weren't looking for much help from her, and we pretty much told her that!

Truth be told, services like a social worker might be completely new to a lot of patients who come here, but we've been fortunate enough to have that type of support back home. We realize we shouldn't take that for granted. Being here for just over twenty-four hours, it's obvious to see that people come from all over the country, and from all walks of life, to this hospital to try and save their children.

Our last appointment of the day was the best one yet. We met Dr. Wetmore and connected immediately. She and Shannon talked about hockey, they talked about teachers at Willow Creek, and they talked about the staff at the Mayo Clinic. Lots of comfort in the familiarity that Dr. Wetmore has with the journey we have taken to get to this point. She spent ten years at Mayo, so she understands us Yankees!

We are making progress on some of the logistics here. Tomorrow we are hoping to finalize some housing that will allow Sunny (oh, yeah, and Grandma and Grandpa) to join us this weekend. Dr. Wetmore is also planning to let us return home for a long holiday break—hopefully coming home from Christmas through New Year's—then returning the first week of January to complete the four-week protocol. We are being given this latitude because of Dr. Wetmore's familiarity with Dr. Rao and Mayo. The Mayo Clinic will instead do the labs and check-ups that week that otherwise would have been done by St. Jude in Memphis. How lucky are we that we happen to live in Rochester? Unbelievable.

We finished our night off with a family dinner here at Grizzlie House. Various corporations sponsor these free events, and tonight it was southern comfort food provided by Gus's Famous Fried Chicken. This is stick-to-your-bones kind of food: fried chicken, grilled cheese sandwiches, mac and cheese, bread, and baked beans. Oh, and a little coleslaw if you need something green on your plate! It was delicious. And to top if off, the in-house movie they were playing was *Miracle*, Shannon's favorite movie about the 1980 Olympic men's hockey team. Ironic, to say the least.

Tomorrow brings a lengthy MRI for Shannon. Advanced imaging to look not only at the tumor, but also at the nerves surrounding it and the blood pathways leading to it. After that, we will meet with Dr. Wetmore to look at results and sign off on participating in the clinical trial. Shannon should receive her first dose of the drug on Thursday. Time is ticking as Shannon continues to be more symptomatic each day.

Thanks to all of you back home who are keeping tabs on us and supporting us on this journey.

POSTED BY JEN

WEDNESDAY, DECEMBER 7, 2011

We awoke to something that made us feel right at home this morning—snow! The people of Memphis are not accustomed to the white stuff, and a few St. Jude staffers tried to blame us for bringing it with us from Minnesota.

Dan and the girls were able to sleep in a bit this morning. I was up early, drinking coffee and reading the protocol for the experimental drug. Our first appointment of the day was Shannon's MRI. We are feeling more comfortable with our surroundings now. Comfortable enough that Erin stayed at Grizzlie House to work on homework while we headed over to the Chili's Care Center, the building where all the scans take place.

We had been told that this was an extensive MRI and Shannon was prepared. Luckily the IV went in easily today, no feeling faint like yesterday. But, by the end of the scan, seventy-five minutes in the tube had Shannon feeling really claustrophobic. As always, she is such a trooper and made it through it.

By the time we came out of the MRI, Erin had joined us. After finishing her homework and checking in with Mrs. Nielsen and some of her friends by telephone, Erin checked out the shuttle schedule, saw that she could catch the 11:45, and texted her dad that she was coming over to the patient care building. She got on the shuttle—alone— and then navigated her way through the building—alone—to find Dan doing some work near the Starbuck's. Completely confident that she knew her way around and could handle herself. Not bad for a ten-year-old.

After a quick lunch, we met with Dr. Wetmore. She didn't have time to show us the scan today but told us she had taken a look at it, and while she saw some small changes she didn't see much tumor growth since the scan done three weeks ago at Mayo. That was good news. We will have more details from her on Friday when we have time to look at the scan together.

Although she was in a hurry to make it to a meeting today, Dr. Wetmore did have time to hear one dog story from the girls. This morning, we FaceTimed with Grandma who was staying with Sunny at our house. The girls had Grandma hold the phone up so they could say hi to Sunny and as soon as the girls started saying her name, Sunny's ears perked up and she licked Grandma's iPhone and disconnected the call! Dr. Wetmore said she hopes she gets to meet Sunny.

Our day finished up with a helpful nurse, Miss Gina, getting us to photography to get Shannon's patient photo done quickly and then showing us where to go for a quick EKG for Shannon (part of the protocol for this trial). After all that, Shannon had earned herself a nice long nap this afternoon.

I am struggling for the words to describe this place. It is amazing and overwhelming at the same time. Everyone here has a story. You don't end up at St. Jude unless you have a story. Some people draw strength from sharing their stories and hearing the same from others, but Shannon is not quite to that point in her journey. She is polite, but she likes it better when people chat with her about other things: her friends, her hockey team, her dog, etc. As always, we continue to try and follow her lead.

Tomorrow starts early. Labs at 7:00 A.M. as Shannon prepares for her first dose of the new chemo tomorrow.

POSTED BY JEN

THURSDAY, DECEMBER 8, 2011

This day deserves a wow!

At the end of the day, a new, highly selective inhibitor drug—a chemo called Crenolanib—is in Shannon's system, and our next fight is underway.

The day started at 7:00 A.M. in the triage unit at St. Jude Children's Research Hospital with an IV inserted in Shannon's left hand that will stay in place until Saturday. The first blood draw provided baseline numbers. The Crenolanib was introduced by 8:50 A.M. Three little tablets that Shannon ingested easily under the guidance of a PK (pharmacokinetics) nurse named Sherry who made us all feel comfortable and safe.

Then Shannon had to give about five tubes of blood after one hour, two hours, four hours, and then the final draw came at about 3:00 P.M. In between, there were meetings with researchers, child-life specialists, Dr. Wetmore's nurse practitioner … and an encounter with Carmen Electra.

I made Jen and Shannon rush out and check out today's celeb spot of the day as Ms. Electra waited to jump on an elevator. They were not

Shannon begins to decline | Needing assistance walking around the St. Jude campus

impressed and headed back into the medicine room. We are learning that the celeb sightings around St. Jude are pretty common, especially around the holidays. So hopefully we can chronicle a few more over the course of the next couple weeks. The girls accused me of being a "creeper," but Carmen didn't notice. A striking woman I have to admit, but she's a little too tall for me.

But our little Shanner had a tough day. She was tired and lethargic and a little nauseated. Lots of chemicals coursing through her blood stream. And lots of blood drawn. We helped her around the campus and tried our best to get her to eat some bland foods and drinks fluids. But we are suspecting she may be worn down from sleep deprivation, the overall stress of being away from home, managing a school load from afar, uncertainty, and—there's no denying it's impact on her energy—the Big C.

Today's day brightener: the sun. It made an appearance in our world for the first time since arriving in Tennessee. Tomorrow's day brightener: Sunny. Our dog should arrive with Grandma and Papa Har-kins mid-day when our appointments are complete. At that time we will pack up and head for a townhome we have rented out near Shelby Farms Park in Germantown, Tennessee. We will set up camp there for the next two weeks. Our pad has king-sized beds, a kitchen, multiple TV rooms, a fitness center and access to tons of green space, trails, and fresh air. We are ready to turn over our room here at Grizzlie House.

We tried to give Erin as much attention as we could today, but it was another all-about-Shannon day here at St. Jude. The staff around the E clinic is getting to know us and warming to our Yankee ways. I think we are a little less invested in relationships at St. Jude, but we have some angels watching over us and helping us negotiate the local culture.

Friday is a new day.

POSTED BY DAN

FRIDAY, DECEMBER 9, 2011

Tonight we are settled in our two-bedroom apartment in the Mem-phis suburb of Germantown that will be home for the next two weeks. It feels really good to be "off campus." Shannon and I hadn't left the confines of St. Jude since Monday when we arrived. Our set-up here is good and gives us a little more breathing room than we had at the Grizzlie House.

The best part of today was seeing our minivan roll in with Grandma, Papa, and Sunny the Wonder Dog in tow. They had an uneventful adventure through Iowa and Missouri, and Sunny enjoyed every min-ute of the ride! The girls were so happy to see Sunny, and the three of them rode together in the backseat of our jam-packed van as we headed out to the burbs.

The worst part of today is how Shannon is feeling. She made it through her blood draw, EKG, and E Clinic visit this morning, but immediately needed a nap. Then after lunch and moving to our new digs, she needed a nap. She doesn't feel up to doing much, and she had a few tears today when it was too hard to concentrate to do her homework. Dizziness, numbness, and fatigue have a grip on her. We hope this is a temporary phase and that she will rebound soon so we can spend some of our free time exploring Memphis.

Tomorrow takes us back to St. Jude for the forty-eight-hour blood draw and EKG, and then Shannon will get her second dose of chemo. The trial protocol calls for one dose, then just blood count measurements until the forty-eight-hour mark, after which the second dose is taken. From here on out, she will take the chemo, named Crenolanib, every day.

Grandma, Erin, and I have plans to do a little shopping tomorrow while Shannon naps, and then the women folk are hoping to do our traditional Christmas cookie baking tomorrow afternoon. Shannon and Erin seem excited about that, so I hope it's a day brightener.

POSTED BY JEN

SATURDAY, DECEMBER 10, 2011

Shannon's condition continues to deteriorate. She looks like she did in late June when the after effects of radiation kicked her butt for about two weeks. She just can't shake the fatigue, and now the numbness is working its way down her right side.

Today the four of us—along with Grandma and Papa Harkins—drove back to the St. Jude campus for labs, another EKG, and a second dose of the Crenolanib. Shannon told me, "If I have to feel like this for the next two years, I don't want to feel like this."

Dr. Wetmore is in the know about Shannon's condition but wants to hold off on pumping up the steroids to make sure it's not just a virus of some kind running its course. The symptoms have been coming on over the last couple weeks. We aren't scheduled to return to St. Jude until Tuesday. Dr. Wetmore suspects—and we are praying—that a dead cell from the tumor or some dead cells may have triggered swelling which is causing pressure on Shannon's fifth cranial nerve.

We had to help Shannon around campus and outside this afternoon to take in some fresh Tennessee air and soak up some vitamin D. The sun is shining bright here in the mid-south. It's cool but the forty degrees felt good to us, and we each took turns getting out and walking.

Grandma and Erin are baking Christmas cookies. It smells good in here. Jen is working on a puzzle. Shannon is out cold on the sofa with a puke bucket close by. No sightseeing today.

POSTED BY DAN

SUNDAY, DECEMBER 11, 2011

Today was a slightly better day, although everything is relative ... our day still started and ended with vomit. TMI, I know.

Shannon woke up hungry today so she took her Decadron, Zofran, and Bactrim and chowed down her breakfast. It didn't stay down for long. After consulting with Dr. Wetmore, we re-took the steroid and anti-nausea, and Shannon was cautious with food choices and movements for the rest of the day.

Shannon slept a little less today and even managed to play a card game with Erin, Grandma, and Papa this afternoon while Dan and I went for a walk. She followed along with texts from one of the hockey moms at today's Rebels game. (Just to update you all, the Rebels suffered their first loss of the season yesterday, but bounced back with a victory today.) The highlight of Shannon's day was a FaceTime call from some of her friends, the Olsons and Langs, from back home.

Shannon continues to be unsteady on her feet as she struggles with numbness down her right side. Today she also has a ringing in her ears that she tells us is "really annoying." Dead cells that are vacating the tumor and touching nerves could cause these symptoms. It's pretty tight quarters inside the brain stem. That's what we're hoping it is. That's the positive spin I'm going with until I learn otherwise. I'm not ready to accept the alternative.

Today we did what we usually do on Sundays, watched a lot of NFL football. We coerced Erin into doing some homework today and got her caught up on her assignments from last week. Shannon has been unable to do any work these past three days, so that's been a bummer for her.

We also offered Erin the chance to escape Memphis for a couple of days since we haven't been able to get out and do things like we had hoped. Grandma and Papa rented a car, and they are going to spend the next week traveling around—maybe Nashville or the Smoky Mountains. They offered to take Erin with them, but, given the option, Erin wants to stay here. She wants to be with us. She wants us to stay together. Erin was in tears tonight after seeing her sister get sick again.

Tonight's episode of nausea came shortly after taking the Bactrim again, so now we are supposing that the Bactrim is not sitting right with Shannon and her new cocktail of medicines. Hard to reconcile that these drugs that are hopefully helping can make her so sick. While we had planned to have a couple of days away from St. Jude, we will head in tomorrow for a consult with Dr. Wetmore.

I would be lying if I said this wasn't hard. It is. Hard for us to be away from home. Hard to be missing our friends. Hard to be missing the pre-Christmas craziness that I always put myself through. Hard to be missing Rebels games. Hard to see Shannon sick. Hard to see Erin sad. Hard to admit that Shannon may never be healthy enough again to enjoy the things she once did ...

But, as the ten-year-old said, we should stay together. And for now, we will keep fighting.

POSTED BY JEN

MONDAY, DECEMBER 12, 2011

Monday was an unscheduled day at St. Jude Children's Research Hospital for Team O'Hara, but we are hopeful the issues addressed today will lead to a rebound.

Shannon has been just clobbered by nausea, fatigue, and—more disturbing—a loss of function to her right side. What started as face numbness has worked its way down her right arm to her right leg. When she talks she sounds severely inebriated. But for most of the day Shannon did not even attempt to talk, she just slept. We transported her around St. Jude in a wheelchair.

The rapid progression of the numbness—along with a couple days of vomiting—sent us back this morning in 9-1-1 mode. Shannon needed fluids, and she needed drugs that she just couldn't keep down on her own. By about 10:30 A.M. she had an IV in place and for the next six hours it was a slow drip, drip, drip. More steroids, more Zofran, more Zantac, and saline.

Dr. Cynthia Wetmore was all over us today. Shannon is the first patient in her trial to get this high a dose of the Crenolanib. Her opinion is that one of two things is happening: one, the tumor is growing, or two, the drug has had an immediate impact, and cell death and edema are causing these problems. The second explanation is not only most hopeful, but it seems most logical.

The MRI taken just last Wednesday did not indicate much change to the tumor, and Dr. Wetmore feels that if there is tumor growth it would not happen that fast. The symptoms would present more gradually.

When Shannon passed the pee test—when she was able to urinate—we were allowed to go home. (OK, home is a stretch, but to our apartment home in Germantown.) That happened at about 5:00 P.M. We will head back tomorrow for further monitoring.

By the time we returned to our pad, Shannon wanted popcorn and mac and cheese. We tried to pace her. But she was hungry. Now she's sleeping again. In a chair, wearing a shamrock blanket given to her by the Rochester 12A girls hockey team. She looks cozy. If she is sleeping, she can't puke.

POSTED BY DAN

TUESDAY, DECEMBER 13, 2011

Another long day of drip, drip, drip at St. Jude, more IV fluids and more steroids given intravenously as well. While the nausea medicines have kept Shannon from getting sick, they have made her very lethargic. It is an inexact science, a bit of trial and error to get the right cocktail that keeps you from throwing up, but doesn't knock you out. Let's say that's a work in progress …

The steroids needed to be increased as well today because Shannon's right side is still not functioning. She can't use her right arm or get her right leg to work properly. It's almost unimaginable that she was skating nine days ago. Now, she needs a wheelchair.

It is likely there is much swelling around the tumor and probably bleeding as well that is irritating the brain. So today, Shannon received 12 mg of Decadron, twice the highest dose she had ever needed in the past. Just like that.

One bright spot today was Dan and Erin taking a break from the medicine room at St. Jude to take Sunny out for a walk on Mud Island, a great park area on the Mississippi River and just minutes from St. Jude. Dan and Erin walked and talked and enjoyed some sweets afterwards at little shop called Miss Cordelia's.

We will reassess again tomorrow at St. Jude with Dr. Wetmore. The goal is to keep Shannon on this high dose of Crenolanib because that gives us the best chance to kill tumor cells. But, Dr. Wetmore is prepared to back off the dosage if Shannon just cannot tolerate it.

It's hard not to feel like we've gone backwards. Looking at Shannon lying in a hospital bed just tears at our hearts. But, we are trying to keep

Mud Island, Memphis | Erin and Sunny take a break from the hospital

the faith that the chemo is killing the tumor. Things have gotten much worse, but that doesn't mean it can't get better again. We could live with Shannon feeling really crappy for a while if there's a return on the other end. We have to believe.

POSTED BY JEN

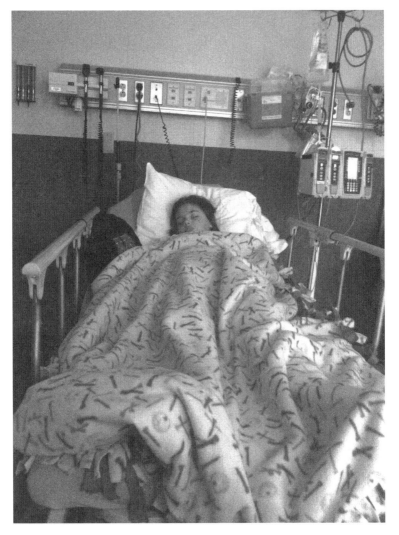

Fight like a girl | Shannon receiving IV fluids and steroids at St. Jude

St. Jude

Our time in Memphis was so short—just seventeen days—but that was plenty of time for St. Jude Children's Research Hospital to make an impact. We knew that going to Memphis was a last ditch effort for Shannon. She was losing function slowly over the course of November, but we couldn't have imagined the rapid decline that would take place over those seventeen days. Looking back, if we knew that Shannon would decline so rapidly, would we have made the decision to leave home and attempt to take part in the clinical trial? I can't say for sure. We will always feel a pang of sadness when we think of our time in Memphis, because it will be associated with the awful period in our journey when we watched Shannon's body betray her. She could no longer dress or feed herself. She became completely dependent on us. Those awful, tearful nights when she told us she didn't want to live that way. Would we have been better off at home, closer to our support network instead of in a rented townhome in Tennessee? Possibly. Hindsight is 20/20, for sure.

But somehow, I believe that we were supposed to go to Memphis. We were suppose to gain an understanding of St. Jude, of this place where science and medicine come together, and battling childhood disease is the priority. We were supposed to realize that some day, in a lab, they would hopefully make advances toward a cure for this terrible tumor. We were supposed to be given the opportunity for Shannon to donate to that very science. We were suppose to meet Dr. Wetmore, who spends countless hours each week trying to care for these patients and improve the science.

St. Jude is a place of both desperation and hope. You can see it on the faces of the families that are walking those halls, eating in the cafeteria, and staying in the lodging provided. Every family there has a story. Every parent there fears for their child's life. But there is help available, even for the worst cases, and that offers hope. And there are success stories to be found. For every kid who is there receiving his or her initial treatment, there is another who is back for a check-up and has survived for months or even years. We met people who started coming to St. Jude when they were infants and now were teenagers back for their yearly check-up. Oh, how I dreamed that we could be one of those families. A success story. But the painful reality was we realized that outcome wasn't in the cards for us. But for many others, St. Jude is the place that saved their child.

True to their word, we didn't pay a penny for the treatment we received at St. Jude, and that included countless physician's visits, two MRI's, a CT scan, and an experimental chemotherapy drug. All costs are covered for each and every child treated there. It is an amazing place, and even though it was too late for Shannon, we will always feel connected to St. Jude and their mission. There are thousands of St. Jude stories with happy endings.

WEDNESDAY, DECEMBER 14, 2011

We have been on a long journey since April with lots of highs and lows. Today is amongst the lows.

Shannon had an emergency MRI today to try to get to the bottom of the loss of function in her right side. We were hoping that we'd see a lot of swelling caused by bleeding in the brain from the Crenolanib doing a number on the tumor. While there is a small amount of bleeding from the tumor, what the MRI showed is that one cystic part of the tumor—kind of like a blister—is expanding. The position is just so that the spinal column is being pinched, and the flow of the spinal fluid is being stopped. Hence, the paralysis.

Dr. Wetmore introduced us to a neurosurgeon today who may perform a procedure to reduce the swelling in the brain by putting in a stent. We will try steroids for a couple more days before making that decision. While this procedure might relieve some of the pressure, it does not access the tumor or improve the right side function.

So, as prepared as we were for this trip to Memphis, we now are dealing with something unexpected. The truth is that this loss of function was coming slowly over our last few days in Rochester. We had seen it in Shannon's facial droop and coordination. It is just a coincidence that it reached this tipping point shortly after our arrival in Memphis. While it is very hard to be away from home at this time, taking Crenolanib gave us the best chance to fight this tumor. And to do that, we had to come to St. Jude.

Shannon told Dr. Wetmore that she wants to do whatever gives her the best chance: drugs, surgery, whatever. She's still trying to fight. She wants to stay on the study for herself and for the kids who come next. So she will keep taking the Crenolanib until we see more results after four weeks. There's still a hope that it will show it can stop tumor growth.

The support from Minnesota is so appreciated. Shannon wishes she could communicate more with her friends, but she just hasn't been capable of it. Texts and emails to each of us remind us of the support we have. The Rochester Athletic Club and the RAC tennis department are putting on a big fundraiser for Shannon this Friday morning. I wish we could be there.

We all cried today, but Shannon cried the least of all of us. She was busy figuring out how to manipulate a wheelchair with only one functioning hand. Thank goodness she's the toughest of us all.

We will try to sleep tonight, hoping for yet another unexpected turn to come our way. If we've learned anything on our cancer journey over these past nine months, it's that you can't predict what will happen next.

POSTED BY JEN

THURSDAY, DECEMBER 15, 2011

We are taking a day off from St. Jude today. Shannon is status quo, and there's nothing they would see today that they couldn't see tomorrow.

She'll keep taking her meds, and we'll keep hoping they work. She is more alert, and the eye patch she is wearing is at least allowing her to watch TV and look around without feeling dizzy.

Grandma and Papa Harkins are returning to Memphis today, cutting short their sightseeing in Nashville. We are planning for some sort of an outing this afternoon if Shannon feels up to it. She said, "Let's do something fun today." That's a good goal.

We are all processing and coping. Dealing with what we see now and what may be ahead. Trying to remain hopeful while being realistic.

POSTED BY JEN

THURSDAY, DECEMBER 15, 2011—NIGHT UPDATE

We had hoped a day off from St. Jude and some fresh air would brighten Shannon's spirit, but Shannon reached rock bottom today.

She is a prisoner in her own body right now, and she told us tonight, "I don't want to give up, but I don't want to live like this. I can't do anything for myself."

The only time she is comfortable right now is when she is sleeping. She is having trouble seeing, hearing, and swallowing.

We are hoping for grace and peace as we make tough decisions in the days ahead.

POSTED BY JEN

FRIDAY, DECEMBER 16, 2011

This is going to come as a shocker (not): Shannon wants to stay in Memphis and keep fighting.

Dr. Wetmore showed us the scans today. You can see why Shannon has been feeling so crummy. The tumor is growing and causing all sorts of challenges. But the kid won't quit.

She was given many options including returning to Rochester immediately.

We will update later with more time to process. Holy schnikes.

POSTED BY DAN

ANOTHER WEEKEND IN MEMPHIS

Our ability to predict what is going to happen on any given day is completely kaput.

Jen and I both woke up today taking glances around our apartment, each wondering to ourselves, "How long is it going to take to pack this place up?" We were pretty sure we were heading back to the 507.

Before we could leave, Shannon was due for labs required as part of the clinical trial we came down to St. Jude to take part in. But before Shannon got another poke, Dr. Wetmore wanted to see us. She came in and announced that it was "time for a new plan. First, let's go look at some pictures." So we were steered into a consult room ... Dr. Wetmore, nurse Vicki Fergus, and Team O'Hara. Pretty cute to see Erin pushing her sister's wheelchair into position in front of a bank of monitors and then holding Shannon's hand. Dr. Wetmore proceeded to pull up image after image of Shannon's brain from scans taken at Mayo in August and November, comparing them to the two scans taken at St. Jude December 7 and December 14.

What jumps out at you ... this ain't no cell death causing some swelling. The tumor is alive and growing, and growing fast. Even from December 7 to December 14 there appears to be significant change of at least 10 percent. So let's just get all our cards on the table before we make any decisions. The reason Shannon has lost her right side—her dominant arm, hand, leg, and foot—the reason her vision is blurry, the reason her ears are constantly ringing, and the reason she feels like shit is because the tumor is growing against key nerve regions in her pons.

So, Dr. Wetmore laid out our options: go home and say enough is enough; stay on the study at a lower dose of Crenolanib, which will keep her in the trial; or stay on the trial at the 220 mg adult-sized dosage that is definitely taxing Shannon's system to the max. Guess which one she picked?

Shannon kept asking, "What gives me the best chance?" Of course, the answer is the 220 mg blast of chemo for twenty-eight straight days. Daydreaming about the mapping of our route back to Rochester, I heard Shannon announce, "Let's stay."

Either way—we decided as a group—we would be home for Christmas. Either Shannon is going to stabilize as the drug gets fully into her system, or we are going to be miserable and pull the plug on the trial anyway and head home. We'll know by next Thursday.

At this point we really want Shannon's data to matter. If we can't complete the trial, her labs are thrown out. Shannon wants to matter. I sense that's a big part of how she's weighing her need to feel good and her want to be around friends and family. To keep going in the clinical trial gives her the best chance to accomplish all goals (and get home for Christmas). It gives her a fight.

By the end of the day we were back in our apartment. We had purchased Shannon a new iPad and she had a renewed determination in her eye. She had been ignoring texts and Facebook requests because she couldn't see them on her phone. She can see the iPad much better. She can see, and with her left hand she can execute replies to her friends. Her Facebook post tonight says it all: "Thanks everyone! I have a whole weekend to myself. No appointments. Yay!!! Can't wait to see Anna Olson on Monday!!"

Yes, one of her BFF's is coming to Memphis to see Shannon. Just what the doctor ordered.

POSTED BY DAN

SATURDAY, DECEMBER 17, 2011

How many times have we written here about adjusting to a new normal? We are attempting to do it again, but this one is really difficult. Our new normal is coming to acceptance that Shannon is disabled. This time the new normal involves navigating the world with a wheelchair in tow everywhere we go. We are learning to use an apparatus called a gait belt to help us move her without fear of dropping her. Another skill, as Shannon said, "they didn't teach you in mom school." We must find small moments of joy amongst the overall sadness.

Shannon talked with a friend of hers on the phone this morning. Listening to her explain what's been going on in her own words and with her impeded speech is so heartbreaking. Yet, her friend made her laugh and sent a text later saying how good it was to talk with Shannon.

I hope that Shannon's friends can remember the wonderful kid that is trapped inside her terrible body. I think they will.

Today it was sunny and fifty degrees, and we ventured out. Shannon's request: to go out to breakfast at the Waffle House. The large dose of steroids—up to 14 mg per day—means Shannon's appetite is healthy. Wanting food is one thing. Being able to feed herself and swallow is proving to be a more difficult task. She is learning to feed herself left handed, but it's made more difficult by the patch on her left eye. Try it, eating with your non-dominant hand with one eye closed. Oh yeah, and with numbness on one side of your mouth and with your brain forgetting to tell your mouth to chew and your throat to swallow. Despite that, she managed to polish off two eggs, toast, hash browns, and a waffle.

Shannon is coming to acceptance too. She lets us wipe her mouth if she can't feel the food on it. She lets us get her in and out of the wheelchair and the van. She lets us help her with her eye patch. She lets us read to her. You can imagine all the other things she needs help doing. She told me, "This is pretty awkward." No kidding.

Sunny the Wonder Dog continues to make us smile. Today we were soaking up some sun outside our apartment, and Erin was pushing the wheelchair a little too fast for Sunny's liking. Sunny tried to protect Shannon by pulling the blanket off her, and in the process almost pulling Shannon out of the chair! The girls made it into a game of taunting Sunny, and Sunny was happy to play her part.

The wheelchair we are using now is just a loaner from St. Jude. It's not fitted to Shannon, and she can't propel herself with only one working arm. We will get her fitted for that next week, and hopefully we will have it before too long. Right now, Erin likes to be in charge of pushing the wheelchair, but I think Shannon will be glad when she can propel herself. We have some thinking to do about how we will navigate things when we get home. A split-level house built in 1984 certainly isn't ideal.

Some of these worries—at least the financial part—were taken care of by the fundraiser the RAC did for Shannon yesterday. Such a wonderful effort by my employer and my fellow tennis pros. Dan and I were amazed at the faces we saw in the photos: friends, family, and even the girls' bus driver, showed their support and made donations to ease our burdens. Let's just say, Shannon can pick out the most mac daddy wheelchair she can find. Saying thanks doesn't seem adequate, but it will have to do ...

Hard to believe that we will be home in a week. Shannon's deterioration will be hard for all to see, but I know family, friends, classmates, and teammates are anxious for a chance to see us, to see Shannon.

The Rebels won again today. They improved their record to 12–1.

It's going to be a different kind of Christmas this year.

POSTED BY JEN

SUNDAY, DECEMBER 18, 2011

Trying to draw inspiration from my iPod to help me through a tough night. John Hiatt's "Have a Little Faith in Me" is helping ...

When the road gets dark
And you can no longer see
Just let my love throw a spark
And have a little faith in me

And when the tears you cry
Are all you can believe
Just give these lovin' arms a try
And have a little faith in me ...

I have been struggling all day, and I don't think it is because of another Vikings drubbing or the last gasp from Dublin Danny's fantasy football season that are bringing me down.

We had friends visit us in Memphis and we were given a preview of what reactions to us will be in the days ahead when more of our loved ones get to be with us, with Shannon possibly for a final time. The visit was wonderful and our relationship with this family predates kids or marriages. Old friends. What was painful was the goodbye, when it just kinda dawned on all of us ... you know. Saying goodbye to people is going to be messy. And now I am listening to Jason Mraz's "A Beautiful Mess."

Saturday was a pretty good day, but Sunday Shannon struggled. Her energy was low, and it was obvious she was struggling to track the action in a busy apartment with dogs, kids, a TV with football on, and lots of conversation and white noise. So she slept. Later in the day she watched *60 Minutes* with just Jen and me and said it was easier watching a show like that than watching football. I know that sucks for her—for us—because she loves watching sports and constantly commenting on everything (just like her mom).

When Shannon was a little girl we used to dance around our Rochester house on 21st Avenue, stereo cranked loud for Marvin Gaye and Tammi Terrell's classic duet, "What You Gave Me":

Like a breath of spring you came
And as you leave I can only sigh your name
Cries of anguish echo from way down
But never reach my lips to make a sound

Though it seems my world is crumblin'
Honey, you don't owe me anything
Cause what you gave me, girl
Is more than enough to last ...

Monday we're back at St. Jude to see Dr. Wetmore and our team at E clinic. Nothing major. Just a check of vitals and a pee test for the trial. I think there is stabilization. The higher dose of steroids is probably making a difference. But it's still a shocker to see the little battler so helpless. Maybe the chemo is zapping all her energy. Maybe it will get better ...

POSTED BY DAN

MONDAY, DECEMBER 19, 2011

Things are status quo for Shannon. No right side improvement, and the fatigue continues to beat her down. But no vomiting or nausea, and she is tolerating the Crenolanib. We had a short day at St. Jude: just a visit to E Clinic for Dr. Wetmore to eyeball Shannon. We are still on target to come home this weekend for Christmas, but our plans going forward are in flux. Dr. Wetmore has some trepidation about us being home for eleven days with the condition that Shannon is in, and rightfully so. It might be time for another new plan ... we will keep you posted.

The highlight today was the arrival of friends Anna, Hallie, and Tommy Olson in time to meet us at St. Jude. Anna is one of Shannon's BFF's, and Erin and Hallie are school and basketball buddies too. Lots of smiles from Erin as she and Hallie enjoyed some outdoor time, including a great hike with their dads and Sunny at a nearby park.

Anna was content to hang with Shannon, watching her sleep and upon waking, reading her all the cards and well wishes the Olsons had transported from friends back home. No appointments scheduled tomorrow, so we are hoping to do a little sightseeing with a trip to the National Civil Rights Museum. That's the plan. Here's hoping Shannon's energy level and comfort allow.

POSTED BY JEN

TUESDAY, DECEMBER 20, 2012

I should never write here about no vomiting, because as soon as I do ... shortly after my post last night, Shannon awoke and wasn't feeling well. You know what happened next, and the rest of the night and early this morning, Shannon was uncomfortable and struggling with it all.

But, our day got better as Shannon fired up to spend time with the Olsons. Another trip to the Waffle House, followed by some sightseeing in the minivan. While Shannon slept through some of it, we were all awake and eyes wide open when we reached the Lorraine Motel, the sight where Martin Luther King Jr. was assassinated.

We carried on our Memphis car tour with a drive by Graceland and then allowed ourselves some down time this afternoon. Upon waking from a nap, Shannon announced that she wanted to go to a movie with the other girls. So, off to *Alvin and the Chipmunks* for Erin, Hallie, Anna, and Shannon.

I have to admit, I was a little nervous leaving my child, in a wheelchair, in the care of someone else. Shannon was OK with it, though,

Sightseeing from a wheelchair | The Lorraine Motel, the site where Martin Luther King Jr. was assassinated.

Laughter and sadness | Out for ice cream in Memphis with Hallie, Erin, Anna, and Shannon

because Anna was by her side. So, let go, Mom, let go. We finished our night with pizza and ice cream, saying goodbye to the Olsons and thanking them for bringing a little bit of sunshine to these dark days.

Shannon is learning acceptance and so are we. Acceptance that her disease is progressing, acceptance that she is physically very limited, acceptance that she has limited energy. Acceptance that this great plan to be home for the entire holiday season needs to be adjusted. We will be returning to Memphis between Christmas and New Year's and staying until the four-week MRI scan takes place January 4 or 5.

Shannon found a little joy tonight listening to the other girls tell jokes and make fun of their dads. Straining to form the words with her slurred speech, she managed to join in on the fun. Cracking a joke that made us all laugh, and calling her dad a "dork." Just like the good ol' days.

Little moments of happiness amidst the sadness.

POSTED BY JEN

WEDNESDAY, DECEMBER 21, 2011

At this writing we are packing up and ready to pull up stakes in Germantown, Tennessee. Thursday morning Shannon is due for lab work for the trial. We will leave in the morning, packed for the road trip, and as soon as we are dismissed from St. Jude, we will cross the bridge into Arkansas and head north for Christmas.

Shannon was wiped out today. She never really left the sofa. Not until bath time and then it was right to bed. We are hopeful a patch stuck to Shannon's right arm Wednesday will keep nausea under control. The challenge of keeping an oral six-hour anti-nausea drug into a patient sleeping twenty hours a day made the patch a necessity.

Erin and I had another tearful pillow talk last night. She told me she is done with Memphis. When we come home she wants to stay home. She's sad. She wants her big sister back the way she was, but E knows that is unlikely and she's trying to sound out how our lives will look together in the future. When you get that one figured out, kid, let us know. She's processing. Way not fair.

Erin's decision means Team O'Hara will skate shorthanded for next week's return to Memphis for Shannon's labs and exam. So Shannon, Mom, and Dad will party like rock stars and celebrate New Year's in Memphis. (Yeah right ... midnight is a foreign concept!)

Jen and Shannon will stay in Memphis through the first week of January; a key MRI is set for January 4. I will make sales calls in Wisconsin that week, and Erin will return to school (speaking of foreign concepts). Sunny's Tennessee run is over.

OK, so now I'm selling hope ... it's possible the reason Shannon is wiped out is there is a fight going on, and ground zero is her brain stem. If the Crenolanib is starving cells—as it is designed to—a reaction could be extreme exhaustion. Either that or the Olsons just made us eat too much.

"Memphis Lives in Me," from *Memphis*, the Tony Award winning musical we took in together in New York City at the end of March, is a really meaningful song to this family. Two weeks later they found the tumor. Ironic that now here we are in Memphis fighting for Shannon's life.

POSTED BY DAN

THURSDAY, DECEMBER 22, 2011

Greetings from US Highway 218 just around Mt. Pleasant, Iowa. Don't worry, Jen is driving.

We are making our way. Shannon is resting comfortably. Erin is watching *Mr. Popper's Penguins* on Shannon's iPad.

We left St. Jude at around 11:30 A.M. Hope to be back on Willow Lane in Rochester around midnight.

Shannon's condition is not improving. Fatigue continues to keep the little battler pinned down. We had some frank discussions with Dr. Wetmore. When we said goodbye to our sweet team, Dr. Wetmore, nurse Vicki, and nurse practitioner Valerie, we were hugging goodbye maybe forever.

However, our appointments are still on the books next week and with any kind of rebound we will go back. Shannon wants to stay on the Crenolanib. The plan is to spend time with our families over the Christmas weekend and see how it goes. The name of the book might have to be *17 Days in Memphis*.

POSTED BY DAN

FRIDAY, DECEMBER 23, 2011

Team O'Hara is home where the heart is. Safe and sound. Took us twelve hours exactly with multiple stops for food, coffee, Red Bull, and puke. Might have to post two-a-days for a while. Our home looks like Christmas. Thanks to all who made that happen. Wow.

POSTED BY DAN

FRIDAY, DECEMBER 23, 2011—POST #2

As I sit here by the fire with a glass of wine, the house is quiet. Erin is with her friends. Dan is at the store. Shannon is sleeping. And I am attempting to put thoughts into words ...

The posts about our decisions the past thirty-six hours or so only tell part of the story. So many little pieces of information went into the decision to leave Memphis so we could be home for the holidays. With that, we took a leap of faith as Shannon's condition was deteriorating. But, having a ventriculostomy in Memphis on December 23 would have meant Memphis was home for the holidays. To reiterate, the surgery would have improved Shannon's alertness and relieved the pressure in the brain, but it would not have anything to do with quality of life or improved right side function. And the pressure would most likely eventually build up there again, and we'd be right back where we started.

We made our decision that being at home was most important to us, and Dr. Wetmore supported our choice. She was a rock for us on one of the most difficult days in this eight-month journey. So beyond competent and compassionate. Amazing. I will never forget that.

When Dan said that we had frank discussions with Dr. Wetmore, he wasn't kidding. Discussing the unimaginable. Dr. Wetmore taking the time to talk to Erin. The end could be near. As in, twelve hours in the car near? Yes. Thankfully, as you know, that did not happen.

So we woke up today to a house decorated for the holidays and stocked with food and cards and presents. And yet, there was business to attend to. A wheelchair to pick up. A handicap parking sticker. A conversation with Dr. Rao about more unimaginable stuff. Conversations with Mayo's home hospice. The business of preparing for death.

Amongst all that today, was beauty and grace in being with Shannon. We've invited some family and friends to stop by, different people throughout the day, to see with their own eyes, to talk to Shannon, to cry, to feed her, to hold her hand, to be present.

Shannon feels no pain right now. Her breathing is becoming shallow, but she is eating and sleeping and listening and sometimes saying a few words. She told coach Bart today, "Tell the Rebels good luck." She is aware, but not fully conscious all the time. It could be hours, days, even weeks. We hope to spend the holidays with those we love without attending to the business of dying …

We are so conscious of all who have shared this journey with us, and we want you all to be a part of this stage too. We will try to continue to share, to let you in, as that has been such an important thing for all of us, but especially for Dan and me.

But, our pain is ours to carry. Not yours. And it is Christmas time. A time to focus on those you love. Those dearest to you. That is our plan. Make it yours too.

POSTED BY JEN

The Dumpster

As we wrote our blog each day, we did our best to be honest and share our reality with others. But once in a while, there was an event we just couldn't write about at the time. Dan and I would joke about the untold, classified version we had in our heads. This is the best, most absurd untold story of them all. I can laugh about it now, but at the time, this was anything but funny.

The trip home from Memphis was going smoothly until we got to Cedar Rapids, Iowa. I had just given Shannon her dose of Crenolanib during the drive, and I was keeping the experimental drug in our cooler, as it was to be refrigerated. After giving her the dose, I tossed it into our snack bag and was going to return it to the cooler after a quick stop for fuel and a bathroom break. That's when all hell broke loose.

While pumping gas, I peered into the car to see Shannon was vomiting. All over her clothes and the seatbelt, and even into the snack bag. She was barely conscious enough to even realize it. Our car was packed to the hilt with everything we had brought for a month in Memphis, and I had to dig deep to find a change of clothes for Shannon. I found a pair of Erin's pants and a dirty t-shirt. That would have to do.

Dan jumped in to help. He tossed Shannon's stained clothes into the snack bag and said point blank to me, "I'm just going to chuck this whole thing, OK?" "Go for it," I said.

At this point on the ride home, I began communicating with Dr. Wetmore. We had left Memphis with guidance from her to keep driving and get home before seeking any more medical attention. We didn't want Shannon to be hospitalized in Cedar Rapids.

An email sent to Dr. Wetmore at 10:00 P.M. on a Thursday night was promptly returned. (Thank goodness for iPhones and cell coverage!) Emailing gave way to texting, and Cynthia (during this conversation I feel we reached the first name basis stage) talked me through Iowa, as I administered some steroids to try and relieve some of the brain swelling and alleviate the vomiting.

By the time we returned home, it was midnight. Twelve hours in the van to get from Memphis, Tennessee, to Rochester, Minnesota. We made it. Shannon was home. Alive. After getting the girls to bed, Dan was ready for sleep, but I couldn't quite rest. So, I began unpacking a bit.

Around 1:30 A.M., it dawned on me that I hadn't put the Crenolanib in the refrigerator. Shannon's plan was to keep taking the drug and stay on the clinical trial protocol. I went searching through our luggage looking for the vial. After searching for a half an hour, I realized the Crenolanib was in the snack bag, which was now in a garbage can in Cedar Rapids, Iowa, covered in vomit.

In a panic I woke Dan by crying out hysterically, "We threw the Crenolanib in the f*#@ing dumpster. It's in Iowa. F*#@!" We attempted to call and get the manager of the convenience store. The "manager" of the convenience store at 2:00 A.M. on December 23 is the seventeen-year-old working the overnight shift! I couldn't convince him that if he just dug under the vomit-filled clothes and into the vomit-filled bag of snacks, right next to the Pringles, he would find two vials of chemotherapy. He just told us the trash cans had already been emptied in to the big, giant dumpster, and he couldn't help us.

Dan was wide-awake, and he was ready to jump in the car, drive two hours, and go dumpster diving. Cooler heads prevailed, and we decided to wait until morning and then figure out our options. My last act before trying to sleep was to send one final text to Dr. Wetmore's phone.

"Call me first thing tomorrow. We accidentally threw the Crenolanib away in Iowa."

Oh, I had some explaining to do! Cynthia has a good sense of humor, so she laughed at the absurdity of the situation. But, she also went to work to try and right our wrong.

She spent Friday, December 23 haggling with the pharmacists to get a new supply of the experimental drug sent to us. See, the drug needs to be refrigerated. But, FedEx couldn't guarantee that a temperature-controlled package would arrive on December 24, so the pharmacist was reluctant. Dr. Wetmore is a persuasive woman, and she convinced the pharmacist that it's cold in Minnesota in December. Put the drugs in an envelope and overnight it.

On Christmas Eve, two things were delivered: A FedEx envelope with a vial of Crenolanib and a bouquet of flowers from Dr. Cynthia Wetmore, wishing us a peaceful Christmas.

CHRISTMAS EVE

It's the best night of the year for young children. And for parents of young children. As I watch Shannon lying here, I can't help but think of those early Christmases. Shannon was our first-born, the first grandchild, and first niece on my side of the family. On the other end of the spectrum (the O'Hara side), she is grandchild number eighteen. She truly has the best of both worlds: one side to spoil her rotten with attention, and the other side that fills a room with voices of love and laughter.

I think back to the craziness of trying to have the "perfect" gift for Shannon from Santa each year. One year it was the toy kitchen, complete with pots and pans and all the little toy food you could imagine. One year it was the toy vanity with makeup and a mirror that had a button you could push to make it light up, and this little voice would say phrases like, "You are pretty!" or "Oh, how beautiful you are!"

Toy kitchen, toy vanity ... and I thought of myself as a feminist! But, at the time, it seemed important to get her what she wanted. I was trying to be a good mom. The wow of Christmas morning ... it would make those big, beautiful brown eyes light up.

I also reflect on these memories because as she grew into a preteen and then a teenager, she wasn't bound by the traditional. She wasn't afraid to be herself. She doesn't wear makeup, has never asked to. (It's comforting to me that I didn't scar her with that toy vanity thing!) She's avoided middle school girl drama by just being a good person, being kind, by believing in herself, and not needing to prove herself to anyone. We heard such beautiful words today from a couple of Shannon's teachers about the kind of person she is and what she's meant to them. Those words brought us to tears.

I find myself sitting here thinking about Erin. An old soul. Thank goodness for that. She is watching her sister slip away and handling it with courage and grace. She will feel the love and the pain of this Christmas forever. She will be the one in our family to carry on our memories.

But, she's been preparing for that job since she was a toddler. Those early Christmases would play out like this: Shannon, a ball of energy, bouncing off the walls with excitement. And Erin, idolizing her sister, sitting back, observing, taking it all in. She gathered a lot of information by being quiet, being still, listening. She still does.

We spent today with a few close friends this morning and then my family this afternoon. For my brother Eric, his wife, Jen, and their kids, Laurynn and Jack, this was a tough day. Shannon is slipping further. Less time awake today. Less responsive today. Slipping ...

So now it's time to tuck in on another Christmas Eve. There is nothing I could put under the tree this year to make those big, brown eyes light up. So, give us another day. Give us Christmas Day with the O'Haras.

Sleep tight, everyone.

POSTED BY JEN

CHRISTMAS MORNING

Dan and I sat with Shannon at 3:00 A.M. and talked about some favorite memories. She would squeeze Dan's hand to acknowledge our words. It was a moment of beauty.

Shannon is sleeping again now, saving up energy for those O'Hara cousins, aunts, and uncles who will be arriving in a few hours.

Thinking back to better days | Christmas, 2004

There is no Christmas card or photo coming from us this year. Instead, here's one from the archives. Christmas 2004: Shannon, age 6 and Erin, age 3½. Merry Christmas, everyone.

POSTED BY JEN

CHRISTMAS, 2011

Shannon O'Hara spent Christmas Eve and Christmas Day smothered by love. Cousins, aunts, uncles, and both sets of grandparents took turns holding her hands, telling her stories, laughing, and crying ... together. All weekend our home was packed to the roof with love.

While Shannon never really opened her eyes, she responded with approving nods of her head and squeezes of her left hand. Fr. Mahon— our pastor from St. John the Evangelist—sat with Shannon and lead a family service that has to rank among the most spiritual moments of my life. Even Shannon gave it a good squeeze. Thirty-four of us crowded around Shannon in our family room and prayed for a peaceful transition to her next life. Another beautiful moment in our journey.

Now it is quiet in our house, and Erin is taking her turn crying on her sister's chest. Through sobs she told us, "I am not ready for her to go away." We are all taking turns today. Sometimes the tears help you power back up for more fight. It's a Christmas none of us will ever forget.

POSTED BY DAN

Christmas Day | Cousins gather to sit vigil with Shannon

MONDAY, DECEMBER 26, 2011

We are holding steady. Shannon is still requiring pretty close monitoring. A labor of love truly as friends and family take turns holding her hand, chatting with her. Her nods and headshakes acknowledge that she is tracking.

A meeting was called tonight to address our beloved Rebels—Shannon's hockey team. All players and all parents lined the benches in locker room #3 in Graham #2 tonight. Jen and I told the girls and their parents about Shannon's status and her future ... our future as a family. Our friend Kelli P—who has a day job as a Mayo Clinic social worker—volunteered to come along for the meeting. The message to the girls was this: What would Shannon do? She would want them to play hard, have fun, win games, and be kind to each other. Not necessarily in that order. Kelli told them it is OK to feel sad, sick, sleepless. Erin O'Hara even chimed in to tell the group that Shannon is not having much fun right now, and that the next stage will be a good one for her sister. Damn. We love those Rebels.

Tuesday we will meet with hospice people from Mayo Clinic.

POSTED BY DAN

TUESDAY, DECEMBER 27, 2011

Home hospice was set up today and practical matters needed to be discussed, details of which are not for blogging. We have a plan and will attempt to honor Shannon's wishes to the best of our abilities.

Shannon has had a mostly restful day, but she has tried to say a few more words. It is very difficult to understand her and you can feel her frustration as she curls the toes on her left foot when we can't decipher the syllables that come from her mouth. She can hear and understand everything we say, but it's a bit of a one-way street right now. She can't open her eyes very easily, so using a keyboard to type or pointing to things isn't an option. I can't imagine what is going on inside her head. Tonight Dan is reading stories to her to help occupy her mind ...

Today a few words came out more clearly than others: Jell-O, egg ... and she's taken in a few bites of each of those and let it slide down her throat. She's also sipping some water from a syringe to keep her mouth and throat wet. These may seem like boring details, but this is the reality that we are living right now. Tiny little moments of interaction amidst hours of holding her hand and watching her rest.

Lots of time on our hands. Time to think. We are here, being present, and waiting ... it is surreal ...

POSTED BY JEN

WEDNESDAY, DECEMBER 28, 2011

There have certainly been some changes in Shannon's breathing patterns, but she remains stable and—most importantly—resting peacefully. Our hospice nurse, Diane, came and spent time here today. O'Hara visits are on her schedule for Thursday and Friday as well. I almost wrote "God willing." But God's will is a real mystery to us right now.

Some of our dearest friends are trickling through and taking turns holding Shannon and sitting with her. She is less responsive, and the squeeze replies are less frequent. Our friends keep apologizing for their tears, and we keep telling them it is OK. Truly, there is something comforting about seeing people weep for you and your child. They care so deeply. Oddly, I draw strength from it. Every once in a while Jen, Erin, and I will join in. But you can't really be like that all day, so you take turns.

Erin took off to hang out with some basketball buds—holiday tournament time for the high schoolers—so the girls are hanging out at Mayo Auditorium. She needs this. She is well tended to. Erin may choose to sleep away from home. That's her call.

It's a bizzarro world we are living in today. All I know is that people seem better when they leave than when they get here. Shannon still has that way about her.

POSTED BY DAN

THURSDAY, DECEMBER 29, 2011

Today marks one week since we left Memphis. We were unsure whether Shannon would even make it home. But here we are seven days later, and she's still with us.

Last night she showed her first signs of distress and finally said yes to some pain medication. Eight months since diagnosis, and last night was the first time we used anything for pain. So a couple of small doses of morphine helped the lungs to relax and not work so hard to clear themselves. She slept soundly through the night last night in the leather recliner that kept her more upright and allowed her to breathe more easily. I suspect feeling relaxed is the best she can feel right now.

Yesterday brought a steady stream of visitors and a couple of them were really poignant, memory-filled visits. The most emotional point yesterday was a visit from our old neighbors, the Gushulaks. When we moved into this house on Shannon's second birthday, there were two little girls living just across the street. When Erin was born the following year, we had a foursome: Abby, a year older than Shannon, and Tessa, a year older than little E.

The pictures and stories we shared yesterday brought back so many of those early childhood memories. Your kids' first best friends. The ones who spent hours playing school, drawing on the driveways with chalk, and selling really lousy lemonade to the neighbors. These girls show up in a lot of our home videos. Nikki was the mom I could call and say, "Please take my kids for an hour because they are driving me crazy!" and she wouldn't question my skills as a mother. And vice versa. Our girls haven't spent as much time together since the Gushulaks moved from the neighborhood several years ago, but the memories came flooding back yesterday as Abby held Shannon's hand and cried.

Another day is upon us.

POSTED BY JEN

THURSDAY, DECEMBER 29, 2011—POST #2

Shannon has had a pretty good rebound day. Heaven can wait.

There were eyes-open responses and more attempts at commu-

Water girls | Erin and friend Lexie help out the Mayo High School boys basketball team

nicating words. Her sock was bugging her, and it took about five tries before we realized she was saying, "toe." Really frustrating for me and Jen, but I can't imagine the agony Shannon must feel trying to get enough air in her lungs to create a sound. Only to have us respond, "I didn't understand you, Sweetie." Shocking stuff if you had interacted with her within the last month or two. Tonight she was able to communicate that she was craving a Diet Coke. Morphine and Diet Coke. Did we mention that we are living in a bizzaro world?

The Wild game is on the TV, and Shannon seems to be looking in that direction. We have the sound up. The Wild are playing Edmonton at the X. Thirty-four days ago Shannon and I watched the Wild play Edmonton at the X—sweet seats too. That was the Friday after Thanksgiving. Might as well have been a million years ago.

I wanted to take a second to talk about Erin O, who had a great little getaway from our home hospice to hangout with her friend Lexie. Lexie's dad, Shaun, is the boys basketball coach at Mayo High School, so the girls were able to sit on the bench and tend to water duties as the Spartans scored a win over JM.

Ms. Erin continues to carry around an amazing amount of confidence and perspective considering that her heart is being ripped in two as her big sister keeps slipping away right in front of her eyes. But she loves friends and fun—as a ten-year-old should—and her time with the Langs lasted through two basketball games, a sleepover, and a baking session. Not once did she call to say she was sad or wanted to come home. From all indications, Erin is going to be OK.

POSTED BY DAN

FRIDAY, DECEMBER 30, 2011

We are having a really tough time keeping our chins up today. This journey has taken yet another unexpected turn, and our hearts are conflicted. One thing Shannon didn't want was to suffer or end up in a hospital bed. While we're still at home tonight, a hospital bed was delivered to our door today.

Shannon's rebound day from yesterday continued into the wee hours of the night. At 3:00 A.M. I was awakened by Shannon saying "What ... time ... is ... it?" I came to her side in the leather chair and explained that it was the middle of the night. She was wide-awake and wanted to drink water and ask about the whereabouts of Erin and Dan. The mind was hard at work.

So when our hospice nurse, Diane, arrived today, she was startled at the uptick in Shannon. While that would seem like a good thing, there are complications; if death was no longer imminent, some needs had to be addressed. We decided it was time for a hospital bed for Shannon's comfort and to ease the difficult transfers we have been making. Dan's rotator cuff has taken a beating as he's been using a fireman's carry to move her from a bed to the couch to the chair.

Why the changes? Dan and I had a long conversation with Dr. Wetmore (on her day off!) this morning and explained the changes we've seen. As we talked about what we were seeing, she was rattling off the different cranial nerves that are affected, and trying to get a mental picture of Shannon and what might be going on with the tumor. Dr.

Wetmore had told us before we left Memphis that there was always a chance that the cystic area of the tumor could decrease due to pressure on it. Without a CT or an MRI, we can't be completely sure, but it appears that is what most likely has happened. Fluid in Shannon's brain is flowing more freely than it was. An uptick in alertness like this would have been the result of the surgery we declined to have one week ago.

So, where does that leave us tonight? The pressure in her head has reduced, and it is less likely that will be the cause of her life ending. She is more alert, but the right side function is non-existent and she can't hold her own head up. We have possibly entered a longer stretch of comfort care, and we now have to think about how to keep her hydrated and fed when swallowing is still very difficult.

We are exhausted from the steady stream of visitors, but being alone with our thoughts is no picnic either. We must find some more strength to carry on and keep honoring Shannon's wishes as best we can. Today was a hard day.

Shannon is alive, but this is not living.

POSTED BY JEN

SATURDAY, DECEMBER 31, 2011—REALLY EARLY

Shannon seems to be settling into a pattern of finding peak alertness at 3:00 A.M. So here I am taking a shift. She's back asleep, and I am stuck here with my thoughts. She just clearly told me, "Food ... shake ... shake."

So, I'm up making a milk shake at 3:30 in the morning. I sprinkled a little hot cocoa packet with some peppermint flavoring in with some ice cream and skim milk, and the kid just killed it. Before dozing back to sleep she mustered up a slurred "thank you." How great is that?

I'm going to make some observations about human nature. I do not want people to overreact. I'm reminded of the big voice out of the sky from *Field of Dreams*, "If you blog it, they will come." So I have to be a little careful of what I write so as not to offend. But maybe it will offer some insight into our view of the world from our Willow Lane hospice.

People like to bring stuff. They don't know what else to do to help ease your burden, so they drop off nuts, pasta, desserts, breads, chickens, chocolate bars, peanut brittle, fudge, sodas. Nobody brings beer anymore. I guess that's OK.

People need to tell you, "We are thinking of you and your family constantly." I guess that's a good thing too. There's really no downside to telling us that. We really can't believe people are thinking about us as much as they are, but they are. Heck, I'm not thinking about us that much.

People are compelled to fill "dead air." Talking is sometimes a release for nervous energy. I spent thirteen years in broadcasting, and in that business, "dead air" is the enemy. But in our world, sometimes some quiet reflection is OK. We don't always need to be talking. Sometimes just sharing the same air, the same space, enjoying a moment in time is good enough.

People are really sad for us. There is so much compassion for our situation out there that it blows you away. People are kind.

I truly believe I am the lucky one, because I get to be with Shannon, Erin, and Jen each and every day. Our families and friends seem to feel better when they get to be around the girls and their energy. They generally give off a pretty peaceful vibe. Shannon is stirring again … "More water …"

POSTED BY DAN

NEW YEAR'S EVE

Shannon is resting a little more peacefully after a rough start this morning. Her breathing became shallow and raspy sounding, possibly due to increased cranial pressure again. She has been asking for water all day as she tries to clear her chest. It has taken a while for the morphine and Ativan to help calm her down and allow her lungs to relax. We're hoping for a more restful night, no 3:00 A.M. milkshake! But we'll take it as it comes …

It's New Year's Eve, a night where we always reflect on the past year and think about the one ahead. I could never have anticipated what would happen to us in 2011.

Last year at this time, we were busy with all the normal life things: school, jobs, hockey, and basketball. Life was sailing along, and we were busy planning our big family spring break trip to New York City and Washington D.C.

Our trip was one of those where you do all the legwork to prepare for how to spend your time and what sights to see, and then, magically, things go just as you had hoped they would. We have a couple hundred photos from the trip, pictures of our "perfect" little family with the girls at just the right ages to enjoy it. Shannon and Erin smiling in Times Square, goofing in Central Park, taking in the history at the U.S. Capitol, and the obligatory pose outside the White House. Not a clue that two weeks later, Shannon would be diagnosed.

So now I sit here and reflect on that time B.D.—before diagnosis—and the ensuing eight months that bring us to today. Those carefree spring break days are a moment in time, but the lessons we've learned since April 15 changed us, changed me, in ways I couldn't imagine.

We learned new medical terminology, and we learned our way around the campus of the Mayo Clinic. We learned about perseverance and a positive attitude from our own child. We learned that people are kind and generous beyond belief. We learned that people like our kids and they like us. We learned to take each day as it comes. We learned to enjoy the good days. We learned to battle through the bad days and stay together no matter where life takes us—even to Tennessee.

I learned some things about myself too. I learned that writing is cathartic for me. I learned that I could make good friends. I learned that I could be strong. I learned that having things planned and staying on schedule isn't as important as I thought. I learned that I love being a mother.

The year 2012 is almost here. Happy New Year.

POSTED BY JEN

SUNDAY, JANUARY 1, 2012

Norah Jones is providing accompaniment on a somber New Year's Day. The Shannon O'Hara Victory Tour is drawing to a close. Most everyone that needed to hold her, hold us, has been through. We're not feeling too social anymore.

Shannon still reflexively asks for "water," but there's no way she knows what she wants. She was able to get out the word "bored" early Sunday morning. Now with midday approaching she is back to sleep. Thank God. Her ability to swallow is more limited than ever. She managed to communicate to my sister Molly that the feeling of hunger never goes away. Hungry and bored. Can that suck anymore?

We need to find a way to capture the ground swell of Shannon support and keep it going and channeled into something sustainable. Something productive for all of us to feel like we fought a good fight and will carry on fighting. I suppose this is what all families that lose a loved one to cancer go through. So I guess that is my New Year's resolution.

Earlier this week, Thursday I believe, Shannon was asking what day it a was and asked about "football?" Today, the NFL regular season draws to a close, and I'm not sure our little angel knows the difference.

Norah Jones is crooning "What Am I to You?"

When you are feeling low
To whom else do you go?
See I cry if you hurt
I'd give you my last shirt
Because I love you so ...

Not much more to say folks. Prayers for strength and mercy.

POSTED BY DAN

MONDAY, JANUARY 2, 2012

Shannon is holding true to form. Up at 5:00 A.M. ready to drink water and converse as best she can. She is still tracking and comprehending what we say, and in these early morning hours, she tries to get her bearings on what will happen in the day ahead.

Yesterday's weather here was ominous and befitting our mood— low, grey clouds, and cold whipping winds made you want to curl up in the fetal position. Dan and I, feeling emotionally tapped out, were having trouble managing our anger and sadness yesterday. By last night, we had to just ask our families to give us some space and let the four of us be alone in our own home. Family, of course, obliged. They would do anything, I mean anything, we asked. And that's part of the problem. There is nothing to be done. Watch and wait and hope for resolution. Sometimes having more people to help you do that isn't a comfort. But, sometimes it is. Sometimes you just need to be alone with your thoughts. And sometimes you need support. It is a roller coaster ride that is keeping everyone around us on their toes.

While these days are lingering now, I'm trying to have faith that in the future, this will be just one tiny piece of our journey. It is all consuming at the moment, but it will pass. We need to stay strong and believe that we can get through this stage, just like we have so many others.

Today brings us to the end of winter break. Tomorrow, normal daily life should begin again. Dan has some work to do. Erin has to go to school. It's time to carry on as best we can, all while still keeping Shannon as safe and warm and as comfortable as she can be. I'm not sure how Dan or Erin will concentrate on the tasks at hand, but they have to try.

I'm hoping for a better day today. I'm pretending I don't hear that cold wind outside the window.

POSTED BY JEN

TUESDAY, JANUARY 3, 2012—MIDNIGHT

My body is not interested in sleep at this time. No doubt, there are some whacked out physiological characteristics taking hold of all of us. My sweet Jennifer appears to be getting some good rest—she was asleep quickly after going up around 9:00. I am sitting here watching Shannon sleep peacefully. I know I should be taking advantage of this time and resting, but it just ain't happenin' for me.

We have all sorts of literature around us about the dying experience. Good resources. But I just can't pull the trigger and read. Instead I want to look at pictures.

There are games on. I should be scouting Andrew Luck. But I just don't care. I heard the Badgers lost. And the Timberwolves got another

How quickly things changed | Shannon taking her first turn mowing the lawn, just six months prior to decline

win. But I just can't care. Michelle Bachmann's campaign is on life support in Iowa. But I just don't care. OK, that was a joke.

Erin was able to get out of the house for a two-hour basketball practice Monday. She came home in good spirits, exhilarated from the combo of exercise and love from her teammates on the Mayo Spartans sixth grade team. She has tournament games each of the next three Saturdays. So, January will be a busy month for her. Tuesday morning E will get on the school bus and return to Willow Creek Middle School for the first time in over a month. I think she is excited and a little anxious about how far behind she will be. But, she's a bright child and will catch up quickly. She also has a staff at Willow that will be watching her closely.

As for Jen and me, Tuesday we will attend to the business of planning a funeral service. Maybe that's why I can't sleep.

Saturday, Shannon was sleeping, and we were surfing around

and stumbled across the NHL's Winter Classic old-timer's game on TV. Within two minutes of our recognizing what we were watching, our buddy Shjon Podein scored a goal for the Flyers' alumni squad. Tonight, as I was sitting here blogging, I got a text from Shjon with the

The smile | Shannon with Junior and former NHL goalie Carl Wetzel at the Minnesota Wild game

attached photo of Shannon with Podes' son Junior (along with former North Stars goalie Carl Wetzel).

I'm going to miss that smile. A lot of people will.

I keep catching good songs while I blog ... I swear I don't plan this out ... this morning I leave you with Crosby, Stills, Nash & Young and Neil Young's haunting voice singing "Feel Your Love":

I really want the night to end
I really want the sun to rise
I really want to feel
Want to feel your love
I want to feel your love

POSTED BY DAN

TUESDAY, JANUARY 3, 2012

The days are dragging on. And while the end is near, near is a relative term ...

Shannon continues to slip away from us, but it is slow and very difficult to watch. We have now added a pain medication patch to ensure that she has an even dosing of pain meds throughout the day to try and keep her comfortable. She was much less responsive today, eyes slightly open, mouth agape. I'm not sure how much she comprehends at this point. Sorry to be so graphic, but we've been honest here before, so why stop now ...

Dan and I talked today about how hard this is. That may seem silly to say. Of course it's hard to watch your child die. But I mean, the actual "doing," doing the things that need doing so that the end goes as smoothly as possible. Providing hospice, making funeral arrangements, etc.

Dan and I laughed today too. Laughed at the territory that we have covered in our nineteen years together, seventeen of them married. Man, nothing prepares you for this, but we are doing all right. One of the tasks we did today was to go through old pictures for use in a memorial service. There are some wonderful memories tied to those pictures of our kids at their various stages.

We sometimes think that Shannon's illness turned her into the person we all have admired through these last eight months since her diagnosis. But, truth is, she was that person a long time ago. We got a nice note today from Jamie Berry, who both of our girls had for a first grade teacher. Mrs. Berry wrote us these words today about Shannon:

"She walked into my classroom and lit up the room with her positive energy and fantastic sense of humor. Your precious baby had such an aura even as a first grader. She is truly a gift...."

That's what I want to remember. Not the image I see before me lying in a hospital bed, but the girl that Mrs. Berry described, the girl I saw in those photographs today. Like the day she came home from that first grade classroom, smiling from ear to ear, carrying a tiny plastic treasure box because she had lost a tooth at school. I'm going to try and remember that day ahead of this one ...

POSTED BY JEN

Toothless | So proud to come home from first grade having lost her first tooth!

ETO – Born Wise

Erin has such a different disposition from her sister, even at a young age. She is an observer of the world around her, and more cautious before jumping in. She is always assessing the situation and reading the mood. Erin has had a sense of the people around her and their needs since she was very young. I remember when her preschool teacher even commented on her compassion.

To go along with the emotional compassion, Erin is whip smart. She was reading before kindergarten, and by the first grade, she needed a challenge. Luckily, Erin had our favorite first grade teacher, Mrs. Berry, and she was in tune with Erin's needs and pushed her to work above grade level. Mrs. Berry also opened our eyes to the possibility of grade acceleration. Erin went through a series of IQ and aptitude tests, and it was determined that she could benefit from skipping second grade and moving right on to the third grade in order to keep her engaged and challenged.

This was not an easy decision, and we were worried about how Shannon would react. Erin was especially worried about her big sister's reaction. But Shannon was on board and told Erin that she was cool with it. Erin's next concern was the fact that she'd be younger and smaller than her new classmates. Shannon again had her sister's back and reassured her, "Erin, you're an O'Hara. You're always going to be little!" So, off to third grade she went.

Thank goodness for Erin's maturity. She was as equipped as any ten-year-old could be to watch her sister fight for her life. Throughout the journey, Erin attended doctor's appointments and discussed medications and procedures. She talked with doctors, nurses, and hospice personnel as if she were Shannon's guardian. And she was. Erin would be there at the end, holding her big sister's hand.

THURSDAY, JANUARY 5, 2012

First off, big props to Ms. Erin for suiting up and showing up. She rallied today to climb out of bed in the dark and dress for school. Ate some breakfast. Took the bus at 6:47. I know kids do this everyday. But this kid is facing some extraordinary circumstances and still finding a way to face the world. On her basketball team her nickname is "Smiley." Love that kid.

Jen and I were able to get more sleep last night, just because Shannon has slept. Pretty non-responsive again this morning. Please God, let today be her day to come to heaven.

People are doing a pretty good job of giving us space. The text messages and emails slowed, but that's also because people are back at work and school. I have no problem with those types of communications. I like them, and they give me strength.

I have forced myself to read up on the dying experience. Shannon is following the script. Eyes now glassy, teary, and slightly opened, even at rest. Breathing is shallow and intermittent. But here we are standing (or sitting) vigil for another day. Knowing Shannon, she is probably still negotiating the terms of her next life.

I made contact with three dear friends Wednesday. All three reached out understanding where we are in this process. All three lived our hell. In different ways, each watched loved ones die. They just wanted us to know that they were feeling our pain. Misery loves company, I guess. Again, strength comes from many sources, and right now we are trying to find another vein.

POSTED BY DAN

THURSDAY, JANUARY 5, 2011—LATER

Today has been a better day than yesterday; not without its moments, but better. People and their words of kindness and support have buoyed us. Reminders of what a great kid Shannon is help us to carry on. We received an email from a mother of one of Shannon's class-mates this morning. We don't know her, and she didn't really know Shannon, except through her son's words. And he spoke highly of our girl. This mother's note brought us to tears, but then it lifted us up by reminding us of Shannon's spirit.

So, we trudge on in this state of limbo. Shannon's vital signs have shown an ever so slight decline from one day to the next, and the kid hasn't eaten in eleven days, but her heart and lungs keep working. She continues to fight, even though we've said it's OK to give in. We should have known she wouldn't give in easily. This has been her pattern her whole life, why would she change now?

This is the kid who, as a two-year-old, bloodied her lip by banging herself against her crib rail until someone would come and pick her up. She wasn't going to bed until she was ready.

This is the kid who wouldn't give up her pacifier until we bribed her with a boom box for her room. I'm pretty sure if you're old enough to operate a boom box, you shouldn't still have a pacifier!

I think Shannon got the stubborn gene from both sides of her fam-ily tree. But, sometimes stubbornness is an asset.

This is the kid who, when given a terminal diagnosis, wouldn't take any shortcuts. She did every school assignment, attended every sports practice, and carried on with all her responsibilities, even when every-one around her was telling her it was OK to take a pass.

Which brings us to today. With barely enough strength to muster a cough, and taking in one small swab full of water at a time, Shannon worked and worked and worked to try and clear the secretions from her lungs. After all the effort she could muster and ninety long minutes of wheezing, mission accomplished. Shannon can't really communi-cate with us anymore, but she's still showing determination.

If only a strong will was enough. If only prayers and well wishes added up to extra good days on this earth. If only ... but it isn't so ...

Instead, another night of watching and waiting is ahead, keeping vigil at the bedside of Shannon the Cannon ...

POSTED BY JEN

FRIDAY, JANUARY 6, 2012

Shannon O'Hara lost her nine-month battle with brain cancer today.

We announce this with tremendous sadness and relief as our little angel was suffering terribly over the last thirty days.

She died with Jen, Erin, and me holding her. Sunny the Wonder Dog was at our feet.

Grieve without shame.

POSTED BY DAN

MORE THOUGHTS

January 6, 2012. Etched in our family's memory forever. Is it possible to be preparing and wishing for something, and still be surprised and shocked when it happens? That's how I feel about the events of today. We wanted mercy for our dear Shannon, but still, it was a quick end to a short life.

Dan drove Erin to basketball practice last night, and they took in a beautiful sunset on their way. This morning, I drove Erin to school and we saw the brightest pink sky as the sun rose. Omens, perhaps.

We cannot begin to delve into the emotions we are feeling tonight— relief, sadness, anger, grief, fatigue. They are all wound together, and we are not yet ready to peel away the layers. We will continue to write in the coming days and sort through our thoughts in due time.

POSTED BY JEN

SATURDAY, JANUARY 7, 2012

This first day of the rest of our lives has been peaceful. There's a calmness. Relief really. Just not as intense with Shannon gone from the hospital bed that occupied our family room. The hospital bed is gone too.

Our families and friends have given us space to regroup and recharge for the busy days ahead.

Jen's BFF, Teri, arrived from Michigan, and we are watching the Lions and Saints wildcard game. Erin is hunkered down in her room with BFF, Emily, over for a sleepover. Erin is always happy with Emily around. There is peace.

Since Shannon's death, O'Haras have been congregating in subsets to share stories, tears, and just be together. This will have to do until we all come together Sunday, Monday, and Tuesday. But no one has felt like being alone.

Shannon's passing was well documented in our local paper, the *Rochester Post-Bulletin*. I have to tell you, it is completely surreal to read your child's obituary in print. I'm not sure how to process that. I have only been able to look at it once.

We did manage to accomplish a few things Saturday. Jen and Erin snuck around Apache Mall to finalize dress-up clothes shopping. I snuck around Hy-Vee to get us some groceries. None of us looked to make too many contacts with outside world types. However, we did drop in on a Rebels team pasta feed. Had a couple drinks, shared some yucks ... continuing the healing process for all.

Our friend Mike Dougherty, a PB columnist and editor, contacted us earlier this week to see if we would mind him mentioning this blog in his "Saturday Digital Mike" column. Jen and I spent a fair amount of energy early in Shannon's journey keeping our blog off Facebook. But when she got really sick—around the time we were heading for St. Jude—the blog went viral as friends and friends of friends posted and re-posted our blog link, and there was no stopping the runaway train that is social media. So the *Post-Bulletin* pub is not really going to make a difference.

I think we are still writing for us. And for our families. And for our friends who want to know how we are managing on a day-to-day basis. The truth is, we are day-to-day.

POSTED BY DAN

SUNDAY, JANUARY 8, 2012—MORNING

Did anyone notice the atmospheric tussle that took place over the final days of Shannon's life on this earth?

As the cancer in her brain took control, the winds howled. Blew down the "We heart Shannon" Christmas sign on our deck three times. We pieced it back together with some nails and used heavy objects to keep it in place only to wake up to find it blown down again.

Thursday night, in Shannon O'Hara's final hours on this earth, the sunset created a most spectacular canopy of color to the west. And Friday morning's sunrise was breathtaking.

And since Shannon left this life on Friday morning there has been calm. The forecast through Tuesday looks fabulous. The wee hours of this morning are so bright. I just did a quick Google search to check moon phases. The first article I find explains, "As the full moon approaches, the brightness of the moon tends to grab our attention." The moon will be full Monday, January 9.

And on the seventh day, actually Sunday is January 8, it is going to be sunny and forty with light south winds. We have no snow on the ground. In Minnesota. In January.

I don't know, maybe I'm overthinking it.

And just now, the *Minneapolis StarTribune* is being delivered to our mailbox. Today's edition of the Sunday Strib includes Shannon's obit.

POSTED BY DAN

SUNDAY, JANUARY 8, 2012

There were a few tears shed today, but it was a mostly good day. I think we need to get used to that—mostly good. We had our moments, though, especially this morning over coffee.

Dan awoke thinking about Shannon's best buddies. They were headed to Faribault to play basketball, and Dan wanted to check in and see how they were doing. Hearing their voices—and their pain—brought tears to our eyes. They have all suffered a great loss in their lives too. Dan did his best to encourage and console them.

I awoke thinking about milestones, those markers in time that our children reach, and the sobering reality that Shannon's journey is over. I was thinking about those same best buddies—and all of Shannon's classmates—and what it will feel like when they reach one of these milestones: next fall when they enter high school, or when they turn sixteen and I see them driving around town, or when they graduate. Watching the class of 2016 graduate will be tough. Shannon will be thirteen forever.

After our somber morning, things improved. Walks in the unseasonably warm January weather with Sunny helped us to clear our minds and invigorate our bodies. A steady stream of family began arriving, and those who live far away were glad to see us and hug us.

The final preparations we did today for the upcoming services have us feeling like we are as ready as we can be for what's ahead. Another day behind us. We are holding up and holding on ...

POSTED BY JEN

MONDAY, JANUARY 9, 2012

First off, happy birthday to Papa Harkins today. Sorry, Dad.

Kids at Mayo High School and Willow Creek Middle School dressed in green in Shannon's honor today. A lotta love coming our way.

Dan, Erin, and I are ready to head to the funeral home. Ready to mourn the loss of Shannon and celebrate her life and spirit.

POSTED BY JEN

Green out | Mayo High School students pay their respects by wearing Shannon's favorite color

TUESDAY, JANUARY 10, 2012 — EARLY

I am awake waiting for the sun. It's supposed to be a record high temp here in Minnesota today—possibly fifty degrees. One more day for family and friends to mourn, honor, and celebrate at Shannon's funeral.

Last night's visitation was an amazing event. The line of people who came to pay their respects weaved all the way out the door of the funeral home. The displays our friends designed with all of Shannon's pictures and memorabilia brought people to tears as they waited in line. Dan and I found strength we didn't know we had. Must have been from Shannon. In an odd way, it was invigorating to see these people— people from our past and present—and to hear the impact that Shannon's fight has had on them. I had been dreading standing there for hours greeting and consoling people, but as each person came, we drew comfort and strength from their words about our kid.

The hardest part for me was seeing the body. It didn't really look like Shannon. It was her, with those long eyelashes and beautiful hands and fingernails, but death takes it's toll on a person's appearance! I don't mean to be glib, but I want to remember Shannon not the way she looked last night, but the way she was: big, brown eyes aglow and smiling from ear to ear.

The other most difficult thing was seeing Shannon's peers absolutely breaking down. Girls and boys sobbing at the loss of their friend. There were all kinds of kids there—the popular kids, the quiet kids, the jocks, the loners—each one trying to make sense of it all through their pain. Another testament to Shannon and the way she treated people. She didn't discriminate.

The family's final goodbye and the closing of the casket were emotional. It was all too much for Erin who sobbed the whole way home asking, "Why?" She is sad and mad and scared. She's endured more than a ten-year-old should have to endure over these past nine months. We got home and stood in our kitchen together, the three of us hugging, and Erin said, "This sucks." I teased her saying, "You're not allowed to say that word." And she responded, "I am today!" No kidding. I hope she can find strength for one more day on this journey.

The funeral is today at 4:30 at St. John's. One more celebration, and then the hard part begins ...

POSTED BY JEN

FAMILY WALK

Sixty or so family members took a walk around the reservoir today. Thinking about Shannon all the way around. It's fifty-four degrees. On January 10. Shannon must be shining down on us already. We are off to St. John's ...

POSTED BY JEN

The Reservoir Walk | Family and friends hike together before the funeral

WEDNESDAY, JANUARY 11, 2012

The events of the last few days since Shannon left our world can only be explained as an out-of-body experience. Heck, how about the last nine months? A blink of an eye. From diagnosis to death. Went way too fast.

Participation in the ritual of ceremony—as anyone that has survived a wedding ceremony can attest—brings with it intense scrutiny. The eyes of your world are on you, and you either embrace it or it makes you sick to your stomach. Fortunately, Jen and I were able to embrace it.

When we met with Fr. Mahon at the end of November, he gave us some insight into how a funeral can go down. We knew it was in our future. Without telling each other, Jen and I had each visualized the ceremony in our head dozens of times since April. Fr. Mahon said that you will draw strength from the mourners around you. He said you might even enjoy it—if that's possible. He was right. Tim Macken from the funeral home told us the same thing. You just find strength to carry you through.

As we entered St. John the Evangelist Church for the funeral ceremony of Shannon Anne O'Hara at 4:30 P.M. on January 10, 2012, the eyes of our world were on us. We could feel them. But we could feel the love too. Jen and I both felt pretty darn good. Really strong. Erin maybe didn't embrace the attention quite as comfortably as we did. But she did well. She is a beauty. A child of God.

But—damn—there were a lot of eyes. I have never seen our church so full. Shannon would have been so embarrassed. She never liked much attention. Especially as she embodied a fight that turned her into a disciple of God. Shannon and Erin never asked us to "blog about it."

But the blog allowed us to share our journey with family and close friends without needing to be on the phone every night talking to people. The blog allowed us to summarize the events of the day at a time when the girls were asleep or busy at school. It allowed us to turn insomnia into a productive session on our counselor's couch. But Shannon and Erin never signed up for the blog. Never knew what it would become. Neither did we. No idea that it would turn into 30,000 page views … in a day. You kiddin' me?

So that's probably why there were so many sets of eyes on us. As we joked with family, you don't get to pair down an invitation list to a funeral. If they were touched by the life, they are free to come celebrate the end of it.

Back to the out-of-body experience. Marching in with family. Looking over at the choir. Making eye contact with so many friends ... important people in our lives ... looking you right in the eye. Then you get used to it and just begin to absorb the ritual. My brother Mike's eulogy captured Shannon's spirit so perfectly. I'm proud to be Mike's brother.

Our St. John's community has played such a tremendous role in our journey. I will never forget the Sunday two days after diagnosis when Erin and Shannon sobbed in each other's arms (and all our friends in our section did the same), or Easter Sunday when we were asked to bring up the gifts, or Sunday, December 4, when our parish community raised hands over our family as Shannon was given the Catholic Sacrament of Anointing of the Sick (formerly known as Last Rites ... I think I like Anointing of the Sick better).

St. John's is home. We don't always agree with the politics of Catholicism. But weighed against the sense of community we feel at our home parish, it's not even close. To Jen and me, those people are our family. We watch over each other. We watch our kids grow up together.

So to say they rose to the occasion is an understatement of epic proportions. St. John's rocks. Our friend, Fr. Jerry Mahon, made Shannon's service so personal, involving hundreds of kids in the ceremony. Holy buckets there were a lot of kids. At least a couple hundred. Maybe three hundred invited up on the altar. Hockey players, golfers, basketball players, friends, just normal tweens and teens, boys and girls of all sizes and shapes that have been touched by Shannon's journey. Fr. Mahon brought them up and talked to them about how God could take Shannon this way. Unthinkable, really, that a kind God could do it. But it happened. And now it is up to each of them to figure out a meaning.

The music made me cry. Music Director Sebastian Modarelli, and the choir, and our friend and cantor Nora O'Sullivan, and the piano, and organ, and the instruments ... they brought their "A" game. Nailed it.

I still need some time to process the events of these last few days. But just like after a great wedding party, family comes together and feels together. They share. They want to keep going over events and do some talking. Nobody wants to board jets and head back to lives. But today is that day. So lots of goodbyes coming this morning. Power up for one more session. I don't think Erin is going to make it to school again today.

But there's time to catch up. For the first time ever last night, I referred to my kids as "our girl." Singular.

POSTED BY DAN

THURSDAY, JANUARY 12, 2012

We are dipping our toes back into reality. We started last night with basketball practice for Erin, or "Smiley" as her teammates call her. She was quiet on the way there, but once she was surrounded by her friends, she relaxed and maybe realized that they are carrying on and she can too. Yet another new normal. This one the hardest of them all.

Today marks the first day back to school. While Erin is apprehensive about the attention and the "pity" as she described it, we must take these baby steps back into life. Dan is planning to travel for work next week. As for me, well, I haven't figured out what's next. I guess for now, I'm here encouraging and supporting Erin and Dan as they forge ahead. Is that enough?

We are still working through opening all the cards and gifts we received. Absolutely amazing. The funeral home directors said they've never seen anything like it. All these cards and the handwritten messages inside—especially the ones from friends and classmates of Shannon's—are bringing us to tears. All part of the process, I suppose.

Dan and I have been discussing this blog and what to do with it. We still feel we have things to say as we sort through the end of Shannon's life and the beginning of life without her, but it feels a bit narcissistic to continue writing now that she's gone. We are torn because this blog has been such a big part of our journey and such a big coping mechanism for us. It feels too soon to stop. We won't blog forever, but we are not quite finished ...

POSTED BY JEN

FRIDAY, JANUARY 13, 2012

It's Friday the thirteenth and we have a long way to go. A week ago, at this very moment, Shannon was struggling through her final painful moments on this earth. Probably TMI. But, impossible to ignore.

Erin shows flashes of her old form. At basketball practice last night she was good ol' Smiley. When we got home the three of us snacked on a frozen pizza and watched the Gophers hold on for a win at Indiana. It was OK. Felt right. (BTW, I caught myself caring about a sporting event … baby steps. Sports indifference has been the rule around here for a while. And we are pretty huge sports geeks.) Then around 9:30 we tucked Erin in and she fell asleep without much of a fight. Until about midnight.

Just around midnight Erin came up to our room crying. At our bedside, she told us Sunny the Wonder Dog woke her with a bark and then led her into Shannon's room. Sunny was acting funny. So Erin was kind of freakin' about that. When I came down, Sunny led me to the door and then went outside and pooped. So you tell me … either the spirits were moving throughout our home … or Sunny really had to go.

Since she was a pup, Sunny has slept at the foot of our bed on her dog bed. So while laying and talking with Erin it dawned on me that maybe it was time for a change. I brought Sunny's bed down to Erin's room, plunked it in the corner, and within a few minutes Sunny was curled up on it. When Erin awoke in the morning, Sunny was on her bed with her. There is no doubt this dog knows something is different. She carefully reads and studies our emotions and moods and reacts accordingly. So we will see how it goes tonight. But I think Erin having her dog sleep by her would be a tremendous comfort. We'll see if Sunny remembers.

In the middle of the night, Erin sobbed through some painful admissions about her relationship with God at this time. When I asked if she wanted to say a little prayer she told me, "I prayed and then the tumor came back and then Shannon died!" She was pissed off. And I had no wisdom to offer … didn't even try.

Try listening to The Proclaimers, "If There's a God."

If there's a God
Why does He let
People die slowly
Wracked by pain?

And if there's a God
Who blesses with children
Why does He steal
Some back again?

I don't know
Can you tell me? Oh
Can you tell me? Oh

Saturday morning we are off for a Mayo sixth grade basketball day in Albert Lea. E's Spartans will play four games, and then we are booked at the Country Inn and Suites in Albert Lea with some of the families on the team. Erin and her buds will run around the hotel while parents visit and hang together. Might be just what this family needs to keep us busy, distracted, and laughing. Erin always had to come on Rebel road trips. But this one will be all about her. I'm excited ... a little anxious too.

Erin allowed us to drop her at school again this morning. She has been taking the bus home with her pals. Today at 1:00 she will participate in a sixth grade band concert at Willow Creek Middle School. I'm pretty certain Erin has had the fewest rehearsal sessions of anyone in the band. But I'm also pretty certain her French horn will not be the only instrument slightly off through "Twinkle, Twinkle" and "Camptown Races."

POSTED BY DAN

SATURDAY, JANUARY 14, 2012

We are off for Albert Lea where the Spartan sixth graders will play four games today. Wish us luck.

POSTED BY DAN

SUNDAY, JANUARY 15, 2012

Erin and the sixth grade Spartans basketball team had a good day yesterday. Playing four games and then hanging out with her teammates was just what the doctor ordered to put a smile on Smiley's face.

Dan and I enjoyed seeing that: seeing her active, seeing her focused on something other than what's happened in her life the last week. Hell, how about the last nine months? Dan and I are trying to focus on the present and the future, but sometimes we are more successful at that than others.

Friday, I had a terrible day. Maybe it was the one-week marker since Shannon's passing. Maybe it was Friday the thirteenth. Maybe it was that everywhere I looked in our house, there were pictures of Shannon (and Erin). I've had many people tell me, "You'll always have those happy memories," but right now when I look at images of those happy times, I just feel sad. We weren't done making those memories. I wasn't done being her mother. I think on Friday, I finally let down. All the momentum and activity surrounding the end of Shannon's life and the celebrations that took place are over now, and it's time to go on. This is the hard part ...

So Saturday we headed to Albert Lea and gave Erin all of our attention. People are rooting hard for us, and the families of Erin's teammates all acknowledged our loss and were glad to have us back. A couple of Shannon's good friends were along, rooting on their little sisters. Just as Shannon would have been. I like these kids and I like to be with them, but it was hard. The anticipation of their futures—conversations about going to high school next year—made me feel envious. That's not how I want to feel. Will it get better with time? I believe it will. Will that heartache ever completely go away? I doubt it.

It's another day and another chance to take a tiny step forward. Trying hard to stay in the present and cope today, and yet peek into the future and make plans in hopes of even better days ahead. We are off to St. John's this morning for mass and then to the KTTC Eagles Cancer Telethon to make a donation in Shannon's memory.

POSTED BY JEN

SUNDAY, JANUARY 15, 2012—EVENING

I guess as a family we are in recovery. The hard work is underway. I was just reading about Minnesota Wild Coach Mike Yeo who has a phrase he comes back to often: "Whatever it takes, right?"

In terms of the hard work we are doing to keep plugging along, it's almost as though we are starting over. We need to go face everyone and every situation as a threesome. We need to find our stride as a family of three. Just like a dog with one of its limbs amputated, we are a little out of balance. But eventually we will pick up speed and become deft again. Whatever it takes, right?

We returned to St. John's for mass Sunday morning—back for the first time since Shannon's funeral. (Putting those two words together still seems surreal.) Our mood was somber. It seemed as though the whole mass was a little dour. At least with the people sitting around us there was not much kidding around. Normally, there is a fair amount of friendly banter, joking around, and smiles. And maybe our perception is completely skewed. I just know Jen and Erin both agreed mass was a pain cave.

At the end of mass Fr. Mahon mentioned the funeral service and thanked the many volunteers that stepped up to help park cars, bake cookies, clean up, etc. I just wanted to jump out of my pew and scream, "YES, THANK YOU!" because the parish outpouring was nothing short of incredible. We are extremely grateful. Fr. Mahon also acknowledged that he has received much feedback on what an incredible spiritual experience the funeral was for families of all denominations. He did a great job.

Showing up for 9:30 mass this morning was a painful but necessary step in the process. Suit up and show up. After mass we hung out to chat with some friends. It was nice, pleasant. One friend—who is wise and knows all too well about the grieving process—offered us some sound advice. For one, take it one day at a time. But also she recommended at the end of each day try to think back on something good that happened that day. So Jane, here's what I'm hanging my hat on for this Sunday. On January 15, the Green Bay Packers lost.

Bruce Springsteen is singing in my headphones. *"Hey pretty darling don't wait up for me, it's going to be a long walk home..."*

POSTED BY DAN

The Letters

We knew that Shannon's life had impacted us, our families, and our close friends. But the events of the visitation and funeral opened our eyes a bit. There were so many kids in attendance who were affected by her, who called her a friend. She had reached so many people just by being herself. She had avoided the middle school drama by being kind to everyone, no matter their "status."

During the visitation, there was a boy waiting in line to pay his respects. He was holding a white teddy bear. I didn't know the boy, but you could see and hear from his speech that he was developmentally disabled. When he reached me and Dan, he shook our hands and introduced himself. He told us, "I was in Shannon's physical education class, and she was always nice to me. People aren't always nice to me, but Shannon was my friend." When he reached her casket he placed the teddy bear inside, and then stood and cried. Etched in my memory forever.

Notes of condolence came from people we knew, and some we had never met. Cards, letters, and emails. Expressing their love for our daughter and for the way she lived. Sharing with us how Shannon had touched their lives. Kids and adults alike expressing what their experiences with Shannon meant to them. We received a three-ring binder with letters from over two hundred of Shannon's eighth grade classmates, including this one:

Dear Jen, Dan, and Erin,
    Shannon was my good friend. I met her on our sixth grade soccer team, I had transfered to that team, and Shannon was the only one who talked to me. I never told her how much that meant to me, I wish I would have. The best way I can describe her is, she was like a sun. This may sound cheesey but it's the truth, her smile was always real and completely genuine and she laughed easily and with fervor. She could light up a room. In seventh grade we had social studies together, our class was quiet-ish and she and I were the only ones who really ever asked questions. She had a passion for learning, one that I greatly admired. She was responsible when it came to her school work, and creative with everything she did. During class we talked a lot about soccer, sometimes she'd ask me about tennis. She was always so excited about sports, and even if we knew we were going to lose a game, she would never give up. Last year I went to Kate Glynn's birthday party, there was only three people there including myself. Shannon was coming later because she had a doctor's appointment. We waited and talked a little until she came in. She told us about the tumor, we all started crying, and afterwords she asked us to not tell anyone, she didn't want anyone to treat her differently. People found out anyway, but I admire her so much for keeping ruitine and living her life to the fullest. That was the kind of person she was, selfless, compassionate, and so kind. She was the strongest person I knew, and probably she will be the bravest person I'll ever know.
    I am so sorry for your loss,
                Caroline Groves

The letters | One of many letters we received from Shannon's classmates that touched us and lifted us up

And this from her English teacher:

I was amazed at Shannon's daily determination to persevere and be "normal" ... She is just one of those people you meet who makes you better—a better teacher, a better parent, and a better person.... She has taught me the importance of not complaining about trivial things, about not taking moments with my children for granted, and about how important it is to get up every day and live a good life.

245

Please know that your daughter has changed my life and the lives of so many others. And, I guess, that's what we all want—to make a positive difference with our lives, to enter the world and leave it knowing that we did our part to make it a better place for God's people.

Peace to you, Chris Harmon

And the letters Shannon's Rebel teammates wrote us, sharing their thoughts and feelings about her, were so touching that they brought us to tears.

When I think or see the number 9, I think of Shannon. When I see lime green I think of Shannon. Also when I hear the song "Don't Stop Believein'" I think of Shannon and how she never stopped believing. Shannon taught me how not to be just a teammate but a friend. She taught me the value of friends and friendship and how important they both are. When I look at the goalie stick in my room I remember how nice to people she always ways (except for when your on the other team.) When I looked at her black jersey hanging on the bench I remembered how hard she worked for things not just in hockey. Mostly when I think of Shannon I think of her kindness and her passion for hockey. But to me Shannon is more than that, more than words alone can say. Lastly I want to say what an amazing opportunity it was to have Shannon on my team, she is an amazing friend, teacher, and leader. Shannon has inspired me to never give up no matter what!

Shannon the Cannon

Fight Like a Girl!

From,
Clare Brunn

A letter from a hockey teammate

We shared our journey, but we received so much in return. Not many people get to find out what their child meant to the world. We know that Shannon made a difference in this world, and that is a gift.

TUESDAY, JANUARY 17, 2012

Since Shannon's death, winter has certainly reared its ugly head. Seems fitting, though. I ventured back out into the world today to run a few errands, and I came in contact with a couple of people who wanted to acknowledge our loss. We are "that family" and people have a certain sad look on their faces when they see me. It's hard to bear the weight of it all.

Then there's the flip side—the cheery bank teller who is just trying to make polite conversation and asks, "Has your new year gotten off to a good start?" Wow. I could have ruined her day, but I just bit my tongue and politely smiled. How do I go out in the world and pretend that life is normal? It's hard when people acknowledge Shannon's passing, and it's hard when they don't ...

Today is one week since Shannon's funeral, and I don't want to get any further away from it without officially saying thank you. The outpouring was amazing and we received well over a thousand cards and many donations. The sincerity in each of your messages was greatly appreciated. Please know that Dan and I sat and read every single one. We were brought to tears many times. Due to the sheer volume, we are not going to attempt to acknowledge each of them personally, so please accept this electronic thank you from us.

I had a friend tell me that grief is hard work. I never imagined. I am attempting to keep the mind occupied while allowing time and space for the heart to heal.

"It is the nature of grace always to fill the spaces that have been empty."
—Goethe

POSTED BY JEN

THURSDAY, JANUARY 19, 2012

We are doing the tough, but necessary tasks. For Dan, that means being in Utah all week and training with the newly formed company. The days are busy for him, but the nights in a hotel are lonely. Not easy, but necessary.

For Erin, that means getting up each day and going to school. Trying to focus and concentrate and find some contentment in being around friends and teachers who care for her. Not easy, but necessary.

For me, this means dealing with Shannon's belongings. Tasks like shutting down her Facebook, and disconnecting her email and cell phone. Erasing the little traces of her. Is it too soon? Is it the right time? It felt right to me. It felt like progress. There is no handbook for how to do any of this. Yesterday, I tackled the big one: Shannon's room. Not easy, but necessary.

All those team pictures and trophies and jerseys, her favorite t-shirts, her favorite hat. They are all stored neatly away in a couple of plastic bins for safekeeping. Two of Shannon's prized possessions were passed on to her friends: one pal has a new loft bed and another pal has a new iPhone. Passing those things on felt good. Shannon would be happy for them.

So, physically, we are doing what needs doing. Coping and taking baby steps forward. The mental part of grieving, that's the more difficult part. Erin and I met with our social worker yesterday. Erin is so sad and lonely, and the rhythm of our household has changed. We need to find ways to fill the void that's in our lives now. We need to be willing to change our patterns and try new things. What will bring our downsized Team O'Hara some joy?

The trick is staying busy, but also allowing ourselves time and space for grief. It's OK for us to be sad and to have bad days and to let the grieving continue. You can't just "get over" a loss like this. People keep reminding us to be kind to ourselves. Not easy, but necessary …

POSTED BY JEN

SMILEY

Today's after school trick for putting a smile on Erin's face: warm, chocolate chip cookies and pre-algebra homework ... well, at least one of those two things made her smile!

POSTED BY JEN

THURSDAY, JANUARY 19, 2012—LATE

I'm blogging tonight from 31,000 feet somewhere over Nebraska. Purchased the Wi-Fi on tonight's flight back to the tundra. US Airways Airbus 321—a pretty nice aircraft and for $9.95 you can surf the web and blog. Not exactly the Mile High Club, but kind of cool.

I have been away from Erin and Jen since Monday, and it has been a challenge. Staying busy while learning about the new EFS offering was just fine. Exciting, in fact. I'm pretty fortunate to have landed on the "A Team" of our new company. We merged with a competitor, and together we are formidable. We are going to be a huge factor in the fuel card market. I feel as though my experience and this opportunity have come together at a really interesting time in my life.

While working and learning was invigorating, the after-hours social times were really work. I mean everyone is nice, and they are just living their lives talking about their kids and school and milestones and such things that normal people talk about. And then people let their hair down a little and have some fun and yucks like normal people do, and I just can't get away fast enough. I used to be the guy that closed down the party.

I don't want to be Danny Downer. And professionally, there's no doubt when you miss out on those after-hours events, you stunt the growth of relationships.

I guess I just need to be patient. This is going to be a slow recovery. The good news is I have a great job. Our company is going to kick ass, and I'm good at what I do. Baby steps. But I need to start selling stuff. My sales body clock is itching to do some deals.

I can't wait to see my girls. We have a busy weekend together. Busy is good.

POSTED BY DAN

SATURDAY, JANUARY 21, 2012

I've developed a serious case of bleacher butt over the past twenty-four hours. We attended the Mayo varsity games last night, and Erin and her friend worked as the water girls for the boys game and honorary ball girls during the girls game.

Big 9 Champs | Erin and her sixth grade team take home the title

Then today, it was four games to finish up the Big 9 season for Erin's team. The sixth grade Spartans avenged their two losses by beating Mankato West in the semifinals and then taking out top seed Owatonna in an exciting championship game. Lil' E played some minutes in every game and left the court smiling. We'll take that. Anything that brings moments of happiness and occupies our minds—even just for a little while—is welcomed.

POSTED BY JEN

SUNDAY, JANUARY 22, 2012

A sleep-in Sunday morning at Casa O'Hara. It seems as though we have been on the go from the moment the alarm sounds. Erin might sleep 'til 10:00. She's earned it.

Jen and I are in separate parts of the house because of a media blackout—she has Roger Federer's Aussie Open third round match on DVR. She just told me Fed is rolling. So I suspect she will be up shortly.

Quiet reflection is feeling good so far. My music shuffle has been finding some mellow tunes. Hall and Oates "Abandoned Luncheonette" is currently playing. *"Day-to-day, today, today ..."*

For the past two weekends we have been in gyms—not rinks—following Erin's basketball team. And while it has represented a major shift, it has been fun. Like Shannon, Erin loves being on a team. Loves the social. And like Shannon, Erin is a natural leader. Being a sixth grader is the easiest part of her new gig.

Saturday the Spartans really showed some guts winning a semifinal and then in the Big 9 Championship they gutted out a win against a team they were dominated by last weekend. That's fun. Good teams find ways to win even when they are over matched. We have a few weekends of tourney play left in the season. It will be over in the blink of an eye.

Our Rebels squad continues to struggle to win games, but I suspect they have developed a bond that will live within them for a long time. They are playing in a tournament in St. Paul this weekend. We've been getting texts with game updates. I told Coach Bart this week that I will not be returning to the Rebels bench—I need to give Erin everything I have at this time in her life. A sad realization, but I think the right thing to do. Jen and I will attend as many Rebels games as we can here down the stretch. Love those girls.

Erin has some homework to attend to today. The second quarter ends this week at Willow Creek Middle School. Have a good thought for E as I know she is anxious about how this will end—we were gone for a good portion of the quarter.

I'm going to ease into some sales travel this week. But I'm just not quite ready for another four-day week on the road. Baby steps. That will come. This business of healing, coping, grieving is a process, and we are just getting started. I feel pretty good today so far.

"Day-to-day, to-day, to-day ..."

POSTED BY DAN

MONDAY, JANUARY 23, 2012

I am up early and we just received notification that school is on a two-hour delayed start due to the freezing drizzle we had overnight. Erin will be happy about that, and a little extra sleep won't hurt.

I worry that there is less good to share in this blog nowadays. We attempt to be honest here, and right now that means admitting that, at least part of each day, we feel kinda shitty. Little things set us off. Emotion comes out when we least expect it. It's like we are on a roller coaster in the dark so we can't anticipate when the next up or down is coming.

Sunday was a mostly good day: sleeping in, being productive around the house, and doing some shopping. Then it was off to our friend's house to watch the first football game of the afternoon. It was fun and social and felt good in the moment. I feel for our friends, for our family, for anyone who tries to interact with us right now. It is hard to know what to do or say. Words are completely inadequate, but silence hurts as well. How much do you talk about Shannon? About the events of the past few weeks? Is it insensitive to bring it up? Is it insensitive not to? People want to ask the question, "How are you?" and I don't have an answer. Even we don't know what we want or need, so how is anybody on the outside supposed to figure out what to do or say?

So, we got home from watching the game, and we all sort of let down. On some level, feeling pleasure—like laughing with friends—made me feel guilty, I think. Shannon would have loved being in that room, watching the game, and talking smack. How could we go on and do it without her? Happiness may now always come with a sense of longing for what we have lost, for the one who is not there.

But, on the bright side, we did it: we got out there, we interacted, and there was some pleasure in that. It's a start. Things are never going to be the same. We are never going to return to the path we were on. That path doesn't exist anymore. We have been re-routed and we are trying to find our way ...

POSTED BY JEN

WEDNESDAY, JANUARY 25, 2012

"Mourning is the constant reawakening that things are now different."
—Stephanie Ericsson

Things are different. We are here in the same space, the same town, the same house, taking the same routes, but things are different, we are different. We can keep the mind busy with activities, and we do manage to laugh a bit each and every day. But, we also feel the deep, deep ache of loss that will take a long time to dull. Working through the loss of a child is a long process—not measured in days or weeks or even months.

Erin is doing some hard work on her thoughts and emotions and journaling a bit herself to help her sound out what she's feeling. She misses her best friend and their usual day-to-day interactions. There's no one to watch the latest Disney episode with. But, she's coping and going to school each day, and her friends are stepping up and making plans to help keep things moving. Thank goodness she's got such good friends from good families who would do anything for our little E.

Dan is doing some local travel this week, but has been able to stay home each night, which is nice after a long week out last week. Next week it will be back out on the road. He is able to concentrate long enough to do some work each day and prepare for the travels ahead. That's pretty impressive as I'm not sure I could do the same.

We've been occupying some of our time with making decisions on a family room remodel. We have had this in the plans and always knew that after a home hospice scenario, we would be ready to make some changes in that room. The way that room sits now, I can still picture the hospital bed … so, now is the time. New carpet, new sofa, new paint and a fireplace update are on the wish list. It's fun to have a project on the docket, and it's giving my idle mind a little content …

Speaking of home hospice, we received cards from our hospice nurse, Diane. One to Dan and me, and more importantly, one to Erin. Diane thanked Erin for snuggling with her during Shannon's final hours. Diane told Erin, "I really needed that." So kind.

Praise and kindness are pretty key for the three of us right now, especially toward each other. It's easy to pick out the things that we aren't doing well or to notice the struggles, but it's more important to look for the little triumphs. We tend toward sarcasm around here (no

kidding!), but a little sincerity goes a long way right now. We are making a concerted effort to recognize the little bits of good in each day.
POSTED BY JEN

THURSDAY, JANUARY 26, 2012
There is a pairing of bald eagles that live in the neighborhood. There is much green space in close proximity, lots of trees to perch but most important the Willow Creek Reservoir just to the west, fed by streams and creeks. Our street—Willow Lane—is a flyway for the beautiful birds to get to the reservoir from their nest just about a half-mile east of our home.

It seems as though the eagles show up in some of my most spiritual moments. Tuesday I was hiking around the reservoir with Coach Bart, and the male was perched in a tree just off the path we were walking, no more than twenty feet up in the tree. As we approached, I was sure he was going to flee. But he never did. He just looked at us as we walked by. We stopped in our tracks and just looked up, and I said, "How ya doin', Shannon?"

To me, the eagles represent Shannon's spirit set free and watching over us.

This morning Erin pulled the covers over her head when I came down the second time to get her out of bed. When she came up for breakfast she was quiet and told us she was sad. We tried to rally her with mini-waffles and some light conversation about the school day ahead and our plans for the next day or two. But she was struggling.

So we drove Erin to school—all three of us together—and as we took a left out of Willow Lane, the eagle soared right over us ... low to the ground ... Shannon was there as we embarked on another day.
POSTED BY DAN

SATURDAY, JANUARY 28, 2012—EARLY
Three weeks. Has it been a lifetime or a blink of an eye since Shannon passed? It depends on the day, the hour, the minute. We can talk about

her and reminisce oftentimes without tears, but some things set me off.

Yesterday, I returned to Graham Arena for the first time since Shannon's last skate on December 4. Graham Arena might have been Shannon's favorite place on earth.

The U14 Rochester tournament is taking place this weekend, and several of Shannon's classmates are on that team. These girls wanted to honor Shannon and help us start to raise funds for a scholarship bearing Shannon's name, which we hope to be able to award in future years. So, we wanted to show our support. Seeing all these girls walking around with green stickers with Shannon's name and number was heart warming and gut wrenching at the same time. There are t-shirts being sold that say "I skate for Shannon," and a big poster displayed with Shannon's story and picture on it. Seeing that was just a little too much for me, and I had a public teary moment. Not a complete meltdown, but the tears came.

The tears flowed for the kindness of these girls and their families. But, as I watched those girls skate and compete, my tears also flowed for Shannon. She loved these tournaments where you spend all weekend at the rink with your friends and you play some hockey too. That was her happy place. My tears flowed for Dan and me too. We really enjoyed watching our kid play hockey and being a part of the hockey community. We've admitted this week that losing hockey as a part of our lives is really tough for the two of us. That was one of our happy places too.

Next weekend it's the Rebels turn with the Rochester U12 tournament taking place. The fundraising efforts will continue, and we will be there at the rink supporting those girls as best we can. I better be prepared for a few more public tears.

But, while we spend some time thinking back, we are also trying to put some energy into moving forward. Erin spent yesterday with two different groups of friends, staying busy and having fun. Today, we are off to Faribault for some more basketball. More activity, more motion.

We applied for a passport for Erin yesterday. No definite plans, but we want to have options to do something different and make new

memories with our little E. Forging ahead while still mourning, honoring, and reminiscing. Two steps forward, one step back ...
POSTED BY JEN

SUNDAY, JANUARY 29, 2012

Another weekend filled with activity and emotion. A little bit of each of those things is good. Too much of either of them leaves you feeling exhausted ...

It's hard to describe the emotional part of the weekend—sadness, anger, and helplessness hits each of us at different times and in different ways. We do our best to carry on with the tasks at hand, but idle time, reflective time, can start the waterworks. Dan, Erin, and I each took our turn. It's a balancing act to stay busy enough to keep the mind occupied, but not so busy that you wear yourself out. Like everything else in our world, this is a work in progress.

As for the activities, we kept things moving with a basketball tournament, some time with family, and emptying out our family room in preparation for the remodel. Erin and the Spartan sixth graders enjoyed another tournament championship in Faribault on Saturday. Fun to see Erin working hard on the court and smiling on the bench. Coach Olson even ran a sweet set play for her, allowing Erin to score on a great backdoor layup. That one was for you, little E.

We had dinner with Dan's brother Tim and his wife, Suzie, on Friday, and lunch today with my brother, Eric, and his family. We're trying our best to keep in contact and share a little bit of ourselves with family when we feel up to it. There are no words to ease the pain that we all feel, but just eyeballing each other sometimes helps.

Today was a busy day of preparations. Moving eleven years worth of stuff off the family room shelves and removing all the furniture so the remodel project can start bright and early tomorrow. We're excited to get it going.

Finally tonight, Dan and I tackled another "first" in our journey. We went to see the Rebels play. Shannon's #9 jersey was hanging behind the bench. Those parents and girls were happy to see us. The Rebels pulled out a 3–1 victory tonight for their third win in a row. They've survived a rocky stretch, and maybe they will find their mojo just in time for an end of the year run. A bond has been formed amongst those families after what they've been through together. Just another little gift that Shannon left behind. She'd be proud of them.

POSTED BY JEN

TUESDAY, JANUARY 31, 2012

I am up in the middle of the night in room 100 at the Courtyard by Marriott in Bloomington, Illinois. I tossed and turned for a while but gave up and now will write a little and then get some work done. Maybe even jump on the treadmill for a few miles. Haven't been doing that enough.

I was asleep for about five hours before a really vivid Shannon dream woke me. She was getting dropped off in the driveway after a practice of some kind. I couldn't wait to tell her about one of her friends who had survived local qualifying for the US Open. But then I woke up ...

Sunday I read through some of letters presented to us in a three-ring binder by the eighth graders at Willow Creek Middle School. The "I heart Shannon" logo on the cover has been staring at me for days. So I started paging through them. It didn't take long before I was covered in tears. I went to Erin for comfort when I got to full sob. She held my hand.

I have been absorbing bits and pieces of the many books and grieving resources we have been sent. I don't know, maybe I have been floating down the river denial—I am trying to face this thing as often as I can. But those letters just got me. Over and over the same theme ... "that smile," "what a fighter," "she always made me laugh," "she was so smart."

I'm reading that grief can overtake you at anytime and without warning. For the first time Sunday I experienced that—the physical ache. So, I got that going for me ... which is nice.

Steely Dan playing on the iPod now ... "Only a Fool Would Say That."

Team O'Hara is transitioning into a new day. Our downstairs remodel is underway. The wood pellet fireplace is gone. The brown paneling is next.

I have a couple meetings today in the Land of Lincoln, but will return to sleep in my own bed tonight. Expecting a high temp around fifty-six. Carole King's classic "Home Again" is up now.

> *Sometimes I wonder if I am ever going to make it home again*
> *It's so far and out of sight*
> *I really need someone to talk to, and nobody else*
> *Knows how to comfort me tonight*

I know, I need to update my playlist ... but the Steely Dan, Elton John, Hall and Oates, Bob Seger, and Springsteen vinyl I wore out as a kid are like comfort food to me right now.

Time for some exercise. I have about 120 days to train for the Med City Half.

POSTED BY DAN

WEDNESDAY, FEBRUARY 1, 2012

The family room remodel carries on. Things must be torn down to be built back up again: the fireplace has been demolished, paneling covered up, walls skimmed, and carpet torn out. Chaos often precedes progress ...

A metaphor for our lives? Possibly. The three of us are doing some serious deconstructing—we are in a period of chaos. We are doing the tough work of sharing our emotions and thoughts and fears with each other in the hopes that we can make progress—progress toward fulfillment, contentment, and hopefully some happiness.

Erin has been emotional this past week, but that's not necessarily a bad thing. She is willing to share her feelings with Dan and me, although sometimes we are not quite ready to receive the full brunt of them! Some days we barely have the mental capacity to deal with our own emotions. But, on the bright side, Erin's not bottling things up or shutting us out. She's telling us when she's mad or sad or lonely. She's dealing as best as any ten-year-old can. It's almost too much to bear, but there is no other option. So, she carries on.

She admitted to us that going to school is really difficult. Passing by Shannon's locker or seeing Shannon's group of friends—those things are really hard for E. But again, what are the options? She has to go to school. So, we make her get up each day and try to keep moving forward.

The chaos in our hearts and minds means we are grieving, but the fact that we manage each day to go out into the world and do the best we can means we are coping. There is no right way. Even baby steps can add up, and eventually you get where you want to go.

We've been reading a daily meditation as a family each morning over breakfast. Today's passage comes from a Chinese proverb: *"The man who removed mountains began by carrying away small stones."*
POSTED BY JEN

SATURDAY, FEBRUARY 4, 2012
Another Friday has come and gone, and I wonder how long I will do "the count" on Friday mornings: it has now been four weeks since Shannon's passing ...

Erin made it through a full week of school. I wasn't sure that would happen with the way things were going this week, so it's a hell of an accomplishment on her part. We spent Friday afternoon doing some shopping as Erin has been growing like a weed and growing out of her clothes. Then Dan and I took her to see some furniture we like for the family room, and it got Erin's stamp of approval as well. After that, we let Erin pick a dinner destination and the three of us celebrated making it through another week.

This week was a pretty emotional one as we try to find balance between solitude and being social. We need some of each, and what we want depends on the day or the hour or the minute. We have heard from all our close family and friends that they would do anything for us, if they just knew what to do. You cannot take our grief away, but you shouldn't pretend it isn't there. It will lessen in time, but it is a process we must go through and there is no timetable. The future is unknow-able, as we have learned.

We had some good chats at dinner about what's ahead this week-end. Today we will go and watch the Rebels play in their home tour-nament. Before the game this afternoon, there will be a dedication ceremony as all the Rochester Youth Hockey girls tournaments have now been named "The Shannon Cup." This weekend, not only do the 12B's play, but the 12A team and two 10B teams are playing their home tournaments and competing for the Cup. We are off and running with a fundraising effort so that starting next year, we can give scholarships to graduating seniors in Shannon's memory. We want to be able to pay it forward and honor Shannon's spirit in this way.

I awoke this morning thinking that Shannon would have been so pumped for this weekend. Damn. Little bits of heartache each day as we carry on ... Hopefully balanced out by little bits of joy as we move forward.

Go Rebels!

POSTED BY JEN

SUNDAY, FEBRUARY 5, 2012

Blogging about events that make the hairs on your arms stand up is impossible and unjust. It's just too hard to capture the energy.

So many times along our journey a day has come together in a way that the only possible explanation is that a higher power is in charge.

Diagnosis day, our first Sunday at St. John's with cancer, the day our families came together at the Med City 5K, the stormy night in South Haven, Michigan, water skiing at Lake Hubert, Christmas weekend with family, the final sunset and sunrise of Shannon's life on earth, the funeral walk around the reservoir, and the service St. John's.

But of all those events, Shannon's favorite "hair-raiser" was the weekend it all came together for the Rebels at a hockey tournament in Hopkins, Minnesota. That weekend the Rebels won a tournament with Shannon's team winning two overtime thrillers including a classic in the championship against the host team Hopkins.

Saturday's events at Graham Arena in Rochester would have to be added to that list.

Before the Rebels played Centennial, Shannon was honored with a ceremony that will rename the annual Rochester tournament "The Shannon Cup." The stands were packed with friends, family, people who have supported us along the way, and people who just wanted to honor her—honor us.

Shannon's life—or the awakening that her life sparked—seemed to unite the Rochester hockey community. The girls on the 14A's hangin' out with the girls on the 12B's and 12A's—working together to collect donations. Parents collaborating to start the Shannon Scholarship and organizing fundraising events, t-shirt sales, chuck-a-puck signage, volunteer schedules, etc.

Jen, Erin, and I were called onto the ice where the 14A's presented us with the Shannon Cup—their name already engraved on the trophy from last weekend. The 12A Ice Cats then presented us with a giant check (like the winner of a golf tournament is awarded) with the funds from last weekend's t-shirt sales and chuck-a-puck. Then a special surprise as the Rebels skated over to us with a portfolio from Fidelity Charitable, already funded through donations made by Rochester businesses to get the Shannon Scholarship account started.

What followed was a hockey game that reminded us all of the effort the Rebels gave that November weekend in Hopkins. The Rebels were out shot 32–2 against a bigger, faster team from Centennial. Shannon's teams played Centennial teams maybe four times over her hockey career and never won.

Saturday the Rebels skated to a thrilling 0–0 tie (round-robin pool play format). The Rebels played so hard: forwards getting back to help out on D, the D cleaning up and making smart plays, and goalie Clare Brunn was simply a beast. Incredible intensity. The shrieks from the stands on every close play … the hairs on our arms tingling … no doubt Shannon was there …

Centennial ended up winning the Shannon Cup in the 12B bracket. A goal differential was the tiebreaker, but Shannon's teammates should feel great about how they are playing heading into the district playoffs.

Impossible to send out thank-yous to all the volunteers and folks that helped us get this fund started. You know who you are. Thank you.

We will carry her name forward and start handing out the Shannon Scholarship in 2013.

POSTED BY DAN

MONDAY, FEBRUARY 6, 2012

Today I would have to put in the shitty column. Pardon my language. The one month anniversary was going to be a tough day, but more so than I expected. We were rocked today with news that a friend of ours—a man in his early thirties—had a seizure yesterday, and a preliminary CT scan showed a tumor in his brain. Oh, how we are feeling for him in these early days of trying to get your bearings and figuring out what's ahead. He doesn't yet know the type of tumor or prognosis. We are holding some good thoughts for him …

Erin had an emotional weekend, and she was quiet this morning, but was doing better by tonight. We are lucky that our ten-year-old is able to articulate her feelings. She is smart, but she is also wise. Yesterday we'd had a few blow-ups with her through the course of the day, but by the time we lay down last night to tuck her in, she had calmed down and become more rational. She told Dan and me that she knew she was being mean and that she was angry and she just had "zero tolerance" for any advice or comments from us. Wow. That pretty much cut right through the bullshit, didn't it? Dan and I were using that as a catchphrase all day. It seems that there were a lot of things we had zero tolerance for today!

Emotion hits us at different times and in different ways. It got Erin this weekend with all the activity surrounding the Shannon Cup dedication. It got me as I walked Sunny around the golf course today and thought about Shannon. It got to Dan today when he had a tender moment with one of Shannon's best buds who had obviously been crying. We cannot escape it, and we cannot deny it. We must persevere through it. The way out is in.

POSTED BY JEN

TUESDAY, FEBRUARY 7, 2012

I am happy to report today was less shitty than yesterday! Actually, today felt like progress. Progress on the work front for Dan as he organized his travels for the rest of the month. Progress on the home front as I checked things off the to-do list. Progress on the emotional front as Dan and I each lunched with a friend and shared some thoughts and feelings. Progress for Erin as she also shared her feelings in a less angry manner. Even some progress on the family room as paint started going up on the walls. So far, we are really happy with what we see.

We've started thinking about our happiness level, for lack of a better term. We know we will never go back to the carefree joy that we used to have—something we now describe as our one hundred percent happiness level. But, what level can we get to? Seventy percent? Eighty percent? Really hard to quantify. We are helping Erin come to terms with the fact we can't go back, and our lives will never be the way they once were. But, we can work our way back to some level of happiness. We can cope. We can persevere. It will be a slow climb, with steps forward and sometimes backward, but we have to have hope that we will again find happiness in our lives. And it will be a new kind of happiness, hard earned. We have to believe we can get there.

POSTED BY JEN

THURSDAY, FEBRUARY 9, 2012

Smiley was all fired up this morning. A sixth grade field trip to the Brownsdale Roller Rink will do that to a kid.

Our daily meditation entry offered this nugget: *"Light griefs can speak; great ones are dumb."*

Our reflex is to feel the need to carry conversation—to make sure the flow of it goes well so that everyone is comfortable in our presence. Today's reading highlighted the fact that sometimes the silence is golden, and it is not our responsibility to talk. Especially, to talk about the grief issues that are bogging us down.

As a former broadcaster turned sales guy, that is really hard. Dead air makes me uncomfortable, makes us uncomfortable. But it is OK.

And carrying the conversation is not our job. Our job is to find a "new normal."

So be on guard to listen. Sometimes I might go off if you give me your ear. But if I don't talk I'm not mad at you. And please, no worries.

POSTED BY DAN

FRIDAY, FEBRUARY 10, 2012

This week has been an up and down, and up and down, and up and … well, you get the idea. It is such a strange roller coaster that we three are on. Even living together, Dan, Erin, and I don't seem to be in the same place at the same time on this journey. I may awaken feeling OK only to have Erin stare into her bowl of cereal, not sure she can face the day. Or Dan may return home from a productive meeting feeling motivated only to find that I have been sitting in the same chair reading the same book for hours. We continue to try to cut each other slack and accept that this journey is different for each of us.

That includes the outside world. I read a book this week (I'm just going to keep reading until I figure this all out!) written by nine mothers who had lost their own children, and they came to call people who had not experienced the loss of a child "civilians." It is important for Dan, Erin, and me to accept that the "civilians," no matter how much they care about us, can never completely understand. It's not their fault. You must live it to know it.

This week we've spent a lot of time talking with Erin, talking to Erin, and forcing Erin to talk. She's fed up with it. In fact, one night this week, she called me on my B.S. and then she said point blank to me, "See I can just be my own psychologist." Oh boy. But, we're not going to let her shut down. We're going to be diligent and persevere. When she's angry and we're vulnerable, that's a bad mix. But, we all know it and we get through …

Emotions lie just under the surface—oftentimes there is no explanation or warning. Today I laughed so hard that I cried. We were being silly at Target and things just got away from me … then I felt guilty for laughing. Earlier today, I opened a cupboard and came across Shannon's hockey water bottle. All taped up with her hockey tape and her name on it in her printing. I couldn't bring myself to throw it out. As I put it away with her things, it made me cry ... then I felt silly for crying over a water bottle. Sometimes it's the little things.

Grief work has no rules. Whatever we feel, we feel, and we have to just be OK with it. We must be kind and gentle with ourselves as best we can. Within the confines of our home, that's not too difficult. But, out in the real world that's a whole different animal. Nobody wants to have a breakdown in the grocery store. And, we're not always prepared to see people who give us "the look." We have come to know the nod, the sad eyes that say, "Oh boy, you guys had a really bad thing happen to you." We do our best to smile and say hello ...

Some positive things did take place this week. Good progress on the remodel. One week from right now, I plan to be lounging in our new space.

The most positive news of all came today from my friend Mike. The mass that showed up on his CT scan last Sunday turned out to be an infection and not a brain tumor as originally thought. A four-hour surgery yesterday at St. Mary's removed the infection that was behind his left eye, eating away a part of his skull, and pressing against his brain. I spoke to him this afternoon, and while brain surgery is no picnic, he's relieved to not be heading on a journey that no one wants to take.

POSTED BY JEN

SUNDAY, FEBRUARY 12, 2012—EVENING

Music's big night to celebrate and remember got off to a rousing start with The Boss showing—once again—why he's one of the best live performers ever. After Bruce's "We Take Care of Our Own" grabbed the audience's attention, LL Cool J stepped up and offered an incredibly appropriate and heartfelt prayer to recognize a "death in the family." Whitney ... oh, Whitney ...

So with Erin and Jen locked in on the Grammy's, I snuck into seclusion to write about a pretty terrific weekend. We hung out with friends, skated, took in a Rebels playoff game, went to church, hung out with family and watched as Erin's Spartan sixth graders took down the Owatonna Invitational. Way to go, Smiley!

Over the course of three Spartan wins Sunday, Erin logged minutes at all five positions, including post and point guard. No wisecracks, please. Of course, she's the first O'Hara ever to play the post ... come to think of it ... she's the first O'Hara ever to run the point (not counting her mom who was not yet an O'Hara when she played point guard for the Rochester John Marshall Rockets a million years ago). Good yucks. Good wins. More hardware for Smiley's Spartans.

Saturday night when I tucked her into bed, Erin expressed a slight tinge of guilt for laughing and having fun. But I know Shannon would approve. I know it. Still, it is odd to separate from the sadness. Even for a short time. We all know that separation is temporary.

The kid said she wanted her life to mean something to someone someday. The cards, notes, and reminders keep trickling in from people that knew Shannon, and many that didn't but have been impacted by her life. I wanted to leave you tonight with an excerpt from a neighbor's note to us about Shannon ... it just came today ... and it touched us very much:

> Even from my distance, this whole episode has been a tragic reminder that love is always a setup for heartache. It hurts to fall in love with someone who doesn't love you back. It hurts when your teenage kids push your love away for the independence they need to take on life without you. And, it dearly hurts when someone you love dies. But, this untimely loss of your precious little girl who seemed to embody all of life's most positive energies in one tiny package is too much to bear alone. That's what I'm trying to say: you do not suffer alone. No one can help the fact that you bear the most pain, but Shannon is missed by people she was barely even aware of in her wonderfully busy life. I think love is worth the pain, though. I hope you can feel that way. I'm profoundly thankful to you for bringing Shannon into our lives, and bringing so much happiness to hers. Shannon enriched everything and everyone around her. She still does.

POSTED BY DAN

TUESDAY, FEBRUARY 14, 2012

Happy Valentine's Day. Today is the first of many "firsts" when it comes to holidays. Good to start with a minor one, in my opinion. (Dan will be happy to read that I consider this a minor holiday, because he didn't get me anything. I shouldn't throw him under the bus, I didn't get him anything either!)

I did my usual mommy ritual of having a gift bag of goodies to surprise our children—our child—when she woke up today. I have to admit that shopping for only one of each thing was hard; I am in the habit of buying two ...

Dan and I have found ourselves missing Shannon, missing her physical presence. I suppose as time passes and we get further away from her actual time here on Earth, we will struggle to keep those images of her as a living, moving being in our mind's eye. Dan had a vivid memory of her striding ahead of us through the Gonda Building at Mayo, confident and assured as she headed off to another appointment. I was walking Sunny on the golf course yesterday, and I could picture Shannon focusing on hitting the golf ball and reacting with a big smile when she hit a good shot. (Interesting that my memory chose that image instead of the frustrated look she would get when the golf ball didn't cooperate!)

I can never say that thirteen years with Shannon was enough, but it has to be. That's what we had. It was wonderful, and we made the most of it. Isn't that our hope as humans, to make the most of our time on this earth and live a good life? She did. And so I struggle to make peace with that thought. It has to be enough so that we can continue on our journey and not be stuck wanting something that can never be again ... We know that intellectually, and yet emotionally we ache and miss her so.

Being a glutton for punishment, I am spending today organizing and putting away the cards, letters, and gifts we've received over these past few weeks. Actually, re-reading the many kind words seems appropriate today. Of course, it is painful and heartwarming at the same time. Oh, sweet Shannon. In your short time on this earth, you did good.

"I've learned that people will forget what you said, people will forget what you did, but people will never forget how you made them feel."
—*Maya Angelou*
POSTED BY JEN

FRIDAY, FEBRUARY 17, 2012—EVENING

The Rebels win! Friday night at the District 9 Tournament our squad beat Fairmont 2–1 to keep the season alive. Damn, we should be there; we should be partying with those families at the hotel in Mankato.

With a win Saturday, the Rebels will advance to the next round—a region tournament in two weeks in Waseca.

Personally, I'm not ready for the last hockey season Shannon will ever be a part of to come to an end. In a card we received today, someone referred to the six degrees of Shannon. With each passing of seasons, school years, holidays, Mondays … with each day that passes, we are further separated from her life. You can tell me all day that she will always be part of us—and she will—but with each sunset and sunrise, the space between her days on earth and today grows wider.

My music has not been fulfilling me lately. The songs that were bringing me strength and hope and generating emotion are now leaving me feeling empty, bored. I'm trying some Pandora Internet Radio tonight as we relax in our new family living space. It's pretty sweet. We have a contractor named Mark Borgen. You might need to keep him in mind if you are looking for any remodel projects. Anal and affordable.

Erin is back behind the bench with Coach Lang's Mayo Spartans tonight filling water bottles with her friend Lexie as the Mayo boys take on Mankato West. Sunday we will sneak her away for a couple days with BFF, Emily, for some water park fun in the Dells. Trying to keep her moving in a positive direction—giving her some things to look forward to. Erin has been stringing together some better days.

Jen and I attended her school conferences Thursday, and the reports we were given left us hopeful that she is doing OK. Can you imagine being Erin? She has to walk by Shannon's locker every day, she has to see Shannon's friends sitting together across the lunchroom, and every day she has to see all of the teachers that loved Shannon. Every once in awhile I need to take a look at the world through her glasses. And she's just ten.

So if you have an extra prayer tonight when you lay your head down, have a good thought for Erin O'Hara. And a good thought for the Rebels to beat Northfield Saturday to keep the season alive.

POSTED BY DAN

SUNDAY, FEBRUARY 19, 2012

Dan and I are sitting in a hotel room in the Wisconsin Dells, and we are crying like babies because the Rebels season lives on. We couldn't be prouder of those girls. We've been receiving text updates all day as the Rebels faced two elimination games in the District 9 Tournament. After a tight 1–0 victory over Dodge County this morning, the Rebs had to face Mankato on their home ice this afternoon with the winner advancing.

As we sat at Kalahari watching Erin and her pal Emily enjoy the water park, our minds and hearts were focused on those girls on that sheet of ice in Mankato. After jumping out to a 3–0 lead in the first period, the Rebs had to hang on at the end to come away with a 3–2 victory. We heard that the girls gave a thumbs-up raised to heaven during the post game celebration. Well done girls, well done.

So Dan and I find ourselves so happy and proud, and yet aching so badly, selfishly, for our loss. Shannon would have been over the moon. I can picture her big, brown eyes all aglow as she would have recounted each shift and how dicey it was out there. I can just picture it. And yet, it wasn't meant to be for us. But, our hope was for Shannon's last hockey team to extend their season, and that's exactly what they did. Those fifteen girls have been through so much this season, and they've persevered—together. The Rebels will fight with all their heart until the end. Just like Shannon …

POSTED BY JEN

BFF | Erin's friend Emily is there with her through it all

PRESIDENT'S DAY

We did our best to make the most of this long weekend by taking a road trip to the Wisconsin Dells. As surreal as it still seems, it's time to develop a new pattern now that Erin is an only child, so Erin's pal Emily joined us on our adventure.

We rode the body slides and the tube rides and floated on the lazy river. Dan and the girls even convinced me to go with them on The Hurricane, a family raft ride that drops you fifty-eight feet into a funnel where you go back and forth like you are in a half pipe. My stomach hasn't felt quite right the rest of the day!

So, another first. Away for some family fun. A threesome now. Plus one, this time. So far, so good. Emily was easy and Erin was happy.

POSTED BY JEN

WEDNESDAY, FEBRUARY 22, 2012

It's a good thing I ran all my errands yesterday, because my car won't start this morning! Luckily, I have good friends who will jump in their car at 7:15 A.M. to come get Erin and get her to school. (Erin might feel differently about that!)

So, I'm sitting here waiting for AAA, and I'm not that worked up about it. I'm hoping it's something minor. It's only a car, and it's only money, right? Ah, perspective—you are a new companion, and I kind of like you ...

Grandma and Papa Harkins arrive in Rochester today. They came to Minnesota for some grandkid activities, including Laurynn's band concert in Shakopee earlier this week and Erin's basketball tournament in Rochester this weekend. We're looking forward to showing them our room remodel and having some time together. February is speeding by, and that's always a good thing here in Minnesota.

POSTED BY JEN

SATURDAY, FEBRUARY 25, 2012

First off, Jen's van is fine. Don't know what happened. Our guy Roger at Auto Techs cleaned out the fuel line but wasn't able to pinpoint a specific issue that would have kept it from starting. Who knows? It's a 2002 Chrysler with 180,000 miles. Let's just say, we will be keeping our AAA membership current.

As a family we continue to do the hard work required to get better. Each morning at breakfast, we try to read from the daily reflection book *Healing After Loss, Daily Meditation for Working Through Grief.* The entry from Friday, February 24 delivered this timely message:

> *One of the greatest gifts we can give ourselves (and we'll know we've passed a milestone when we are able to do this) is to remember, with delight and laughter, the funny times we shared with our loved one. At first we have little heart for laughter. Later, when we do, it may seem disrespectful to the dead. Perhaps, we even feel guilty. But think—which would your loved one rejoice in more— seeing you sad, or seeing you reveling in the memory of a wonderful, hilarious time together? 'A merry heart doeth good like medicine.'*
> *—Proverbs 17:22*

This week, while I was on the road for work, I found myself in a bit of a funk. Didn't feel much like talking. I thought I took a couple steps backwards after stringing together some good time.

The quote in our daily reflections book for today reminds me that is OK, "I am feeling down today, it doesn't mean I will forever."

So we continue to heal. Slowly. I've learned feeding the soul with readings and music and quiet reflection becomes part of the discipline required for recovery. Doesn't mean it doesn't suck some days.

But we can do this ... Shannon would insist.

This weekend Erin's Spartans play in the Rochester Youth Basketball Tournament. Grandma and Papa Harkins are along for the ride. We have laughed and cried together. That will continue.

I can tell I am in a better state of mind today as my music is working well this morning. Bill Withers, "Lovely Day" just shuffled up:

When the day that lies ahead of me
Seems impossible to face
When someone else instead of me
Always seems to know the way

Then I look at you
And the world's alright with me
Just one look at you
And I know it's gonna be a lovely day

POSTED BY DAN

SUNDAY, FEBRUARY 26, 2012

Another weekend spent watching basketball comes to a close. Erin's Spartans rebounded from a first game loss to win their next three games and take home the consolation championship at the Rochester tourney.

Smiley played hard every minute she was out there, and loved the time spent with her teammates. She is happy when she's with these girls. And we're happy when we see her happy. Thank goodness we've had basketball to keep us busy and keep us moving.

Grandma and Papa Harkins were able to spend some time with us and see two basketball games before heading back to Las Vegas today. I think they enjoyed their visit, and they could see with their own eyes that the three of us are doing the best we can. Some days—some hours—are better than others. They probably already realized that, though. They are living that way too.

We have another "normal" week ahead; it's a full school week for Erin and the last week of the basketball season. It will be a full work-week for Dan too, including more travel. As he likes to say, "The customers don't come visit you."

To the hoop | Basketball keeps Erin occupied, thank goodness

Today our other favorite team, the Rebels, saw their season come to an end. So sad for those girls that this special season is over. But so proud of them too. What an up and down year they had, and what an end of the season run. I know in my heart those girls have been changed by what they experienced together this year.

Dan and I will watch from a distance as they all grow and progress as people and as hockey players, and they will always have a special place in our hearts as Shannon's last team. We love you, Rebels. We always will.

POSTED BY JEN

Shannon's last team | The Rebels finish their season by carrying Shannon's jersey onto the ice to accept their trophy. These girls will be forever connected to each other—and to us.

Grief

There is no term for someone who loses a child. It goes against the natural order of things. If you lose your parents, you are orphaned, and if you lose a spouse you are widowed. But to lose a child ... it's unthinkable.

One of the hardest parts is accepting that there is a random element to things in the universe. We want the world to make sense. We want to have explanations for why things happen. We want to believe that we have some control over our own destiny. So how do you reconcile an innocent child being given a terminal diagnosis? I could never buy into the idea that it was all part of a plan, part of God's plan, for me, for us. What God would do that? In my mind there is no explanation, no reason for what happened. It just happened. We didn't have control over it. We just have to accept it and realize the only thing we can control is how we react to it. Some days that is easier said than done, for sure. But each day, I have a choice to make a conscious effort to get up and live. Be present. Do my best. The past is in the past and out of my control. What I can control is the attitude I choose toward what's right here in front of me now.

There are plenty of books on grief, and I spent a great deal of time reading and gathering information. Some were helpful, while others didn't speak to me, but knowledge is power. Reading of other's experiences showed me one thing: whatever you feel, it's fine. There is no right way to grieve. If you're having a bad day, it's fine. If you're having a good day, that's fine too. The bottom line is, there's no predictable pattern to grief. Healing doesn't take place in an upward and linear fashion. It's more like a roller coaster.

You miss the one who is not there. We miss Shannon's physical presence. We miss her place in the pecking order of our family. We miss her laugh, her smile, and her energy. We miss her future, and we will continue to grieve the milestones that pass. There will be birthdays and anniversaries of diagnosis and death. There will be summer vacations and Christmases, and we will miss her. We will watch her peers grow up, go to high school, learn to drive, and graduate, and we will miss her. But, life does go on, and we have to forge ahead and make the most of what the future holds for us.

Learning to trust that whatever feelings you have are OK is a process. Sometimes we will have a good day or laugh at something, and then feel that pang of guilt. How could we be laughing when our kid just died? Are we crazy? Are we in denial?

As I move through the days and the weeks and the months, it is sometimes hard to accept that life—the normal, everyday stuff—still happens. You mean I still have to do the laundry and shop for groceries even though my kid is dead? You mean other bad things can happen? The refrigerator will quit running and my minivan will break down? Haven't I suffered enough? Yes, the same stuff that happens to "normal" people can happen to me too. This horrible experience in my life won't save me from the things the rest of the world experiences. But there is something comforting in the everyday life stuff, I suppose.

As we learned to live our new life and do the day-to-day tasks that needed doing, I also recognized that there is a fine line between letting go of the little things and giving up. When you have suffered a great loss, it is easy to feel that nothing can scare you now. What could possibly happen that would make me feel any worse than losing a child? Nothing. But, the danger is the flip side of that coin. What could possibly make me feel good again after losing a child? We had to find those moments of joy amidst the grief. That is the delicate balance that we tried to find as we navigated the days and weeks and months after Shannon had passed.

LEAP DAY

There is no daily meditation to read in our book today. I guess they didn't plan for you to use it in a leap year!

Erin is home sick today; lots of crud going around school, and this cold and cough finally got the best of her. Hopefully a day of sleeping in and rest will help her fight it off. She's been a trooper this winter and hasn't missed a day of school since Shannon's funeral. It hasn't been easy.

Erin has been struggling with memories, and music has been a source of many tears this week. And, as you know, we love our music around here. Songs and lyrics seem to constantly remind Erin of Shannon. Where Dan and I have mostly found solace and comfort in listening to our tunes, Erin has felt pain. Maybe that's the difference between being in your forties and being ten.

So, yesterday afternoon I cranked up the iPod, and Erin and I listened to show tunes from some of our favorite musicals: everything from *West Side Story* and *Annie*, to *Wicked* and *Memphis*, with a little *Hairspray* and *Mama Mia* mixed in. There may have been dancing involved. I'll spare you the details, but let's just say in my next life I'm coming back as an ensemble member in a Broadway hit. Erin laughed and cringed, and asked me to stop dancing.

I tried to frame for Erin the good memories that are associated with these songs. The time we saw *Mama Mia* from the front row in Vegas when we could see right into the orchestra pit. Or when we saw *Wicked* from the balcony at the Orpheum in Minneapolis. Or, the night we saw the Tony Award winning, *Memphis*; it was the "real deal" on Broadway in NYC.

Those are good memories, but it's a hard realization at age ten that you don't get to make any more good memories with your sister. Erin told me the other night that the bad memories of the end of Shannon's life are so close for her, but the good memories are getting farther away.

So, for Erin the goal is to keep the good memories alive and carry Shannon's spirit within her while still looking forward, forging ahead, and finding her own path in life. That is a hard but necessary goal. Erin can't quite comprehend how to make that happen, and that makes her frustrated and sad. My only motherly advice is to try and do it one day at a time.

At the end of the musical *Wicked*, there is a song about the life-altering friendship between the two main characters. While one of them is dying, the other must carry on and carry her friend's spirit with her. From the song "For Good":

> *I've heard it said*
> *That people come into our lives*
> *for a reason*
> *Bringing something we must learn*
> *And we are led to those*
> *Who help us most to grow*
> *If we let them*
> *And we help them in return*
> *But I don't know if I believe that's true*
> *But I know I'm who I am today*
> *Because I knew you ...*
>
> *So let me say before we part*
> *So much of me*
> *Is made of what I learned from you*
> *You'll be with me*
> *Like a handprint on my heart ...*
>
> *Because I knew you*
> *I have been changed for good.*

POSTED BY JEN

FRIDAY, MARCH 2, 2012

Another weekend is upon us, and this one will bring the basketball season to a close. The sixth grade Spartans will play in the Grade State Basketball Tournament up in Prior Lake. Erin is heading to the cities this afternoon with the Olson mafia, as we affectionately refer to them: Tom and Brooke and their three kids, Anna, Hallie, and Siri, along with cousin Lexie. Why not throw in an O'Hara for good measure! Should be entertaining. Dan is not looking to spend extra nights in hotels, so we are lucky that the Olsons are willing to let Smiley tag along so she doesn't miss out on any of the fun. Dan and I will join them in the morning in time for the first game and then stay tomorrow night with the whole team.

Erin has had a good couple of days. Always nice to have something fun to look forward to, and Dan returning home from his travels last night also brightened her spirit. He brings the energy and fun around here. Erin may tease her dad about liking it when he's away, but truth be told, she's happy when he returns.

While there is no right or wrong way to grieve, we've talked a lot with Erin about the things we can control and the things we can't. We couldn't stop the tumor, and we can't bring Shannon back. Those things were beyond our control. And that brings us sadness and grief. We still catch ourselves at some point every day thinking, "I can't believe that Shannon is gone." Sometimes that makes us cry, and sometimes that makes us mad. Depends on the day, depends on the moment, actually …

But, the three of us are still here. We are going on living, and it is possible to carry on and to find bits of joy and happiness amidst the pain. This weekend will be fun, and we are all looking forward to it. I read a quote recently from Helen Keller that said, *"Although the world is full of suffering, it is full also of overcoming it."* That is our job and that is our goal. To keep on keepin' on … even if some days we have to fake it to make it …

POSTED BY JEN

SUNDAY, MARCH 4, 2012

We wrapped up the basketball season as Erin's team went 1-and-2 at the Grade State Tournament in Prior Lake. The Spartan sixth grade and eighth grade teams became a great source of strength and distraction for all three of us as we plowed through a winter that we will never forget.

Coach Olson's eighth graders—many of them Shannon's friends from Willow Creek Middle School—practiced with, and after, Smiley's sixth grade squad every week through the season. So many of them seem to have adopted Erin as their own little sister. Our teams shared a hotel, a party room potluck, and a Bruegger's bagel session Sunday morning. It just felt right to be part of something—part of a family. Count Mayo Spartans girls basketball families among the "healers" for Team O'Hara. All we can say is thank you. We love you.

Getting better one day at a time. Before heading back to Rochester on Sunday, Erin, Jen, and I shopped at IKEA for stuff for Erin's room and laughed frequently. We are settling into a rhythm that is our family of three, plus Sunny. Two months without Shannon in our lives. We still look at each other some days and ask, "Did this really happen?" Yepper.

John Mayer's "Dreaming with a Broken Heart" is in my head as I head for bed … *"When you're dreaming with a broken heart, the waking up is the hardest part."*

POSTED BY DAN

TUESDAY, MARCH 6, 2012

It was a beautiful, unseasonably warm day here today that gave way to a bright, almost full moon tonight. Little hints from the universe that we are just tiny players in the big picture.

On this two-month marker since Shannon's passing, I found myself feeling pretty good about the ground we've covered. A dear friend sent me a note today that reminded me that on this day, while we think about Shannon, we should also recognize that the three of us are functioning quite well. We are coping. So far, we are making it.

Erin continues to go to school, hang with her friends, and sees her psychologist to help her work through the tough stuff. Erin showed some confidence in herself by trying a new activity this week; she went to her first ever volleyball practice on Monday. She loved it, and she's going back tomorrow. All her basketball buddies are volleyball players, and Erin wants to stay busy and stay in the loop with her peeps. So she will give volleyball a try and see where it goes.

Dan continues to travel and stay busy with work. This week he's in Michigan, which is new territory for him. He is out there doing it, even though being away from home isn't ideal, and making small talk with customers sometimes leads to uncomfortable conversations, like the one he had today. Imagine: potential customer, trying to get to know sales rep guy, asks benign question, "How many kids do you have?" I'm not sure we will ever again know the correct answer to that question ...

I continue to manage things around the house, and I am starting to think about what's next for me. I sent my first inquiry into the publishing world this week, wondering if this twelve-month long blog could potentially be something more ...

So, we made it through another sixth of the month. We didn't do it alone. Our dear friends and families are there for us by checking in, and encouraging us. While the loss of Shannon can still bring me to tears without warning, I am finding more joy and more happiness in the memories of her. And we find we are happiest when we are with people who are comfortable hearing Shannon's name. Maybe it's all a part of grieving—realizing that we don't want to forget, but that we want to remember ...

POSTED BY JEN

FRIDAY, MARCH 9, 2012

The people in my house are happy it's Friday. A long week of travels for Dan and a busy week of activity for Erin are coming to a close. I've been fighting a doozie of a head cold that's kept my eyes watering and my nose running, but at least it's made my voice sound really sexy! We don't have a lot on our agenda for the weekend, which is just fine with all of us.

It seems silly that just a couple of weeks ago I was worried that Erin and I would have too much idle time on our hands once basketball season ended. Ha! This week she started a new sport with two volleyball practices, resumed piano lessons for the first time in five months, had a friend over to hang out one afternoon, and did her water girl duty at the last home game for the Mayo boys basketball team. Erin has kept us busy, and busy is good.

She is really liking volleyball, but what's not to like? Time spent with your buddies and a cool coach who makes it fun. So, she wants to stick with it for this spring season. Of course, a new sport requires some new gear, so we will be shopping this weekend! Glad to do it—I'd buy that kid the world if I could.

I find myself thinking about this shift in priorities for Erin. She was always our child who wanted downtime and just needed to chill out at home. As we've said before, she's finding less satisfaction in that because it's less fun doing it all alone. But, I think there's something else. I think she learned from Shannon that making connections with others makes the world a happier place. Spending time with good friends makes for good fun. Erin has had to grow up so quickly and navigate a path that no one wants to travel. But, seeing her laugh and smile at volleyball practice or confidently make her way around the Mayo gymnasium during the boys basketball game gives me hope that she's got the chops to survive this.

That leads me to thinking about myself and my own path. I also learned something from Shannon about sharing yourself with the world. I never would have believed that my circle of friends and acquaintances would expand the way it has. A definite silver lining to this tragedy. It took me almost forty-three years to learn that if you look for the good in people and are open to sharing yourself with others, friendship and love can come your way. My thirteen-year-old taught me that. What a gift …

POSTED BY JEN

SUNDAY, MARCH 11, 2012

A weekend with little agenda served us well. Dan returned to a couple of old hobbies, and Erin spent some time practicing a new one.

Golf season is on Dan's mind, and the spring-like temps meant it was time to get the golf cart out and ready for action. The excitement of hitting some golf shots was tempered a bit by what Dan found on the cart. The last person to use the cart was Shannon, and there, on the steering wheel, was her scorecard in her handwriting: Shannon 6, 4, 5, 7 … She was out there practicing, by herself, trying to get better. And her golf bag, just as she left it: her glove, her ball, and her tee tucked in the side pocket. As if to say, "Until next time ..." Gut shot. But, Dan and I are both hoping to find some joy in playing golf this year. It's something we like to do, and we like to do it together. Last summer was such a blur and focusing was a challenge. Maybe this year ...

Erin's new pursuit—volleyball—required a quick trip to the sporting goods store. Believe it or not, there was a type of ball that we did not yet own. So, with a new volleyball in tow and warm temps, we spent some time with Erin in the driveway practicing our bumping, setting, and serving. After only two practices, Erin thinks she is the expert, and she felt completely confident to tell her dad that he was doing it all wrong.

As for Dan's second hobby, I am selfishly glad that Dan felt like cooking this weekend. Dan has always loved to cook. From our early days of courtship, he would make a meal plan and create some magic. Just another sign that we were meant to be together since I can't cook a lick! Over the course of the last year, partly due to living life in fast-forward and partly due to stress and lack of motivation, Dan hasn't felt as much like cooking. But this weekend he said to me, "I'm excited to cook something." So, I'm taking this as a sign of progress, a sign of healing. The menu was fabulous: Saturday we had rib eye steaks, scallops on orzo, and asparagus. Tonight, he grilled chicken and made parsley potatoes and green beans. He's still got the touch.

We continued to try and put ourselves out there this weekend as well: a basketball game at the Civic Arena, a tennis event at the RAC, and mass at St. John's. And we are still seeing people for the "first time." Dan and I discussed how it's hard when people want to tell you how sorry they are or give us "the look," but then we're angry if people don't acknowledge our loss. Damn, we are hard to please. We're a work in progress, for sure. But, we will keep on trying. Each day. Persevere.

POSTED BY JEN

TUESDAY, MARCH 13, 2012

You know that first perfect day of spring? The one where everyone in the neighborhood is out and about? When grills are smoking all through the neighborhood? That was today all across the frozen prairie. Just shy of seventy degrees, sunny, no wind, and no clouds.

I remember making bad choices on these kinds of days in college. Dang, that was great.

Twenty-five years later, I am making more responsible choices, but these kinds of days still trigger all sorts of happy memories. For many reasons, we choose to live in the north. For me, this is where my family is. This is what I know. There are some brutal days to endure in the winter. Almost fascinating that nature can be so harsh.

But when spring has sprung it is as though we find another gear. Hope springs eternal. The only thing missing is one Shannon Anne O'Hara.

Time to put the burgers and brats on the grill for three. So grateful for what I have. What I have had in this life. Grateful that another cruel winter is history.

POSTED BY DAN

Spring has sprung | Erin and Sunny enjoy a warm March day

FRIDAY, MARCH 16, 2012

"How are you doing?" If I had a nickel for every time someone asked me that ...

I don't mean to sound ungrateful. Some people just say it in passing, but a lot of people genuinely want to know. My problem with the question is this: I don't have a good answer. It's an innocuous, common greeting that leaves me perplexed. I guess my answer is too complicated.

Most of the time, I could say, "We're mostly doing pretty well, but ..." There's always a "but ..." We get up every day and try to forge ahead, doing what needs doing. But, I think of Shannon every day. And that means if you catch me at the right moment, then my honest answer would have to be, "I'm struggling right now because my heart just aches, but ... I can get through this moment of sadness and carry on." That's way too much info to share in passing with someone. So I usually just say "We're doing OK, thanks." It's just easier ...

This week we received cards and emails from people who wanted us to know that they are still thinking about us—and about Shannon. The most touching one was a hand-written note on half a piece of notebook paper from an eighth grade boy. He just wanted to let us know that something happened this week at school that reminded him of Shannon, and that it made him happy to remember her that way. Wow. So kind and thoughtful of him to do that.

There's a certain duty we are feeling to carry on in Shannon's spirit: be a good example and hold our heads high, acknowledging those around us. Some days that's a tall order, but when we do, we are reminded of the good in the world. It's out there if our minds and our hearts are open. Wasting our time living any other way seems foolish ...

POSTED BY JEN

ST. PADDY'S WEEKEND, 2012

I am crediting the freakish meteorological conditions to the Irish spirit of Shannon O'Hara. We smashed the record high for St. Patrick's Day in Rochester by fifteen degrees. (It was eighty-one Saturday.) Sunday was also warm and windy, so I honored Shannon's spirit by playing thirty-six holes.

As Erin noted, we had an extremely social weekend with visits from friends and family, and fun in the sun with lots of activity. Lots of golf. Lots of grilling. Lots of laughs. I would have to say, our best weekend as a family of three.

We received extra attention because of the Irish holiday. People recognized that this might be another tough "first." They were right.

But here was the part that kind of got to me: there was so much good sports action on TV, and she would've been sidled up next to us enjoying NCAA hoops, WCHA Final 5, PGA Tour. Whatever was on, Shannon would've loved. (Jen and I chuckled Friday. Shannon would have been really mad at Gopher hockey. North Dakota was not her favorite college hockey team.) I miss her so much.

So even when we are feeling good about our progress, there is a tinge of guilt about feeling that way. And how can we keep writing about Shannon when Erin is alive and well right here in the flesh?

For me, there is a fine line between honoring Shannon's spirit and moving on. Here's what I come back to every time I find myself feeling good about something: Shannon would want us to move on. She would want us to have fun and laugh and make this life all about Erin. She would want us to play golf and go on vacation and enjoy life just as we did with her.

So that's what I feel today. This has been a really good day. I'm feeling good about that.

POSTED BY DAN

MONDAY, MARCH 19, 2012

A quick shout-out to Sunny the Wonder Dog who turned six today. That means, in dog years, she and I are now the same age.

I couldn't sleep last night, and it feels like I can barely breathe today—reminders of Shannon seem to be all around me. While raking the yard, I hear Van Morrison's "Brown Eyed Girl," and I'm a puddle. While trying to plan a spring break trip, I can't make a decision partly because I can't imagine going on a trip like that without her. Then the email comes reminding us it is time to pick our family's week at the cabin ... Uff da ...

Dan has been swamped with work and too busy to let his mind go there too often. So, while I've been the weepy one stuck in slow motion, he's the one keeping it moving and keeping it together. You gotta know that's killing me ...

One more anecdote I wanted to share from our weekend of sports viewing. Shannon and the Rebels went to a Gopher women's hockey game back in November and had a chance to meet a few of the players. One Gopher, Katie Frischmann, is from Rochester and kept up on Shannon's journey. After Shannon's passing, we got a card in the mail with a wonderful condolence note and a photo from Katie and her teammate Megan Bozek letting us know that they were putting Shannon's name on their sticks to honor her for the rest of their season.

Well, that very Gopher women's hockey team just won the National Championship yesterday with a victory over archrival and #1-ranked Wisconsin. I sent Katie a quick note of congrats and received this response:

"On behalf of Megan and I, I want to thank you. We have had Shannon's name on our sticks through the remainder of the season, rewriting it when we got a new stick. It was a nice daily reminder to love every day and to be grateful for the opportunity we've been given. I know Shannon was watching us win that Championship today, and I hope we made her proud...."

National Champs | The University of Minnesota Golden Gophers women's hockey team was inspired by Shannon

No wonder I'm a blubbering idiot these past couple of days ... like a pebble in the ocean, the ripple effects are still surfacing.

POSTED BY JEN

WEDNESDAY, MARCH 21, 2012

Since my last angst-ridden post, we've had a couple of really good days. It appears that Erin has carte blanche to plan things she'd like to do, and she's got quite a list: Volleyball and piano have been on the schedule this week, so has her weekly ice cream date with her high school buddy, Ariana. Tomorrow, there are plans to watch some NCAA hoops over dinner with friends, and then Erin is going to see *The Hunger Games* movie with buddy Emily on Friday. Phew! Not much time to sit around and wallow with that schedule. Basically anything Erin wants to do can be done. There's always someone wanting to make it happen for her, whatever it is ... it's good to have good people in your life.

I've got good people too; the friends who keep dragging me out on the tennis court to play each week. It's always fun once I get there. I've got those family and friends who continue to call and text and write and check in. I've come to realize that I am much more comfortable giving love and support than receiving it. I think I needed to come to terms with the fact that there is no need to keep score—I will never be able to repay all the kindness I've received. I just need to let go and accept it as I navigate my new world.

I've been struck by how quickly time seems to be passing all of a sudden. Maybe it's the fast approaching dates on the calendar that I know will trigger some memories. Golf practice started for the Mayo Spartan girls this week. I can picture Shannon in all her excitement last year as she attended those first couple weeks of practice, blissfully unaware that things wouldn't go as she had planned.

As I wrote the other day, trying to plan spring break really threw me for a loop. (As an aside, Dan stepped up by forcing my hand, and we did make a plan. The three of us will have a nice little getaway sitting on a beach by the ocean in southern Florida for a few days.) It's understandable that I felt so ambivalent about planning it, but it's not just about going on a trip without Shannon, it's also marking the anniversary of that spring break trip last year when we were blissfully unaware of what was to come just a short time later.

Blissfully unaware: there's no better phrase to describe it. There are just a few more weeks to mark the anniversary of that time, the time before diagnosis. Then we will reach the anniversary of the time when we became very aware, acutely aware of what we had. And what we could lose …

POSTED BY JEN

Hope

I have a bracelet with this word on it. We were given many such charms over the course of our journey, but this one word stuck with me. There is always a reason for hope. Even in our darkest moments, there are things we hope for.

When Shannon was diagnosed, we hoped for treatment. Through treatment, we hoped for good results. Post treatment, we hoped for time together. When she began to decline, we hoped for a miracle. When she became incapacitated, we hoped for mercy.

After such a great loss, how can you be hopeful? In those early days, it was very difficult to find the strength to think positively. But, there is always something to look toward and to work toward.

We now hope for healing and for the strength to carry on. We hope that Erin can rise above her great loss and thrive. Much of my energy and worry as we move forward is centered on Erin. She has lost her best friend and sister, and she is left to carry on. It seems as though Shannon was and still is loved by everyone. That is a tough act to follow. The mother in me misses Shannon so, but worries for Erin each day.

Yet, Erin has realized that she has the power to choose happiness in her life. There is a reason her nickname is Smiley. Pretty damn good for a girl her age. We all hope to carry on and move forward while carrying Shannon's spirit with us. We hope to honor and remember her while still becoming what we were meant to be. All of us. It is important not to get so lost in grief that we accidently miss the good stuff that's right here, right now.

If you try, you can find something good in each day. And, there is always hope—hope that tomorrow may be better than today.

SATURDAY, MARCH 24, 2012
Unseasonably warm temperatures (mixed with some rain) this week have turned things green seemingly overnight. Our lawn is growing like crazy, but I refuse to mow the grass while the calendar still says March! Now, I'm not complaining; the early spring weather has given us the ability to get outside often and feel the sun on our faces. If ever there was a year we needed that, this is it.

Dan and I find ourselves looking at each other as if to check and say, "We're doing pretty well, aren't we?" Dan admits that he wakes up every day and thinks about Shannon, but why wouldn't he? Maybe it's the universe's way of reminding us to get up and live. Thinking of Shannon reminds us of what she would want us to do.

So, we are living.

Erin spent last night doing what it seems every teen/tween in the country was doing: going to see the movie *The Hunger Games*. She left with a purse full of candy and a blanket she planned to use to cover her eyes when necessary. She came home saying it was the best movie she's *ever* seen. After seeing some violent and scary images, we asked her if she wanted to sleep with one of us, but she said, "No, I'm fine. I'm just going to sleep on the couch with a little light on." Feeling pretty secure I would say …

Dan finished one busy work week and another one is ahead. Hopefully he can have a relaxing weekend here in between. No doubt he's working hard partly as a coping mechanism to keep his mind busy, but also because he is the breadwinner for our family and that's not a job he takes lightly. Hard work produces results and results produce income! We try to remain grateful for that.

I had an interesting week as I explored what might be next for me. A meeting with a publishing company initiated talk of how to take this blog and possibly make it into a book. It's exciting and scary to think about and, truth be told, a little bit out of my comfort zone. But a friend reminded me that you have to press forward and try things you've never tried before in order to grow.

Some days are still better than others, but we continue to try and forge ahead, each of us, in our own way. While we will never move on, we can move forward …

POSTED BY JEN

SUNDAY, MARCH 25, 2012—EVENING

To the many amazing kids that took the time to author letters to us: I just want to say THANK YOU.

Tonight I sat down to read my Sports Illustrated Baseball Preview, and instead I began paging through the three-ring binders presented to us with hundreds of letters from Willow Creek Middle School students. We also have a book of letters from Shannon's Rebel teammates that I have been reading.

I think I had put my grieving on hold. But after scanning through a couple of the letters, that tremendous burden of grief and loss is back. And I thank you for letting me feel this way again because without Shannon, I am not OK. I will never be the same.

Sometimes it's easy to fall back into life … to fall back into the same attitudes and behaviors I swore off …

But then I read the words and messages from the classmates:

"Shannon I am so fortunate to have met you and be your best friend. You always treated me with respect and kindness. You have touched my life in so many ways."

"When you were first diagnosed you said you were going to beat it. I just wanna say you did good Shannon. You did good. I'm gonna miss you."

"You could flip my day from bad to amazing with only a couple words. When I think of you I think of you as my hero. You were the strongest person I ever met and will probably ever meet."

The words from the Rebels follow the same theme:

"When I think or see the number 9, I think of Shannon. When I see lime green I think of Shannon. Also when I hear the song "Don't Stop Believin'" I think of Shannon. I think of Shannon and how she never stopped believing."

"I think about you so often. Like every night and every time we drive down that big hill, I look down the road that your house is on. I wonder what it would be like if you were still here, like if we would've gone to regionals or farther. But I also think your passing has brought so many people together, especially your Rebel team. Thank you so much for being such a great friend to me and I hope to see you soon!"

So thank you for helping me muster up some tears tonight. I have been avoiding them. When I am forced to reflect back on what we had and what we have lost—well, the tears are not far from the surface. Your words are a gift we will treasure forever and ever.

POSTED BY DAN

WEDNESDAY, MARCH 28, 2012

I wish there were a predictable pattern to grief. It is hard to accept that one day I might feel fine, maybe even consider myself happy on that day, and then the next day I can barely think straight and feel such sadness that it physically hurts. We expect "recovery" and "healing" to follow an upward linear pattern, but grief refuses to do so. It's quite a ride, to say the least ...

Another week is flying by, and if Erin can make it through one more day, her spring break will commence. That's one of those markers in the school year—three quarters down, one to go. The beginning of our break will bring Grandma and Papa Harkins to town so they can be a part of the Bassmasters St. Jude Children's Research Hospital fundraiser on Saturday.

Erin and her schedule continue to pull us forward and keep us moving. It is rewarding to see her blossom and grow and she's becoming quite a bit more social. She must be texting more often because the speed at which she types seems to be increasing each day!

We are learning to take whatever comes our way—whatever feelings, whatever memories—and accept it. The people around us, family and friends, are also accepting this roller coaster. As we work through our grief, we have carte blanche to feel however we feel. In a way, that's liberating. It's OK for us to be happy, and it's OK for us to be sad.

We've referenced our daily meditation book that we read a passage from each morning. The author, Martha Whitmore Hickman, offered this thought: *"Nowhere more than here is it important to be patient with ourselves, not let ourselves be weighed down by the discouragements of yesterday. Each day is a new day, a fresh beginning."*

Grieving or not, those are words to live by.

POSTED BY JEN

SUNDAY, APRIL 1, 2012

The days have gone quickly since my last post. Thursday was a whirlwind of activity as Grandma and Papa Harkins arrived, and Dan returned home from his workweek in Michigan. On Friday, Erin, Grandma, and I had some girl time that involved pedicures, shopping, and lunch. It was some good quality time for Grandma to be with Erin and see that things are mostly going pretty well for Miss E.

On Saturday, Dan and I were able to play a round of golf with Papa and my brother, Eric, while the grandkids hung out with Grandma and had some cousin time. Saturday evening brought the main event: the Zumbro Valley Bassmasters 7th Annual St. Jude Fundraiser.

Dan spoke to over five hundred people last night, many of whom didn't know Shannon and don't know us. Sure, we had some family and friends in the audience, as well as basketball parents and hockey parents who came to hear Dan's speech. Our families were representing. The Harkins clan was all there. Two of my aunts and uncles came to be with us, and Dan's sisters Megan and Bridgid made the trip down from the cities to support their kid brother.

But, for the rest of the crowd, Dan told the tale of who Shannon was and why it matters. We played the tribute video done by Chris Conte after Shannon's passing. Dan told stories about playing JV golf and playing for the Rebels. He told stories about the letters we received from kids who were touched by Shannon and her spirit. He told of our experience at St. Jude and why St. Jude is so important in

Fundraising for St. Jude and the Shannon Scholarship Fund | Shannon's Rebel
teammates help us with t-shirt sales

the fight against pediatric cancer. He told the crowd that Shannon's
cells are alive and growing in a culture, and they are helping in the
research necessary to find a cure.

Dan spent thirty minutes standing at the podium, and I never saw
anyone in the audience get up. They were captivated. Those of us who
knew Shannon were in tears. Those who didn't know her were in awe.
He nailed it. Dan says there's no question, Shannon helped him get
through it.

Erin was in the audience, looking so grown up. It's as if she's skipped
a few stages and gone right to being a teenager. There were tears flowing from Erin as she watched the video and heard her dad talk about
her best friend. The pain is still fresh and real for Miss E ...

The other item on the agenda last night was selling some Shannon
shirts to raise funds for the scholarship. We enlisted the help of the
Rebels, and Shannon's buddies Samantha, Paige, and Olivia were up for
it. Hard to resist three cute girls raising money in honor of their friend.

So, another day in the journey. Another first. Sharing our story to try and help others. It comes back to what Shannon would want us to do, and there's no question she'd want us to make a difference if we could.

Today the calendar says April. Tomorrow morning we will head out on spring break.

POSTED BY JEN

TUESDAY, APRIL 3, 2012

Spring break is in full swing, and we have had a low-key, relaxing day here on Hutchinson Island in southern Florida. Our balcony looks right out at the ocean. The sun coming up over the Atlantic gave way to a perfect, steamy afternoon.

Only child | Spring break in Florida. Our first adventure as a family of three.

We alternated between playing in the ocean waves and swimming in the hotel pool. People watching is always entertaining! Erin looked older than ten sunning herself poolside while listening to tunes and texting with friends. I guess she will be eleven next week …

Dan and I took turns exercising this A.M. and both noted that the solitude allows the mind to wander. That's OK. We need to acknowledge that this is different and we are starting anew.

Shannon is missed. She always will be. But we are relaxing and enjoying a new place. Today was a good day. Tonight we are headed out for some seafood. Not too shabby.

POSTED BY JEN

THURSDAY, APRIL 5, 2012

The waves crashing into the beach outside our Hutchinson Island room sound like a freight train. Jen and I left the deck door to our bedroom open all week. The power of nature has been alarming. Sometimes the roars are "crackers"—our term for big ones that make a cracking sound when water slaps water.

Wednesday, Erin and I spent hours body surfing and diving into the waves. We are both strong swimmers, but at times you feel a little helpless as the wave energy jostles your body mass like a rag doll. Nevertheless, I am fully aware again of the teeny, tiny place I occupy in this universe.

When you think that the whole time we were completely absorbed in our journey as a family and as a community with Shannon, these waves were still pounding this coastline with no knowledge, care, or concern about our situation. We are bit players. And this trip has given us a healthy perspective on that.

Erin has done her best to keep smiling—but she misses her buddy, her sister, her constant companion. No doubt that has been apparent in our first vacation together as a family of three. This puts pressure on Jen and me to step in and entertain—play swimming games, play in the ocean, just be her play buddy. Sometimes that is annoying when you just want to chill. But the kid still needs to be ten. (Eleven next week!)

The other reality that has been exposed: it is hard to watch cute families enjoy each other like we used to. I would catch myself watching two little girls entertain each other and laugh and fight and compete for the attention of mom and dad, "Mom, watch this!" Erin noticed too.

All a part of the process. We are trying to find our groove. Baby steps.

Our weather was fab. Might've been *too* hot yesterday, but I better keep that to myself. We check out today and return to the 507 tonight, and all three of us are ready. It's Masters weekend, Opening Day, and Easter. We have a few days to recover before returning to the grind Monday.

Music, words, and lyrics are catching my emotions again … I think that is a good thing …

Jack Johnson captures it well:

Shocking but we're just nothing we're just moments
We're clever but we're clueless we're just human
Amusing but confusing but the truth is
All we got is questions we'll never know
Never know, never know

POSTED BY DAN

THREE MONTHS

A quarter of a year has passed since Shannon passed. A season. Winter—which wasn't much of a winter, by the way—has given way to spring. You can see things turning green and plants beginning to bloom. It's Easter weekend. Spring is the season of growth and progress.

A season of progress, you say? So how do we measure ours? We are clicking off days, some of them mostly good. We went on a family vacation as a family of three. But our emotions and sadness and anger are still never far from the surface. Today, on this three-month anniversary, is hard. Shannon's friends are remembering her on their Facebook posts today. It's hard for them too.

Though we've suffered a great loss, we've gained things too. An awareness of the human condition. Deeper friendships. We remember to not sweat the small stuff, and there is a lot of small stuff. We try to do our best each day—whatever we have in us—and then we go to sleep, get up the next day, and try to do our best again. It's a pretty simple formula, really.

Now, of course we would trade all this awareness to have her back. We'd bury our heads right back in the sand if it meant we could hear her laugh and see her smile and listen to her enthusiastically tell a story. Why isn't she here watching the Twins home opener with us today? Her absence is painful.

But she is gone, so we must take what we have learned, to accept this knowledge that we've gained, and continue on. We are better people, more aware of others, and more aware of ourselves because of Shannon. That is an incredible gift we have been given ...

POSTED BY JEN

EASTER

The best-laid plans ... today our emotional state derailed us. We just couldn't do what we intended to do. We made it to church as planned, but that was harder than we anticipated. Easter. Celebrating life. Families together. People watching us. Dan and I were both fighting back tears. So as we headed up Highway 52, intending to join the O'Hara gathering at Bridgid's house, we admitted to each other that we didn't have it in us. We just were not up to socializing today. We turned the car around and headed for the safety of our home.

We broke it to Erin that we wouldn't be going to see her cousins. She gets it. She understands that, right now, sometimes our emotions win out over our best intentions. Erin tearfully admitted to Dan last night that she was sad there would be no Easter egg hunt or coloring of eggs this year. I just wasn't up for it. And she didn't press me on it. Erin may have understood, but it still made her sad.

So, we are home, sitting and watching the Masters. Dan and I had a chuckle today about an Easter Sunday way back when we were newly married, before children. We didn't feel like socializing then, either, for entirely different reasons. We were selfish. We told my family we were going to Dan's family, and told Dan's family we were going to my family. Instead we played thirty-six holes together, and then went home and watched the Masters! We thought we had it all figured out back then. We didn't know much at all, really ...

Chalk it up to another part of the journey. There will be days like this. We've covered some big territory in the last week, and there's more ahead.

Happy Easter, everyone.

POSTED BY JEN

TUESDAY, APRIL 10, 2012—EIO TURNS ELEVEN

It was a good day for Miss E on this, her eleventh birthday. Lots of messages via Facebook, text, and phone helped her feel the love. Thanks to her friend Emily, everyone at Willow Creek Middle School knew it was her birthday. Emily walked around all day carrying a sign that said

"Wish Erin O'Hara a Happy Birthday!" Gotta love that friend who wants to embarrass you a little bit.

After school it was breakfast for dinner—pancakes and bacon—to fuel us up for the spring's first soccer practice. If it's cold and windy, it must be time for soccer! Coach Bart, Coach Dan, and Coach Jen are ready for another season of shaping young minds ...

The best part of the day was the surprise cake and ice cream gathering. Godparents, Uncle Tim and Aunt Suzie, along with cousin Maggie, made yet another trip down Highway 52 to celebrate. That's a big effort on a weeknight and so very thoughtful. Uncle Mike and Aunt Connie came as well as our good buddies the Shives and the Olsons. Erin didn't know any of them were coming, so it was a fun surprise that all of a sudden there were sixteen of us to sing happy birthday to her! After everyone left, Erin gave Dan and me big hugs and a heartfelt "Thanks, you guys." She was surrounded by people who care so deeply for her, and she appreciated it. So did we.

Of course, the day couldn't pass without thoughts of the one who wasn't here. This morning over breakfast we recounted the story of the day Erin was born. Big sister came to the hospital with Grandma and Papa and told everyone that she wanted to hold "my baby." We've got a picture to prove that's exactly what Shannon did.

For Erin's birthday we bought her a TV for her room, something we never would have done before. But, oh well, the rules of engagement have changed. Anyway, the TV has a built in DVD player for movie watching. As I was setting it up this morning, I went to get a DVD to try it out. And when I saw the home videos lying there, I couldn't help myself. I fast-forwarded to video of Erin's second birthday. There was little E, happy as could be, following orders from her big sister on how to open presents. Classic Shannon. And classic Erin.

Those home videos show that E was a patient little sister who allowed Shannon to lead. Now, E is a precious only child, finding her own way.

Happy birthday to my kid, Erin Irene.

POSTED BY JEN

THURSDAY, APRIL 12, 2012

Another week is flying by. In some ways it's the last week before the calendar turns over for us—the calendar that starts with the day our lives changed forever: diagnosis day, April 15 …

But today is a good day. The sun is shining, and soccer practice will be a little more pleasant tonight. I spent my day meeting with book publishers in the Twin Cities. My head is spinning a bit and there are too many details to share right now, but the gist of it is, I believe I'm going to get the chance to tell Shannon's story—our story—by writing a book. I've got a lot to learn and I feel like I'm over my skis a bit, but I'm also confident I'm working with a group of people who can help me. It's exciting and scary as hell. I hope I can do it justice …

So, getting this project going has been occupying my thoughts. So much so that I haven't done any preparations for the birthday sleepover we are hosting tomorrow night. (It shouldn't be called a birth *day*, it's more like we have been celebrating for the whole birth *week*!) I will need to be very productive tomorrow morning to get ready … Erin has five pals coming over to make homemade pizzas and then have a cupcake decorating contest. Erin's favorite shows are *Cake Boss, Cupcake Wars, Sweet Genius*, etc. So that's the inspiration. Dan is threatening to play the role of the mean judge … It should be entertaining!

Friday, April 13 tomorrow … oh my …

POSTED BY JEN

FRIDAY, APRIL 13, 2012

The birthday sleepover extravaganza is in full swing. Here's the cupcake gang: Emily, Erin, Katie, Gretchen, Lexie, and Hallie. Frosting and smiles are everywhere!

POSTED BY JEN

Happy Birthday, Erin! | Celebrating turning eleven with her pals

SUNDAY, APRIL 15, 2012

On Friday, April 15, 2011 we were given news that changed us—and many people in our lives—forever. 365 days later I can still recall in vivid detail the look on Dr. Kotagal's face as he came in to deliver the news. He asked Shannon to leave the room, and I collapsed on Jen's back.

I remember the snowflakes blowing across the window of the exam room in Mayo 16. I remember the quiet ride home and the phone calls we had to make. All the phone calls. 365 days ago. The first time I had ever heard the words brain stem and glioma used together.

So here we are. Changed forever. Changed for the better as people. Not better without Shannon in our lives. But, we go on. And we are doing pretty dang well ... most days. Sunday, we were just a little distracted by the memory of that chilling April day.

We are also a little distracted by a surgical procedure Jennifer will undergo Monday to have an ovarian cyst removed. It will knock her out for a few days. Her doctors are confident she will recover well. We have been unsettled all weekend. Jen is our team captain. Anytime your captain undergoes surgery …

Still we did our best to enjoy Erin's first ever volleyball tournament as her South Side Juniors took to the courts at Minnesota State Mankato. We did our best to let our competitive juices distract. Erin loved it. She is getting better with every point, and I think volleyball has a chance to be her sport of choice. We shall see. Erin chose her uniform and took her sister's favorite #9 …

Checking off another milestone. 365 days since we were changed forever. Damn, that happened fast.

POSTED BY DAN

#9 | Erin carries on, even trying a new sport—volleyball. Wearing #9 in memory of her sister.

ALL IS WELL

Just a quick note to say today's procedure went smoothly, and I am home and resting as comfortably as can be expected. Pathology report showed that the cyst was benign.

Thanks for the notes and well wishes. Give me a few days and I'll be up and at 'em again ...

POSTED BY JEN

WEDNESDAY, APRIL 18, 2012

After a couple of days of recovery, I am starting to feel human again. I managed to shower and drive a car to pick up Erin from volleyball today. It's the little things ...

I am relieved to be done with the procedure and to know that it's nothing to worry about. It is hard to hear a doctor say, "It's most likely nothing, but we need to check it out." Those words will never again be reassuring to us ...

The other difficult part is understanding that I could have a cyst the size of a grapefruit along with a couple of reproductive organs taken out through three small incisions and be home hours later. Shannon had a tumor the size of a shooter marble, and there was little that could be done. Now I know that's comparing apples and oranges, and the abdomen is different than the brain stem. But there's a part of me that wants to make sense of that. Modern medicine is amazing, but it couldn't save Shannon ...

As I look at the date on this entry I am reminded that we posted our first blog entry a year ago on April 18. It was originally an email to family explaining what was ahead as we started Shannon's treatment. As I've been doing some work on putting material together for the book, I've been going back and reading the blog. It's full of optimism and energy and fear. It's hard not to feel like we were a little naive. But, that naivete served us well. We really did want to fight the good fight and enjoy the time we had. If that meant we had to be foolishly optimistic, well, so be it. We didn't know what we didn't know ...

Reaching the point on the calendar where it all began a year ago has been emotional. These were the days one year ago when we learned that the world doesn't always make sense. What happens to us isn't always a result of our actions. Life is arbitrary.

But not all the memories are bad. This is the time one year ago when we began relating to people, to the world, in a different way. We quit sweating the small stuff. Our relationships deepened because we needed them to. We learned that people would be there to help you if you let them. We learned that life could be both painful and beautiful at the same time.

POSTED BY JEN

Lessons Learned

As I think back on the most terrible year of my life, believe it or not, it's not all bad. With Shannon's diagnosis, we went from living an ordinary life to fighting for our daughter's life. The list of lessons learned is long. In no particular order:

I learned that being a mother is the most wonderful, frustrating, rewarding job in the universe. I'm so grateful to be fully aware of how much I love being a mom.

I learned that I don't know everything. As parents, we try to pretend that we have answers and explanations for all of our children's questions. The truth is, sometimes we don't. And it's OK to admit it. Kids are smart, and they will understand if you are honest with them.

I learned that there are medical professionals who have dedicated their lives to fighting terrible diseases. They accept the challenge, offer hope and support, and treat their patients with dignity.

I learned to take stock in what really matters. It's been said before, but don't sweat the small stuff—and most of it is small stuff.

I learned to be grateful for what's right in front of you, today. Tomorrow is unknown.

I learned that people want to be kind and want to help. If you are willing and accepting, people will meet your needs and help you. There are good people all around us, every day. Be open to them.

I learned that teenagers want to be kind and help too. Teenagers get a bad rap, but they can rise to the occasion if we believe in them and give them a chance to express themselves—boys and girls alike.

I learned that having true friends makes life better and makes grieving easier. True friends will laugh with you and cry with you, sometimes in the same moment! True friends will let you talk, or sit with you in silence.

I learned that grief is an ongoing process. You don't "get better" when you lose a child, you change. The world looks different from before. But life does go on, and you can find beauty and happiness amidst the sadness and loss. That's living.

I learned that feeling a loss doesn't mean you have to be consumed by it. Being happy today or making plans for tomorrow doesn't mean you have forgotten yesterday.

I learned that everyone has a story. Once we were open and sharing ours, a lot of people were willing to do the same. Life is hard and everyone is tested. Share your pain and others will too.

I learned that happiness is a choice. We can't always control what happens to us, but we can control our reaction to it. Choose positivity.

I learned that one thirteen-year-old girl could teach a whole family, a whole school, maybe even a whole community how to live. And how to die.

Back to the Start

Shannon was always going to do things on her own terms. Even her own birth. Eight days late, labor was induced, and she still wouldn't come. Two days later, still nothing. Finally, via emergency C-section, on July 29, 1998, Shannon Anne O'Hara was pulled reluctantly into this world. For someone who loved life, she was in no hurry to get hers started.

That day I became a mother. Changed forever, for sure. But I had no idea the journey that baby girl would take. I had no idea the impact she would have on our family, immediate and extended. I had no idea the effect she would have on the people she knew, and even on some who never met her.

Her life was much too short, but she did it right. She taught us all how to live. Dan, Erin, and I shared these final thoughts with all those who attended Shannon's funeral:

> *A silver lining in battling this terrible disease is that we found out how kind people can be. Shannon knew this all along. If you were her classmate or her teammate, you were her friend. She looked for the positive in people. She believed in living life to its fullest with a giant smile on her face. So, how do we honor Shannon as we all move forward? We ask that you continue to be kind, continue to look for the good in people, and continue to smile and laugh and connect with others. We mourn Shannon's death, but we are inspired by her spirit. Carry it on ...*

EPILOGUE

Memorials and Moving On

Some days I still can't believe Shannon is gone. I think it will always feel that way. But time does add perspective, and it puts some space between the acute pain of the end of Shannon's life and the day-to-day living we do. There will be anniversaries of her birth and her death that we will have to navigate each year. There will be milestones that her peers reach when we will feel our loss more poignantly; her buddies will go to high school and soon they will learn to drive and graduate from high school, and on and on ... Those moments will be markers in time for us, markers of what we lost.

But, Dan, Erin, and I continue to try and live our lives, while always remembering our sweet girl. Our hope is that those concentric circles that surround us—family, close friends, community, and acquaintances—will remember Shannon as well. We've made efforts to honor her spirit through scholarships, and through sharing her story—our story—with others.

Memorializing someone is such a personal choice. We took baby steps, first burying some ashes with a new tree in our yard. Grandma and Grandpa Harkins took some ashes to create their own memorial. And Shannon's two favorite places on this earth will hold a piece of her as well.

At Graham Arena, the hockey complex where she learned to play and spent countless hours honing her skills and hanging with teammates, her jersey and picture hang on the wall as a memorial. That #9 will be a reminder to all the hockey players who pass through that building to love the battle, be a good teammate, and enjoy every minute of it. She did.

And a piece of Shannon will rest forever at the O'Hara cabin on Lake Hubert. We as a family chose to do a memorial rock—not a headstone, but a natural boulder—with her name inscribed on it, and the Celtic meaning of the name Shannon: "Small but wise." Who knew when we named our baby all those years ago how well that name would fit her?

Lake Hubert is such a special place in the O'Hara family. O'Hara kids and their kids have been coming there since the 1940s. It's one of Dan's favorite places on this earth, and it became special for me too, over the years. It's a simple cabin on a quiet lake. We don't own any motorized water toys. It's a place for swimming and playing and reflecting. It's been our family summer vacation for a week each year since Shannon was born.

When Shannon was first diagnosed, she went through a list of dreams that she might never get to realize: going to high school, going to college, being a mom, being a grandma. But then, in true Shannon form, she started thinking short term about what she could do in that last summer if her body allowed. First on her wish list was to get to Lake Hubert. We managed to do that twice during Shannon's last summer, and she was feeling good both times. She and Erin played in the lake for hours on end, made trips into town for pizza, candy, and ice cream, and enjoyed sleeping in the beds on the cabin porch while listening to a storm roll in. Perfect.

Six months after Shannon's death, twenty-seven O'Haras gathered to ceremonially help Shannon stay at Lake Hubert forever. As we circled around the Shannon rock, we shared stories and memories, and then each grandparent, aunt, uncle, and cousin placed some of Shannon's ashes beneath the rock. It will be a place for each of them to be with Shannon, always.

One final piece of the ceremony for us was to sprinkle Shannon out in the lake. Out in the spot where she and Erin would spend hours on end playing in the rowboat, swimming, making up silly games, and laughing so loud that it would echo through the trees. Out in the spot that was just deep enough to make me nervous, which, of course, was part of the fun. Giant tears flowed

Rest in peace | Spreading Shannon's ashes in Lake Hubert

from Erin's eyes as the three of us and Sunny sat there in the row-boat. The memories are so vivid and the loss so painful.

The days, weeks, and months since April 15, 2011 taught us so much about ourselves and about others. We know a level of sadness and loss that we couldn't imagine. But we also know about gratitude, grace, kindness, and acceptance. Shannon showed us the way.

Afterword

CYNTHIA WETMORE, M.D., PH.D.
Director of Developmental Therapeutics
Department of Neuro-oncology
St. Jude Children's Research Hospital

Brain tumors are the most common solid tumor, and the leading cause of disease-related mortality in the pediatric population. Approximately 2,500 young people aged 0–19 years are diagnosed with a brain tumor in the United States each year (http://seer.cancer.gov). Only half of these patients will be alive ten years after diagnosis and those that do survive suffer significant cognitive and neurologic sequelae of their treatment.

The type of tumor that Shannon O'Hara battled, diffuse intrinsic pontine glioma (DIPG), comprises about 15% of all pediatric brain tumors and is one of the most aggressive types of cancer. This tumor arises from glial cells—the cells that support and 'insulate' the neurons—in the brain stem. The tumor most commonly arises in children between the ages of 4 and 12 and becomes clinically apparent by exerting pressure on the long nerve pathways that run from the centers of motor control in the brain, to the muscles that control movement of the eyes and face (the cranial nerves), swallowing, speech and other areas of the body. Nearly 95% of children diagnosed with DIPG die of their disease within 9–12 months of diagnosis. The approximately 5–10% that survive likely had a tumor that was of lower grade and had different biologic features, though it resembled DIPG on magnetic resonance imaging (MRI) scan. Diagnosis of DIPG is based primarily upon radiographic findings (appearance on MRI scan), and these tumors are not usually biopsied, unless they have unusual characteristics. While some centers advocate routine biopsy of these tumors, the eloquence of that area of the brain stem and the lack of clinical benefit to the patient render this an approach that has limited widespread utility. Unfortunately, there is no curative therapy for DIPG, and radiation therapy is the only modality that has an effect on temporarily reducing the size of the tumor. Sadly, survival has not improved despite three decades of clinical and basic research.

So, why have we not made more progress in finding cures for pediatric brain tumors? The landscape of some other pediatric malignancies has dramatically improved with current rates of cure for acute lymphoblastic leukemia approaching 94%. One problem is the difficulty in obtaining tumor tissue from the brain. Often, the tumors are in areas where surgical resection is not possible (as in DIPG), so there is not readily available tumor tissue for analysis at diagnosis. The brain is also protected by the tight junctions in the blood vessels that comprise the blood-brain barrier and keep caustic agents, like chemotherapy, from penetrating into brain tissue. While it is relatively straightforward to draw a sample of blood to determine if the chemotherapy agent is killing the leukemia cells, it has not been so easy to determine if the chemotherapy agent is reaching the brain tumor and, if so, if it is killing the tumor cells. Additionally, most clinical trials for pediatric patients with brain tumors have used therapeutic agents that were selected for treating adults with brain tumors. DIPG does not arise in the adult brain. We are learning that the biology of pediatric brain tumors differs significantly from those tumors arising in the mature brain. While the tumor cells appear very similar under the microscope, we now know that the genetic mutations and pathways that initiate and promote tumor growth in a child are very different from those mutations that drive brain tumors in the adult population. Therefore, it is not surprising that moving agents from clinical trials in adults to pediatric trials has been disappointing.

So, where do we go from here? Fortunately, through the sequencing of the entire genome of pediatric tumors and DNA from normal, non-tumor cells, we are able to gain new insights into the biology of these tumors and, for the first time, we are starting to investigate how the mutations present in these tumor cells act to give the cells a growth advantage. Specifically, research conducted at St. Jude Children's Research Hospital and other centers on tumor and normal tissue that were generously donated by patient families has found that over half of the tumor cells show amplification or increased activity of receptors for a potent growth-promoting pathway—Platelet Derived Growth Factor (PDGF). Pharmaceutical companies are developing new small molecule inhibitors that target these pathways, and we are beginning to see a willingness to bring these agents to pediatric clinical trials. Without such collaboration among families, researchers, and the pharmaceutical industry we will never make progress in finding cures for pediatric brain tumors.

I met Shannon and her family on December 6, 2011 when they travelled to Memphis from Rochester, Minnesota, to take part in a Phase I clinical trial of Crenolanib, a potent inhibitor of the PDGF pathway. This was a "first in pediatrics" clinical trial of this agent, and it was only available at St. Jude Children's Research Hospital. Participating in a clinical trial of a new agent requires a significant commitment from the patient and their family. We require the patients to remain in Memphis for the first several weeks of therapy so that we can closely monitor their blood for any changes in electrolytes, blood cell counts, liver, kidney, and other organ function as well as examining them every few days to assure their safety. The O'Haras bounded into the clinic, full of questions and hope. Shannon looked well, had played hockey with her team two days prior, and stressed that she wanted to participate in helping to find a cure for the disease she was battling. The fierce intensity in her eyes engaged me, and I felt a special connection. I, too, had hope.

Shannon died of her disease on January 6, 2012. The Styrofoam box containing her tumor arrived on Saturday morning, January 7, 2012, and I immediately placed the precious cells into culture medium and put them into the incubator, hoping that they would grow as well in the culture flask as they did in her body. The best way to understand what mutations and pathways promote tumor cell growth—and how to halt that growth—is to have the tumor cells available to study. Thanks to the very generous gift of tumor tissue that patient families have donated, we are able to analyze the mutations present in the tumor, and we have realized that there is a heterogeneity of mutations within the different populations of tumor cells that will likely require a full range of several targeted agents to successfully eradicate. With Shannon's cells, we have been able to set up high throughput screening of over 500,000 compounds and small molecule inhibitors to try to discover an agent that will synergize with the PDGF inhibitor to kill the surviving tumor cells. By having access to patient tumor cells, we are also able to move forward to understand how specific mutations give a biological survival advantage and also to understand how tumor cells develop resistance to chemotherapeutic agents. There is new hope and optimism that we are finally on track to develop curative therapy for this deadly disease. Collaboratively, with patients and families, basic and clinical scientists, we come together to learn from those whose impact has far outlasted their brief time on this earth.

Acknowledgments

What are the odds that my husband and I would write a blog that I wanted to turn into a book? And, what are the odds that my sister-in-law would have a friend in the publishing business? Not only that, but that this publisher had been reading the blog all along and so was her brother, who was an editor. They liked it, and they had another friend who could make it happen.

Not only that, this publisher and this editor are connected with fundraising efforts for St. Jude. They feel inspired to help with this project in the hopes that it can make a difference.

So, this woman I had never met, her brother, and their colleague helped and encouraged me, and well, here it is. To Jill Hansen, Paul Abdo, and Nancy Tuminelly, you made me an author. Much gratitude.

Thanks also to all the good people at ABDO Publishing, Scarletta Press, and Mighty Media Inc. who put in the hard work to make this fantasy of mine a reality. To Grace Hansen, Desiree Bussiere, Nora Evans, and Pam Chenevert—we did it.

I want to thank the medical personnel at the Mayo Clinic and at St. Jude Children's Research Hospital for their tireless efforts in treating Shannon. You gave us the precious time we had, time for our story to unfold. We cherished every moment.

If you are a stay-at-home mom who thinks she maybe wants to write a book, you are going to need friends and family who believe in you. I had that everywhere I turned.

Thanks to my girlfriends who told me every step of the way that I could do this, especially Teri Baily and Kula Shives. You believed in me before I believed in myself. You continue to fill up my soul.

To Amy Pankow and Ellen Wente, thank you for all your efforts to help us honor and remember Shannon. To Mary DaRos, the gift of your photographs is everywhere in this book, including the cover. Thanks for sharing your time and talent.

Thanks to Cynthia Wetmore for your treatment of Shannon, your compassion for us, and your continued efforts to help me understand this terrible disease. You started as Shannon's doctor, but you became a dear friend. Another one of Shannon's gifts.

I must give a blanket thank you to the community of Rochester, Minnesota. This is partly a story about our town, our people, and the support they provided our family. We were buoyed all along the way by the kindness of people, some we knew and some we had never met. This town is a great place to raise kids.

To my family, thanks for allowing me to share our story with others. Your encouragement and confidence in me helped me persevere. All of our immediate family deserves to have their names listed here:

To Gwen & Chuck and Ed & Tess, thanks for being the type of parents you are. Dan and I had really good examples to emulate.

To Eric & Jen, Mike & Connie, Mary, Molly & Norv, Tim & Suzie, Pat & Mame, Megan & R.T., Katie & Bill, and Bridgid & H.J., we are blessed to have you as siblings. There was someone there to pick us up at every turn.

And to Shannon and Erin's cousins: Laurynn, Jack, Kevin, Meaghan, Liam, Aracelly, Annie, Nora, Maggie, Doug, Kallie, Brendan, Sean, Leila, Joe, Charlie, Grace, Francie, Tessie, Carey, Ellie, and Teddie. You are all better people because Shannon was in your life. I know you all consider that Shannon's gift.

Of course, Erin deserves a special mention right here. Thanks, my dear girl, for letting your mom spend time looking back when you were ready to move forward. You deserve the world.

And finally, thanks to my husband. Dan, when you asked for my phone number all those years ago, who would have imagined the journey we would take? Along the way, when we were still young and dumb, we decided we wanted to be parents. Best decision ever. I love you.

The Shannon O'Hara Foundation

Shannon lived her life with a positive attitude, always working hard for what she wanted and being a good friend and teammate. In her memory, we have started a foundation that will support youth who carry on those ideals, as well as help to fund brain tumor research.

The Shannon O'Hara Memorial Scholarships will be awarded each year in conjunction with the Rochester Youth Hockey Association. Our hope is to expand and offer more support through donations to youth athletics and other endeavors to support youth here in our community.

In addition, funds will be donated on a yearly basis to Brains Together For a Cure, which funds brain tumor research at the Mayo Clinic, and to St. Jude Children's Research Hospital, where the science necessary to fight these types of tumors is being studied each and every day.

For more information on the Shannon O'Hara Foundation, or if you'd like to make a donation, please check out our website: shannonoharafoundation.org.

About the Authors

Jen O'Hara is a Rochester, Minnesota, native and graduated from the University of St. Thomas in St. Paul, Minnesota, with a BA in broadcast journalism. She has worked as a high school educator teaching television production and as a tennis instructor to students of all ages, while also being at home raising her two daughters, Shannon and Erin. She is an avid Broadway musical fan as well as an enthusiast of all kinds of sports, especially golf and tennis. This is her first published work, adapted from the blog that she co-wrote with her husband, Dan, and it is in memory of her daughter, Shannon.

Dan O'Hara is the husband of Jen O'Hara, father of Shannon & Erin O'Hara, and of course, master of Sunny the Wonder Dog. After earning a BS in mass communications, Dan spent thirteen years in local television as the sports director at KTTC TV, Rochester, Minnesota. Today he is a sales executive in the transportation/trucking industry. Together, Dan and Jen wrote the original blog, and some blog excerpts in the book are credited to him.